DIM

DIMENSIONS OF ADULT LEARNING

ADULT EDUCATION AND TRAINING IN A GLOBAL ERA

edited by

Griff Foley

OPEN UNIVERSITY PRESS

Open University Press
McGraw-Hill Education
McGraw-Hill House
Shoppenhangers Road
Maidenhead
Berkshire
England
SL6 2QL

email: enquiries@openup.co.uk
world wide web: www.openup.co.uk

First published 2004
First published in Australia by
Allen & Unwin

A catalogue record of this book is available from the British Library

ISBN 0 335 21448 7

Library of Congress Cataloging-in-Publication Data
CIP data has been applied for

Typeset by Midland Typesetters, Maryborough, Victoria
Printed by South Wind Production, Singapore

CONTENTS

CONTENTS

PREFACE

Early in 2002, Elizabeth Weiss of Allen & Unwin asked me to edit a third edition of *Understanding Adult Education and Training* (Sydney: Allen & Unwin, 1995, 2000). I started to do this, but soon realised that we had a new and different book. *Dimensions of Adult Learning* is the result. It reflects the radical changes that have occurred in adult education over the past decade. Three changes have been particularly important. First, 'adult education' has been largely displaced by specialist fields— vocational education, human resource development, community-based education and so on—the list is long and growing. Second, adult education theory and scholarship has become more sophisticated and international. Third, there is a growing recognition of the central role of learning in our lives. This third development is by far the most significant. Human life has a learning dimension that is just as important as its economic or political dimensions. Learning, and failure to learn, are central to all aspects of human life. Formal education is a minor part of the learning dimension. Informal and incidental learning and non-formal education are far more significant. This recognition is only just being reflected in research and scholarship. We are, one hopes, at the beginning of a learning revolution in which governments and citizens will come to understand the central role of learning in our lives and the dire consequences of failure to learn.

I develop these points in the first chapter. The rest of the book explores various aspects of the learning dimension. Part I establishes an analytical framework that emphasises the diverse and social nature of learning and the agency of learners. Part II deals in depth with the core knowledge and skills required by adult educators. Part III discusses adult education policy and research, and the history and political economy of adult education and learning. Part IV surveys major innovations and issues in adult education and learning.

The contributors to this book reflect the international character of adult education scholarship. We come from Australia, Canada, New Zealand, South Africa, Malta and the USA. There is a Peruvian who teaches in California, a Swede who moves between Vancouver and the Nordic countries, a Lancashireman who teaches by Internet from northern Alberta, a South African who's likely to pop up anywhere at any time, a smile on her face. We all know each other, either directly or through scholarly networks. We have theoretical and political differences, but we share a passionate concern for adult learning and social justice.

I thank the contributors, who have managed to find time in their hectic lives to write fine chapters. I also thank Elizabeth Weiss, for suggesting a third edition that turned into a new book. I am also grateful to Damon Anderson for his many title suggestions, which led to the final choice. Most of all I thank my wife, Lori Hungerford, for encouraging me to leave the academy and live a more balanced life.

Griff Foley
Merewether, NSW
January 2004

CONTRIBUTORS

Damon Anderson is a research fellow in the Monash-ACER Centre for the Economics of Education and Training, and a lecturer in work and learning studies in the Faculty of Education at Monash University, Melbourne, Australia. Previously he was a senior VET (vocational education and training) policy analyst for state government, and coordinator/teacher of VET programs. Damon has researched and published widely on privatisation, marketisation, student participation, social equity and ecological sustainability in VET. (Damon.Anderson@education.monash.edu.au)

Francesca Beddie is Executive Director of Adult Learning Australia, the peak body representing adult learning in Australia. She is a former diplomat, who served in Indonesia, Russia and Germany. She has also held several senior positions in the Australian Agency for International Development (AusAID). Ms Beddie was a member of the ABC's Advisory Council from 2000 to 2003. She is the author of *Putting Life into Years* (Canberra: Commonwealth of Australia, 2001), a history of the Commonwealth's role in health since Federation, and is a regular reviewer of books on foreign policy and culture in the Asia-Pacific region and Russia. (f.beddie@ala.asn.au)

Carmel Borg is a senior lecturer in Curriculum Studies and Head of the Department of Primary Education at the Faculty of Education, University of Malta. He has written, presented and published extensively on curriculum, critical pedagogy and parental issues. He is the editor of the *Journal of Maltese Education Research*. (carmel.borg@um.edu.mt)

Bob Boughton is a senior lecturer in adult education at the University of New England, Australia (www.une.edu.au). Prior to taking up this position he was an adult educator, a development worker and a social researcher for non-government indigenous peoples' organisations in Central Australia. His chief interests are the traditions and theories of popular education, especially within socialist movements; and indigenous adult education and development issues. (bob.boughton@une.edu.au)

Mike Brown is a senior lecturer in workplace research in the Department of Industry, Professional and Adult Education at RMIT University, Melbourne, Australia. He coordinates and supervises in the higher research degrees 'by project' program. He has spent many years working inside and alongside vocational education and training with a view to changing curriculum and pedagogical practices for working-class learner/workers. (Michael.Brown@rmit.edu.au)

Shauna Butterwick is an assistant professor in the Adult Education Program, Department of Educational Studies, at the University of British Columbia. Her research has focused on feminist approaches to adult education, with particular interest in how employment-related policy and programs shape women's access to and experiences in adult education programs. She is also interested in learning in social movements and the emancipatory possibilities of popular theatre. (shauna.butterwick@ubc.ca)

Tara Fenwick is an associate professor in adult education at the University of Alberta. She studies work as a site for learning, transformation and resistance. Her publications include *Learning Through Experience: Troubling assumptions and intersecting questions* (New York: Krieger, 2003) and *The Art of Evaluation: A handbook for educators and trainers* (Toronto: Thompson, 2000). (tara.fenwick@ualberta.ca)

Laurie Field has worked as a consultant for the past 15 years through his company, Field Learning Pty Ltd, specialising in individual and organisational learning and development. Laurie has written two books, *Skilling Australia* and *Managing Organizational Learning*, and a number of published reports dealing with learning and development issues. His PhD looked at how companies learn about managing pay and performance, and at how this knowledge is retained, transmitted and applied. (orglearn@ozemail.com.au)

Griff Foley is a research associate of the Centre for Popular Education, University of Technology, Sydney. He was formerly an associate professor of adult education at UTS, where he established the masters' degree in adult education, the Aboriginal adult educator professional education program, and the Centre for Popular Education. His publications include *Learning in Social Action: A contribution to understanding informal learning* (London: Zed Books, 1999), and *Strategic Learning: Understanding and facilitating organisational change* (Centre for Popular Education, University of Technology, Sydney, 2001). (Griff.Foley@uts.edu.au)

Keith Forrester is a senior lecturer in the School of Continuing Education at the University of Leeds, England. Dr Forrester works with a variety of labour and community organisations. (forresterkp@yahoo.co.uk)

Vernon Galloway is a lecturer in adult and community education at Edinburgh University. Before joining the university he spent 25 years as a community educator, working in communities across the Edinburgh area. His research is in adult education participation and adult student representative movements. (vernon_galloway@education.ed.ac.uk)

Andrew Gonczi is Dean of Education at UTS. He has published widely in technical and vocational education, and has been heavily involved in research and consultancy related to the development of competency standards in Australia. (Andrew.Gonczi@uts.edu.au)

Nancy Grudens-Schuck is assistant professor in the Department of Agricultural Education and Studies, and in the Graduate Program in Sustainable Agriculture, at Iowa State University, Ames, Iowa. She teaches and studies participatory and qualitative evaluation of adult education. She is author of a forthcoming book, entitled *The Mainstream Environmentalist: Learning through participatory education* (Westport, CT: Greenwood Publishing), which focuses on a large-scale environmental education program for farmers in Ontario, Canada. (ngs@iastate.edu)

Joce Jesson is Director of Research Development in the Faculty Research and Postgraduate Studies at the Auckland College of Education. She is an adviser on education development to the New Zealand Council of Trade Unions and member of a number of national education policy bodies. Her research publications are in the area of education policy, education labour market and union education. (j.jesson@ace.ac.nz)

Linda Leach is a senior lecturer in the College of Education Massey University, Wellington, New Zealand. She has worked as an adult educator in community, polytechnic and university contexts for more than 20 years. Her research and publications focus on adult learning theories and practices and on issues in assessment. (L.J.Leach@massey.ac.nz)

Peter Mayo is an associate professor in the Faculty of Education at the University of Malta, where he coordinates the adult education program and teaches sociology of education. He is the founding editor of the *Journal of Postcolonial Education* and his books include *Beyond Schooling: Adult education in Malta* (coedited with Godfrey Baldacchino, Mireva, 1997), *Gramsci, Freire and Adult Education* (Zed Books, 1999; to be published in German by Argument Verlag) and *Gramsci and Education* (coedited with Carmel Borg & Joseph A. Buttigieg, Rowman & Littlefield, 2002). (peter.mayo@um.edu.mt)

John McIntyre is a former research fellow and director at the Research Centre for Vocational Education and Training in the University of Technology, Sydney, where he specialised in policy and participation in adult education and training. He is currently a member of the NSW Board of Adult Community Education and advises Adult Learning Australia on research matters. He has a particular interest in adult learning and insight meditation. (macjohns@ozemail.com.au)

Paul McTigue is a graduate of the University of Technology, Sydney, master's program in adult education. He has worked in an Australian public service agency, where he is a manager and union activist, for over 25 years. He is especially interested in what people actually learn from organisational change and what that learning means for the future of trade unionism. (paul.mctigue@ato.gov.au)

Tom Nesbit is Director of Continuing Studies at Simon Fraser University in Vancouver, Canada. A former trade union official, his academic interests include labour and workers' education, adult literacy and numeracy, and maintaining and developing the radical adult education tradition. (tnesbit@sfu.ca)

Mike Newman has long and varied experience in adult education. He has published widely in the fields of adult education and trade union training, and has twice won the Cyril Houle Award for literature in adult education. His books include *Defining the Enemy: Adult education in social action* (1994) and *Maeler's Regard: Images of adult learning* (1999). He is currently a senior research fellow in the Centre for Popular Education, University of Technology, Sydney. (Michael.Newman@uts.edu.au)

Kjell Rubenson had the first adult education chair in Sweden before moving to Canada, where he is a professor of education at the University of British Columbia and co-director of the Centre for Policy Studies in Higher Education and Training. He has been the research supervisor for several large national and international projects that have addressed structures, policies and outcomes of adult education and lifelong learning. He is the founding president of the European Society for the Study of Education of Adults. (kjell.rubenson@ubc.ca)

Peter Rushbrook is a senior lecturer and coordinator of VET programs in the School of Education at Charles Sturt University, Wagga Wagga Campus, New South Wales, Australia. Before beginning a second career as a university academic, he was a longstanding Victorian adult educator, TAFE teacher and university-based researcher. His PhD was written on the historical development of Victorian technical and further education. Peter maintains an active research and publications profile in the history of Australian adult and vocational education. (prushbrook@csu.edu.au)

Tom Sork is professor of adult education and graduate adviser in the Department of Educational Studies at the University of British Columbia. His research and writing focus on program planning and professional ethics in adult and continuing education. He is Editor-in-Chief of the *Canadian Journal for the Study of Adult Education/La Revue canadienne pour l'étude de l'éducation des adultes*. (tom.sork@ubc.ca)

Barbara Sparks is an assistant professor of adult education and co-ordinator of the Adult and Community College Program and its affiliate faculty in Women and Gender Studies at North Carolina State University, USA. She has researched and published widely on race, class and gender issues as they relate to adult literacy programming and policy. (barbara_sparks@ncsu.edu)

Bruce Spencer is a professor in the Centre for Work and Community Studies, Athabasca University. Recent publications include *Unions and*

Learning in a Global Economy: International and comparative perspectives (Editor, 2002); *The Purposes of Adult Education: A guide for students* (1998); *Learning for Life: Canadian readings in adult education* (jointly edited, 1998). (bruces@athabascau.ca)

Peter Stephenson is Director of the Regional Integrated Monitoring Centre, a research grouping supporting collaborative decisions for a socially and environmentally sustainable future, and a senior lecturer in environmental health at the University of Western Sydney, Australia. For the past five years he has managed a national education and workforce capacity building program for indigenous Australian environmental health practitioners. (p.stephenson@uws.edu.au)

Nelly Stromquist is a professor in comparative and international education in the Rossier School of Education at the University of Southern California in Los Angeles. She has longstanding interests in gender theory and practices, the intersection of state action and social movements, and ways in which education may serve transformative functions. (nellystromquist@juno.com)

Lucy Taksa is an associate professor in industrial relations and organisational behaviour and Director of the Industrial Relations Research Centre at the University of New South Wales, Sydney. She has written extensively on scientific management, labour and social history, including workers' education and the history of the Eveleigh Railway Workshops in Sydney. (l.taksa@unsw.edu.au)

Mark Tennant is a professor in adult education and Head of the Graduate School at the University of Technology, Sydney. He has written extensively on psychology and adult education, and won the Cyril Houle award for literature in adult education in 1990. (Mark.Tennant@uts.edu.au)

Shirley Walters is a professor of adult and continuing education and Director of the Division for Lifelong Learning at the University of Western Cape, South Africa. She received an honorary doctorate from the University of Linköping, Sweden, in 2001, for her contribution to international adult education. She has written extensively on the politics of adult education and has been an activist within civil society organisations locally and internationally for over 20 years. (ferris@iafrica.com)

Michael Welton is a professor of adult education at Mount St Vincent University in Halifax, Nova Scotia. He has written extensively on adult education history and critical theory. He won the Imogene Okes award for his book, *Little Mosie from the Margaree: a biography of Moses Michael Coady* (Toronto: Thompson Books, 2001). (michael.welton@msvu.ca)

PART I

Our Approach

1

INTRODUCTION: THE STATE OF ADULT EDUCATION AND LEARNING

Griff Foley

This book's progenitor was designed as a text for Australian adult educators doing university-based continuing professional education. It aimed to help adult educators understand their practice. The emphasis was on how theory derived from both experience and study could help adult educators do their work better.

This book retains the original purpose but adds others. It is written not just for adult educators but for the growing range of people who have an interest in adult learning and education.

The changes in the book reflect changes in society and education. In the past 30 years the provision of adult education, and thinking about adult learning, have changed radically. University extension education has all but disappeared, and universities have expanded their professional education offerings. Community-based education has had to become largely self-supporting, and so has become much more businesslike in both its organisation and course offerings. Technical or vocational education has expanded and diversified, adding 'further education' to its title in many countries. Numerous fields of practice have generated their own distinctive forms of education—public health, the environment, community arts, nursing and so on. Human resource development is now concerned not just with training but with broader issues of workplace learning and change, generating a new field of practice and study, organisational learning.

These changes make it harder to publish a meaningful and useful book called *Understanding Adult Education and Training*. The field of 'adult education' is fragmenting, diversifying and expanding. Many people, including some contributors to this book, criticise aspects of this transformation. Such critique is necessary. But we also need to look for opportunities in the changes—spaces in which to do progressive work. Our capacity to do this begins with a sharper and more expansive understanding of adult learning.

THE LEARNING DIMENSION

Learning is central to human life—as essential as work or friendship. As the American experiential learning theorist David Kolb (1984) has noted, learning is human beings' primary mode of adaptation: if we don't learn we may not survive, and we certainly won't prosper. Learning is complex and multifaceted, and should not be equated with formal education.

All human activity has a learning dimension. People learn, continually, informally and formally, in many different settings: in workplaces, in families, through leisure activities, through community activities, and in political action. There are at least four forms of adult learning.

Formal education

This is the form of adult learning with which we are most familiar. Its distinguishing characteristics are that it is organised by professional educators, there is a defined curriculum, and it often leads to a qualification. It includes study in educational institutions such as universities and technical and further education colleges, and sequenced training sessions in workplaces.

Non-formal education

This sort of learning occurs when people see a need for some sort of systematic instruction, but in a one-off or sporadic way. Examples include workers being trained to operate a new machine, or environmental activists undertaking non-violent direct-action training.

Informal learning

This sort of learning occurs when people consciously try to learn from their experience. It involves individual or group reflection and discussion, but does not involve formal instruction. Examples include the management committee of a community centre reviewing the operations of its organisation, or workers redesigning their jobs in consultation with management.

Incidental learning

This type of learning occurs while people perform other activities. So, for example, an experienced mechanic has learned a lot about cars, and elderly gardeners carry a great deal of knowledge of their craft. Such learning is incidental to the activity in which the person is involved, and is often tacit and not seen as learning—at least not at the time of its occurrence.

As people live and work they continually learn. As Stephen Brookfield (1986:150) has noted, most adult learning is not acquired in formal courses but is gained through experience or through participation in an aspect of social life such as work, community action or family activities. Until recently, writers on adult education paid little attention to informal and incidental learning (see Marsick & Watkins 1991; Foley 1999). We are just beginning to study and act on these forms of learning. In what follows, I outline some of the directions we might take.

Learning is often unplanned, is often tacit, and may be constructive or destructive. The content of learning may be technical (about how to do a particular task); or it may be social, cultural and political (about how people relate to each other in a particular situation, about what their actual core values are, or about who has power and how they use it).

If there is learning there is also non-learning. People often fail to learn, or actively resist learning. Consider smokers, who persist with the habit in the face of overwhelming evidence of its harmfulness. Or countries, like Australia, that continue to clear marginal arid land for farming despite the knowledge that this is economically unviable and ecologically destructive. Or a university department that attributes falling enrolments to a shrinking pool of clients in the face of clear evidence of student dissatisfaction with the quality of teaching. (For an extended discussion of failure to learn, see Foley 2001: ch 5.)

If there is education there is also miseducation. Educators like to distinguish between propaganda and education, seeing the one as closed, manipulative and oppressive, and the other as open, democratic and emancipatory. While this distinction has its uses, adult educators also need to become aware of propaganda as a powerful and commonly used form of distorted and distorting education. Propaganda works on simplification: it appeals to fear, hatred, anger and envy. The resources available for corporate and government propaganda, and the scale of it, often make the efforts of adult educators appear puny.

Most learning episodes combine learning and non-learning, education and miseducation. The history of HIV-AIDS education illustrates this complexity.

When it emerged, HIV-AIDS was considered to be a short-term problem, largely confined to the gay community. Workers in the field assumed that medical treatment and education would quickly bring the virus under control. Early education programs were aimed at mass audiences and aimed to motivate individuals to change their behaviour. These programs often sought change by focusing on the negative consequences of practices such as unprotected anal intercourse or the sharing of intravenous needles. This 'social marketing' approach to HIV education, which has also been applied to issues such as road safety and reducing cigarette smoking, assumes that if sound information is transmitted to the 'target' audience in a convincing way then 'customers' or 'consumers' will behave in the way desired by the originator of the message (Foley 1997).

After initial apparent success in western countries in the 1980s it became clear that social marketing education was not reducing risk-taking behaviour. Reviewing their experience, workers and researchers generated a list of reasons why:

- HIV education often concentrated on providing information and neglected behaviour and the social environment that shapes it.
- Many HIV education programs relied on one-way communication.
- HIV education often treated the virus as a single issue, rather than as part of a wider set of problems including poverty, lack of political power and discrimination.
- Few HIV-AIDS services integrated education and treatment.
- Few HIV education programs tackled the distrust that many people feel towards government and science.
- Programs tended to focus on individual behaviour and to neglect the social and political factors that shaped that behaviour.

This last factor points to the basic problem with social marketing education: it simplifies a complex social process. As one HIV researcher put it, 'sexuality and drug use are complicated behaviours, deeply rooted in cultural, social, economic and political ground' (Freudenberg 1990,

p. 591). Another HIV activist/researcher, Bruce Parnell (1996 a & b), articulated the problem more arrestingly. We must, he said, acknowledge the
tension in all gay men, between their rational understanding that unprotected anal sex can lead to HIV transmission, and their desire for this
'warm, moist and intensely human' experience. Educational programs
that simply focus on the mechanics of safe sex, whether it be condoms
themselves or negotiating their use, suppress this tension. The result is
that the tension is buried, and men practice unsafe sex anyway, some
frequently, others less frequently, but all of them, probably, sometime.

Only by reversing this suppressed tension, Parnell argued, by surfacing and discussing the conflict between reason and desire in gay men,
could real education take place. To achieve this, HIV educators need
to use dialogue, not teaching. Educators should see themselves not as
experts bringing answers but as a partner who seeks to act as a catalyst,
prompting and facilitating discussions which will enable gay men to
explore their own experiences, learn from them and make more
informed choices.

In taking this position, Parnell and other HIV educators aligned themselves, often unknowingly, with adult education forms and traditions that
contributors to this book discuss at length. But for too long, too many
practitioners and scholars have failed to grasp the complex, contextual
and often contested nature of adult education and learning. As a professional field, adult education and training has concentrated on developing
practitioners' core skills (teaching/group facilitation, program development) and their knowledge of the psychology of adult learners. As the
field has developed, specialist knowledge-bases have emerged: vocational
education, human resource development, distance education, radical and
popular education, organisational learning, public education. Some attention has also been paid to the history, philosophy and political economy
of adult education, and central issues like research, policy and equity.

All these issues are important and are discussed in this book. But
adult education, as a profession, a field of study and a social movement
could contribute much more. The chapters in this book address aspects
of this larger contribution. But first I need to say something about the
book's conceptual framework.

CONCEPTUAL FRAMEWORK

Because it treats such a diverse and complex field of human activity, this
book needs an organising principle—a coherent conceptual framework.

Practice and theory

I will begin with the distinction between theory and practice. Adult educators do things, and they think about them. When they do things they are engaged in practice; when they are thinking about their practice they are reflecting and theorising.

Theory (systematic thought) and practice (systematic action) are bound up together. One cannot exist without the other. But practitioners do not always act and think systematically. They often act and think rigidly and dogmatically. It is common, for example, for adult educators to have set value positions on teaching and favourite bundles of techniques, often acquired early in their careers and never subjected to rigorous evaluation. An important goal of this book is to encourage adult educators and trainers to critically examine their practice and theory, and to develop frameworks for understanding and acting on their work. Readers will be encouraged to reflect on practice situations, and to theorise.

To theorise is to attempt to make connections between variables, to explain outcomes, and to predict what will happen if particular courses of action are taken in the future. Theorising involves the application of concepts (i.e. systematic ideas) to experience. We can theorise well or badly—in ways that illuminate our experience and help us to act more effectively, or in ways that obscure connections and outcomes and lock us into ineffective action.

FRAMEWORKS

Each of us has a cognitive framework through which we understand the world. In our everyday lives we are bombarded with sense impressions. Our frameworks are filters which allow us to make sense of what we experience. They develop over the years: they change, or should change, as we have new experiences. Frameworks are made up of analytical constructs that help us summarise and systematise experience.

Developing your framework

To become more effective adult educators and trainers, we need to become more aware of and systematically develop our theoretical frameworks, the ways in which we understand and explain our work. We are usually so busy getting on with the job that we don't have time to look at our theories. We need to give ourselves time to do this—to

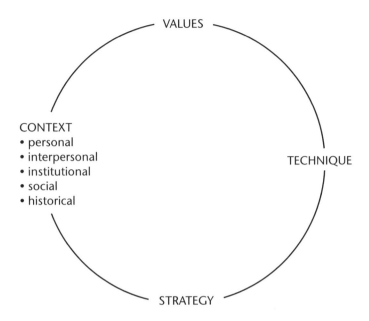

Figure 1.1: A framework for analysing adult education and training

think creatively. We need to seek out and use concepts and theories that strengthen our practice. We also need to identify and allow for our stereotypes and prejudices.

Building a framework is a lifetime job. Because the world is so complex, no-one is ever able to say she/he understands it all. But some frameworks are more useful—and ethical—than others.

A framework for analysing adult education

To be useful, a framework should be comprehensive and rigorous.

Our work is complex. In any situation or context that we work in we are operating at a number of levels at once. First, there are our own feelings and thoughts. Then there are our most intense and immediate interpersonal relations: how we get on with those with whom we live and work. There is also the structure and culture of the institution and/or community in which we work. Then there is the social dimension, the broader economic, political and cultural context of our work. Finally, there is the question of how things got to be the way they are. Here we are talking about the historical dimension.

If we are going to act effectively, we need to be aware of each of these levels or dimensions. But there is another issue: Why are we acting? According to what values? An important assumption of this framework, and of this book, is that anything educators do should be grounded in their values and based on the deepest possible understanding of the context of their work.

We should also act strategically. We should think of the whole campaign and the long-term goals, and ways of attaining them.

We should be technically proficient, too. Technique is important. We need to be sure of our proficiency, particularly in the core adult educator skills of teaching and group work, and program development.

FORMAL AND INFORMAL THEORY

It is useful to distinguish between formal and informal theory. Formal theory is 'organised (and) codified bodies of knowledge—embodied in disciplines and expressed in academic discourse'. Informal theory is the understanding that emerges from and guides practice (Usher 1987: 28-9).

As Usher (1989: 72) points out, 'theory cannot tell us how to practice . . . Most skilled activity does not involve the conscious application of principles . . . [it involves] such things as attending and being sensitive to the situation, anticipating [and] making ad hoc decisions, none of which would be possible if we had to stop and find the appropriate theory before we acted. The question for the practitioner is not "what rules should I apply" but "how ought I to act in this particular situation" ' (Usher & Bryant 1989: 82). Theorising about adult education should therefore be grounded in an understanding of practice and of how adult educators think about their practice (i.e. their informal theories). These informal theories should be tested and reviewed through formal theory. In this way formal theory can challenge and deepen the commonsense understandings we draw from our everyday work experience.

The formal/informal theory distinction can be augmented by the notions of tacit knowledge and reflection. Polanyi argues that some things we 'just know': we have knowledge, which we use, but we do not know it as knowledge; it is buried, unarticulated, implicit. Polanyi, and others, maintain that it is both possible and useful to make tacit knowledge explicit (Grundy 1987: 28-9). Through reflection, we can become aware of our implicit knowledge, our informal theories (Schön 1983; Boud, Keogh & Walker 1985). We can then analyse these understandings

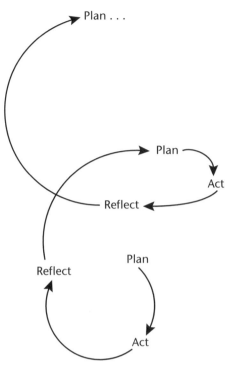

Figure 1.2: A framework for analysing adult education and training

and theories and modify and expand on them through reading, discussion and further reflection.

The notion of informal theory connects with Schön's (1983) concept of 'reflection-in-action'. Schön problematises practice by seeing it as a world of ill-defined problems where ends are often not known in advance. He says that practice situations are confused and tricky and the practitioner has to 'feel' his way through them in a thoughtful way. Through reflection, the practitioner brings to the surface the implicit and tacit knowledge in the action.

Seen in this way, professional work is a cycle, or spiral, of action and reflection. The practitioner acts, reflects on the action and, learning from the reflection, plans new action (Figure 1.2). This, at least, is the theory. Contextual factors, and the rigid mindsets of many practitioners, mean the plan–act–reflect cycle is often interrupted. Nevertheless, a conception of theory and practice that emphasises their mutual dependence is more useful than one that sees theory as prior to practice.

PARADIGMS

In his 1970 book, *The Structure of Scientific Revolutions*, Thomas Kuhn argued that in any science, in any era, a particular conceptual framework or paradigm is dominant. This paradigm defines the boundaries of 'normal science': that is, it defines how knowledge is constructed and how scientists think about scientific problems. In this view there is no pure or objective knowledge: knowledge can be talked about only in relation to a particular social context and particular values (see Carr & Kemmis 1986: 71-5; Usher & Bryant 1989: 14-23).

Kuhn's notion of paradigms was quickly adopted by social scientists, who argued that in the social sciences a number of competing paradigms can exist at the same time. These different paradigms are incompatible: they have such different assumptions about what they are explaining that no agreement is possible (Usher & Bryant 1989: 20). Furthermore, although mutually incompatible paradigms can exist side by side, at any one time a particular paradigm is likely to be dominant and others subordinate.

Education as a science

Behind different schools of thought in education or any other professional field there are radically different views of how knowledge is discovered and used. One view is that knowledge is constructed scientifically. According to this approach, educational knowledge can and should be developed in the same way that knowledge is built in the natural sciences. Knowledge is said to be objective, capable of being discovered empirically, in accordance with the following procedure:

1. State the problem.
2. Formulate a hypothesis.
3. Select research methods.
4. Collect data.
5. Analyse the data.
6. Interpret the data.
7. Reformulate the hypothesis.

This approach aims gradually to discover the 'truth' about the world, the way the world 'really' is. An application of this approach in education is to attempt to uncover the 'rules' of teaching through systematic observation and experiment (see chapter 5).

This 'scientific' approach is supposed to be both rigorous and practical: rigorous because the experimental method enables systematic and controlled research, which allows knowledge claims to be continually modified and refuted; practical because by discovering, for example, what 'actually' goes on in classrooms, teachers will be better able to control classroom behaviour.

The scientific, instrumental, technical or positivist (as it is variously known) approach to education as a field of practice and study was dominant during the first half of the 20th century. But in recent years it has come increasingly under challenge on intellectual, ethical and political grounds. (For further discussion of these issues, see Usher & Bryant 1989: 10–13; Carr & Kemmis 1986: 51–70; Reason & Rowan 1981.)

The interpretive paradigm

It is now generally agreed that in education, in addition to the 'scientific' or positivist framework, there are two other paradigms: the interpretive (sometimes called communicative, practical, humanist, reformist, liberal or progressive, or a mixture of these terms); and the critical (variously named emancipatory, transformative, strategic, socially critical, liberatory, radical or revolutionary). The interpretive paradigm sees knowledge as both subjective and socially constructed; its fundamental assumption is that different individuals understand the world differently. In education and other social activities, it is argued, it is futile to try to discover universal laws. It is more useful to study the different ways people make sense of situations, through language and other symbolic systems. Interpretivists maintain that the way individuals make meanings is not purely subjective or idiosyncratic. The focus in the interpretive framework is on the interaction of self and social structure and culture. It is by studying these interactions that we can come to understand how people make sense of, and act on, the world. There is often a strong emphasis in this framework on communication, on how people's interactions are mediated through language and other symbolic systems (Carr & Kemmis 1986: 83–94; Usher & Bryant 1989: 23–40).

It is possible that the interpretive paradigm is now dominant in Western adult education. Two of the most influential theoretical developments in adult and professional education of the past 50 years—self-directed learning, and reflection-on-action (see chapter 5)—are located within the interpretive paradigm. Both these concepts emphasise the way individuals make meanings and the capacity of individuals to become more proficient learners by 'learning how to learn': that is, by coming to understand and act on their own learning processes.

The critical paradigm

A third framework, the critical paradigm, emphasises the social context of knowledge and education. Critical theory focuses on the relationship of knowledge, power and ideology.

According to Jürgen Habermas, different ways of understanding the world represent different social interests. Habermas identifies three ways of knowing the world. The first of these he calls the technical or instrumental. Here the interest is in knowledge that will help people control nature and society. The second way of knowing is practical or interpretive. Knowledge of this kind serves a 'practical interest', in the sense that it facilitates practical judgement, communication and action by enabling people to understand their own and others' ways of knowing. According to Habermas and other critical theorists, the limitation of the interpretive framework is that it overemphasises the subjective dimension of knowing and learning, and pays insufficient attention to the ways in which our understandings are shaped by the structure and culture of the institutions in which we live and work.

Habermas argues that there is a third or emancipatory knowledge-interest, which arises from 'a basic human interest in rational autonomy and freedom'. This universal human desire causes people to demand 'the intellectual and material conditions in which non-alienated communication and interaction can occur'. This emancipatory drive means that people need both subjective knowledge (i.e. understanding of their own and others' processes) and social knowledge (i.e. understanding of political, economic and cultural processes).

According to Habermas, critical theory takes us beyond the relativism of the interpretive framework, which simply helps us understand that different people see things differently, and helps us realise that our understandings are socially constructed, often in distorted ways. Such distorted understandings, critical theorists argue, can be systematically exposed, explained and eliminated through a process called ideology critique. This notion of critical and emancipatory theory and practice has been influential in adult education over at least the past century (Carr & Kemmis 1989: 137).

The strength of the critical paradigm lies in its recognition of the connections between theory, ideology and power relations. For example, if we are to understand the radical changes currently taking place in workplace education around the world, we certainly need to understand the ideas behind these changes, which are now part of educational discourse. But we also have to understand the historical and social context of these ideas, the political and economic dynamics that have led to workplace education becoming the major current issue in adult education in most countries (see chapters 7, 8, 13 and 14).

CRITICAL THEORIES AND ADULT EDUCATION

For the past 50 years adult education theory in the English-speaking world has been dominated by the US literature. The overwhelming majority of US adult education scholars work within the positivist and/or the interpretive paradigms. Critical scholarship is growing, but it continues to be marginalised in the US adult education academy. Further, US critical scholars tend to work with a theory that emphasises culture, ideology and discourse rather than politics and economics. In other parts of the world, including Europe and Latin America, there is a much more developed body of critical adult education scholarship, much of it springing from the work of activist adult educators. This tradition of activist scholarship, together with the more progressive aspects of interpretive adult education scholarship, informs this book.

SOME THEMES

This book rests on a model of professional education that centres on practitioners' concerns and thinking. I have just outlined some of the characteristics of this approach. Andrew Gonczi discusses it more fully in chapter 2. Practitioners, he says, learn by acting and reflecting. Professional and vocational education should help practitioners understand themselves as actors and learners. It should be seen as an apprenticeship, an educational process in which practitioners learn to exercise judgement and act by participating in a community of practice. It should be work-based and cross-disciplinary. It requires a new relationship to be negotiated between educational institutions and work organisations.

Gonczi argues that this new model of professional and vocational education rests on an activist and holistic conception of learning. We learn by doing, and learning engages our intellects, bodies and emotions. This conception of learning frees professional education from the longstanding Western conception that separates body and mind and sees the latter as a container to be filled with knowledge by experts. It allows the focus of professional and vocational education to shift from training the individual mind, to the social settings in which the individual becomes part of the community of practice. Gonczi discusses recent developments in neuroscience, knowledge management, cognitive science, learning theory and philosophy that support this new conception of learning.

Those of us who have long worked with the practitioner-centred approach to professional education can testify to its effectiveness. It enlivens professional education for a very obvious reason: it deals with the real world of professional practice. Gonczi's chapter provides an intellectual justification for this model. The second part of the book (chapters 4, 5 and 6) takes a pluralist and contextual approach to understanding adult learners, teaching adults and program development. These chapters address practitioners who daily negotiate complexity, giving them alternative ways of understanding the core knowledge and skills of their profession. As Tara Fenwick and Mark Tennant suggest in chapter 4, readers should approach these different theories and techniques with an open mind and judge them on their fit with experience, intellectual coherence and potential effectiveness.

We can add a fourth criterion, 'ethical and political implications'. Every technique you use, every theory you employ, has moral and political effects. For example, if I see learners as containers to be filled with knowledge, I will ignore their experience, knowledge and wisdom. The oppressive and wasteful effects of this 'diffusionist' mindset are legion: bored and alienated students, failed projects in fields such as family planning, religious education, agricultural extension and health education. Crude versions of this mindset underpin colonialism and patriarchy; subtler versions underlie most contemporary management and workplace change theories.

Critical educational theory alerts us to the moral and political implications of educational interventions. It does so with an emancipatory intent. It is interested in learning and education that frees people from exploitation and oppression, and helps them develop their capacities and take control of their lives. It focuses on collective educational efforts in community and worker organisations, social action and social movements.

Critical educational scholarship is strongly represented in this book. Nelly Stromquist (chapter 3) details the emancipatory educational efforts of three Latin American women's organisations. From these empirical accounts she concludes that emancipatory education flourishes in informal settings and requires a critical pedagogy, attentive to power relations and identity formation. Mike Newman and Joce Jesson (chapter 15) elaborate on these themes, surveying various forms and histories of critical and emancipatory education and learning, and discussing issues these raise for educators. Through both conceptual analysis and case studies, Barbara Sparks and Shauna Butterwick (chapter 17) examine relationships of culture, social structure, and attempts to promote social equity through adult education. Chapters 5, 6 and 11 discuss critical as well as other approaches to teaching, program development and on-line learning. Peter Stephenson and Vernon Galloway (chapter 16) take a critical and emancipatory approach in their discussion of problem-based education. The emancipatory commitment of Keith Forrester and Paul McTigue is manifest in their case studies of work-based university education in the UK and informal education in an Australian workplace (chapter 13).

A longstanding negative effect of the US dominance of adult education scholarship has been an overemphasis on educational technique and the psychology of the individual learner. Much US adult education writing is asocial, decontextualised and abstract. In contrast, this book pays careful attention to the contextual and concrete nature of adult education and learning. Mike Welton, Bob Boughton and Lucy Taksa (chapter 7) show how critical histories of adult education, by uncovering buried traditions of learning and countering myth-making about golden eras of adult education, can help develop 'learning movements' 'which study and learn about the world as they work to change it'. By analysing developments in the global economy, and educational policy and practice in Europe and South Africa, Shirley Walters, Carmel Borg, Peter Mayo and Griff Foley (chapter 8) demonstrate that an understanding of the interrelationships of adult education, economics and politics can help adult educators find spaces for progressive work. Through a detailed discussion of the implementation of lifelong learning policy in Scandinavia and Australia, Kjell Rubenson and Francesca Beddie (chapter 9) show that adult education policy is shaped by history and contemporary economics and politics. A crucial message of Nancy Grudens-Schuck and John McIntyre (chapter 10) is that adult education research takes place in a context, and needs to make this context visible in order to create knowledge that is accurate and meaningful. They elaborate this point by discussing the diverse, messy and conflictual history of adult education research and several case studies. Bruce Spencer (chapter 11) and Damon Anderson, Mike Brown and Peter Rushbrook (chapter 14) develop strong contextual analyses of on-line learning and vocational education, fields dogged by decontextualised, technicist theory and practice. Laurie Field (chapter 12) develops a multilayered contextual analysis of organisational learning, taking account of power relations and unconscious dynamics in the workplace, as well as the shaping economic and political context.

2

THE NEW PROFESSIONAL AND VOCATIONAL EDUCATION

Andrew Gonczi

A NEW LEARNING PARADIGM

I argue in this chapter that the way most people think about learning is wrong. For over 2000 years it has been assumed that learning is concerned with the process of individual minds being provided with ideas and that these ideas are the basis of individual competence. This conception rests on a false mind/body dichotomy. I believe that the old learning paradigm needs to be replaced by a new one that links learners to the environment in which learning takes place. Such a learning concept takes account of the affective, moral, physical as well as the cognitive aspects of individuals, and insists that real learning takes place only in and through action. Most action takes place in a social setting such as a workplace or professional association meeting. Hence, there is usually a social aspect to learning.

Learning to become a competent and eventually expert professional can occur only through acting on the world in ways that enhance the capacity to make judgements—presumably over the life span.

CONCEPTIONS OF COMPETENCE

First I will outline how I conceptualise competence. When I and my colleagues undertook work on developing a framework for competency-based education in Australia some 13 years ago (Gonczi et al. 1990), we were drawn into a fierce policy debate. The Australian government had decided that all vocational education should become competency-based, without any real idea of what that might mean—except that education needed to be based on outcomes rather than inputs. What evolved was a highly reductionist and behaviourist concept of competence, on the British model. In education for technicians and tradesmen there were attempts to design curriculum based entirely on an analysis of the various things that they had to do. The essence of each task, it was believed, would be revealed as it was broken down into its various components. This led, in Alison Wolf's evocative phrase, to a 'never ending spiral of specification' (personal communication). Competency standards were designed for occupations consisting of literally many hundreds of fragmented tasks. Curriculum in vocational education was abandoned, and teachers were expected to set up practical situations that would enable students to be observed doing all the things specified in the occupational standards. They would then be ticked off as having achieved the competency. In effect, the tasks became the competency.

In case you are tempted to think that this technique was confined to vocational education, it is instructive to remember that there is a more than 30-year history of reductionist competency-based education in the professional development of teachers in the United States. To be registered in some states, teachers had to be observed undertaking thousands of tasks outlined in sets of 'standards'. This thinking has already done much damage to vocational education in Australia and Britain. Given the recent adoption of competency-based models in many Asian countries, it has the capacity to do further damage.

My colleagues and I conceptualised competence differently. We adopted a relational approach to competence—one which linked attributes of individuals (knowledge, skills, dispositions, values) to the demands and tasks and activities that individuals were undertaking in some aspect of their lives. Competence, we argued, can be inferred from performance and is not directly observable. While the performance of activities and tasks can be observed, the attributes that underline the performance are necessarily inferred. (The implications of this for assessment are profound, and I will come back to these briefly later.)

This concept of competence is best described as the 'integrated approach'.

This approach to competence is also relational, in that it brings together the general and the vocational, the generic and the specific. It posits that the performance of individual tasks and activities rests on more general capacities, such as reasoning and making judgements, as well as specific knowledge and individual dispositions. In this conception there is no dichotomy between specific competencies and key competencies: the capacity to perform specific activities will always entail some combination of knowledge/skills/dispositions/values which when analysed almost always looks like some combination of generic or key competencies. Another way of describing the approach is as holistic. I mean by this that the capacity to be successful in the world, to undertake activities competently, requires people to bring together a range of attributes in the particular context in which they find themselves.[1]

While these ideas have some influence in some higher education courses in Australia, the reductionist view of competence remains the norm.

APPRENTICESHIP

Recent research and scholarly work in a range of seemingly unrelated areas (neuroscience, artificial intelligence, knowledge management, learning theory and philosophy) is now pointing in the same direction, and undermining much of what educators believe: that competence (in jobs, professions, and life more generally) depends on the prior understanding of foundational knowledge codified in the various disciplines. I believe we should accept that the best way to prepare people for occupations and professional practice, and more generally for successful life, is through some form of apprenticeship—an educational process in which the exercise of judgement and the ability to act in the world emerge out of the complex of interactions to be found in a community of practice. The interactions combine cognitive, emotional and bodily processes in the social and cultural setting of the workplace or other social settings. That is, real understanding and competence is essentially a result of social rather than individual activities. While I think this argument has implications for general education in schools (via, for example, a 'cognitive' apprenticeship), I will confine myself here to vocational and professional education.

If my argument stands, the implications for education and work practice are profound. It will mean a need to embed much professional and vocational education in workplaces and other sites of practice. For that part of the educational experience that remains in formal institutions it will mean the growth of cross-disciplinary teaching, problem-based approaches, project work, use of portfolios to gather evidence of competence and so on. There will be extensive clinical and practical experiences, which will be at the very core of any educational program. It will also mean far more elaborate induction programs for new recruits to professions/occupations, with greater obligations on professions/industry associations/workplaces to participate in professional education through coaching and mentoring programs, in association with formal institutions.

LINEAGES

Western educational thinking descends in a direct line from the ancient Greeks through the Enlightenment to the present day. Aristotle distinguished between different types of knowledge. The first is that which is universal and theoretical (which has since been called propositional knowledge, or knowing *that*). The second is knowledge that is instrumental and practical (and context-bound); this has been characterised as knowing *how,* which is mostly tacit and not amenable to expression in language. His third category is knowledge that is related to practical wisdom. Each of these was seen as having independent existence and a different value, the highest being accorded to the theoretical. This thinking, and that of Plato, has had a powerful influence ever since. It is the basis of many of the dichotomies that underpin contemporary educational thought: mental versus manual, theoretical versus practical, mind versus body. The high (or low) point of the mind/body dichotomy is of course the work of René Descartes, who envisaged the mind and body as completely separate. 'I think, therefore I am', Descartes' famous phrase, suggests a thinking, disembodied mind contemplating the world but not involved in it. Descartes' disembodied mind has also had a powerful influence on Western views about the nature of the mind. It has led to what Bereiter and Scardamalia (1996) have termed a 'folk theory of mind'—a belief in society in general, and among educational practitioners in particular, that the mind is akin to a container. In this account, knowledge is thought of as discrete facts, beliefs and ideas: that is, specifiable objects stored in the brain and used as appropriate. The aim of general education in this conceptualisation of the mind is to fill it with appropriate facts, beliefs and ideas and to provide means of accessing them.

In vocational/professional education, while there is greater attention paid to general lessons learnt from practice, the assumption is still that students will be able to acquire and use facts and ideas derived largely from the codified knowledge of the disciplines ('theory') to solve practical problems when they face them. It is assumed that universal, general and timeless theories will provide the basis for practice and competence. There will obviously be differences between educators about what knowledge needs to be inculcated in students, how much time needs to be spent on these ideas and theories, how much on beliefs and so on. But until recently there has been little questioning of the underlying assumptions about the nature of the mind and the need to fill it with knowledge. Where better to do this than the lecture hall and classroom, where those educators who have distilled the universal can pass it on to students uninterrupted by the distractions of the world? Many educators, even in vocational areas, have felt it was enough to let students practise and then apply these objects-in-the-mind at the end of their courses.

DEVELOPMENTS IN KNOWLEDGE

I now survey developments in knowledge which involve a convergence of five intellectual areas and suggest that this conception of knowledge and education needs to change. These are:

- new concepts of knowledge and knowledge management;
- advances in neuroscience;
- developments in cognitive sciences (including genetics, which challenges prevalent ideas of human nature);
- developments in learning theory (particularly the development of a social theory of learning); and
- revival of some philosophical arguments.

New concepts of knowledge and knowledge management

As noted, education in vocational/professional areas has begun to change in recent years. Clinical experiences/practicums have expanded, joint appointments between universities and external organisations have been made, cooperative programs have expanded. Vocational teachers and university lecturers teach (or coach and mentor) in workplaces, not just institutional classrooms. One of the main reasons for this at the higher education level has been the increasing recognition that the creation and production of knowledge is spread across society. While philosophers have been writing about similar matters for many decades (Whitehead 1967), the widespread recognition of this fact appears to have been influenced by the publication of *The New Production of Knowledge* (Gibbons et al. 1994), which focused on research in the sciences and technologies. This book's influence can be explained by the fact that it alerted academics to the extent and nature of research outside the universities.

In brief, Gibbons and his colleagues argue that there are now two distinct modes of knowledge production in developed societies, which they term mode 1 and mode 2 knowledge. Mode 1 is knowledge of the discipline-based type typically produced in universities. Mode 2 is referred to as socially distributed knowledge. It is the knowledge of application and is produced in workplaces and organisations outside the university sector. It is output-driven, specific and transient. It uses methods that might not be seen as legitimate when measured against the traditional university criteria for knowledge production, but it is valuable in economic terms. Much of the knowledge is also tacit and by its nature transdisciplinary.

Not surprisingly, given the view of knowledge inherited from the ancient Greeks, the university sector as a whole has viewed the development of mode 2 knowledge with suspicion (though it must be said that a number of staff in some of the universities have welcomed it). Equally suspicious, for the opposite reason, are governments and industry, which feel that mode 1 knowledge does not serve the wider society in its need for the higher levels of knowledge demanded by the competitive global economy.

The net result has been that universities have on the whole been prepared to accommodate these new developments and to accept that they need to take them into account in planning their courses. All universities in Australia, for example, now have a set of key competencies (often called 'Graduate Attributes') which their courses are supposed to cover. Many, indeed most, of these competencies relate to mode 2 knowledge, and presumably can be developed only in some sort of practical or applied context. The Australian Council of Educational Research has even designed a written test to see how successful universities are in this endeavour. But it appears that universities have made these changes without altering their assumptions about the *primacy* of universal and timeless knowledge (foundational-disciplinary knowledge) and that the minds of students are formed, *in essence*, by the inculcation of this kind of knowledge. There is often a lack of coherence in professional courses, where on the one hand there is an increase in the amount of practical experience students undertake but a stubborn insistence, on the other, of the importance of the teaching of disciplinary knowledge—most often by transmission methods and assessed by formal examinations. Methods for developing the knowledge of application are rarely made explicit and rarely assessed in a rigorous fashion.

The growth in the volume of *both* mode 1 and mode 2 knowledge and the reduction in the 'half-life' of knowledge has presented universities with another problem, however: how to educate students to learn and relearn and also to manage the knowledge of the organisations they will work in. If it is true that mode 2 knowledge is increasing and that more and more of the work of the professional is concentrated on knowledge products and services, as it is widely claimed (see OECD, various publications), then knowledge management becomes an increasingly important part of professional preparation. How do universities teach students to become effective knowledge managers and lifelong learners in the new world of mode 2 knowledge? One reaction has been for some university academics to reassert the value of mode 1 knowledge: in a rapidly changing world only timeless universal knowledge is important, it is argued. But given the dissatisfaction with old forms of professional preparation this return to discipline theory-based knowledge is likely to further diminish the university in the eyes of the professions and wider society.

In Australia, in the technical and further education (TAFE) sector, given the national commitment to an industry-led system, there has been a boom in workplace-based courses, which suggests that this sector has embraced mode 2 knowledge. But there has been very little thinking about how learning occurs in this context and how a teacher or trainer might facilitate a student's learning. Often students are simply left to imitate the work of a colleague, and the only role of the trainer is to assess student competence.

Before we attempt to tease out the implications of mode 2 knowledge and its management for vocational and professional education, we need to turn to the second of the topics mentioned earlier, developments in neuroscience.

Advances in neuroscience

I make no claim to expertise in this area. However, a number of recent books by medical researchers and neuropsychologists have brought breakthroughs in brain research to the non-expert (Damasio 1996, 2000; Greenfield 1996; Edelmann 2001; Goldberg 2001). I believe these developments will have significant implications for our understanding of learning, though much research needs to be done before we can articulate them with any confidence.

One of the major research findings is that reasoning and emotion are vitally connected. Investigations of patients with particular types of brain damage, which take away their capacity to experience emotion but leave intact cognitive processes, demonstrate that while they can discuss things and seemingly are functioning cognitively they are unable to plan for their personal futures: that is, they lose their capacity for successful action in the world. It is true that emotion can have a negative impact on a person's capacity to reason, but in its absence humans cannot reason at all well. Emotion is governed by bodily changes—what Damasio (2000) refers to as the somatic-marker thesis—which are linked by various brain processes. Feelings are the sensors for the match, or the lack of it, between the organism's genetic inheritance and the circumstances in which it finds itself—its environment. Thus emotion can be understood as a biological, evolutionary process. It seems clear that reason depends on many brain systems, including the lower levels that regulate bodily functions. So there is a chain of functions in which the body is intimately involved and which culminates in reasoning, decision making and creativity.

The mind exists in and for the integrated holistic organism and not outside it. Hence, as Damasio puts in neatly, rather than the Cartesian 'I think, therefore I am', in fact we *are* (and have become through evolution) and therefore we think. If it is accepted that the mind is a complex system, in which both the emotions and intellect have been shaped by evolution, the implications for education could be profound, although at the present stage of our knowledge of the mind and brain this is highly speculative.

Pinker (2002) argues that we are equipped with certain intuitions and logics, which have developed through our genetic inheritance—and most likely through the development of our brains in solving problems in our environments. The result is that from a very young age we have a number of intuitions about the world and how it works, what he calls intuitive physics, psychology, engineering and so on. These ways of knowing, while they were suitable for the world of our ancestors, are not adequate for the world we live in. Much modern physics, for example, is counterintuitive.

One implication of this is that in education we need to concentrate on what we are innately bad at. This view goes against both traditional views of the child as an empty vessel to be filled and the more modern constructivist views that learners will be able to solve problems in spontaneous ways through cooperation with others. There will need to be a process of some unlearning before new learning can take place. It is also possible that the logics and intuitions we do possess can be harnessed in the learning of new knowledge.

Developments in cognitive science

Recent developments in artificial intelligence (AI) parallel the theorising and experimentation in brain research. Rumelhart et al. (1986) have established a new paradigm for this research, which they call 'connectionism'. This has moved AI away from a focus on data storage and the logical manipulation of symbols (or at least relegated it to secondary importance) and replaced it with a focus on how the brain has been used for survival as part of a biological system. Another way of describing this is that the old focus was inspired by the 'mind as container' metaphor while the new one sees the mind as a holistic pattern detector.

The battle between these two strands of AI research need not concern us here (they are detailed in Clark 1997). The essential difference, however, is instructive. The old research concentrates on coding items of knowledge and developing rules to manipulate them: it takes artificial situations, such as chess playing, and builds in rules based on precoded information. The new research, by contrast, attempts to model a brain prepared for action. So, for example, robots have been designed to react to their environment without the precoding of information of the old AI. These new robots have sets of circuits working in parallel, and each system receives information from other systems and passes it on. The result is that the robots are able to tolerate imperfect data, are able to complete patterns, and are fast at doing it. They use their environment to solve problems.

To summarise, the old cognitive science conceptualises memory as retrieval from the container. It assumes that cognition is centralised, that the body is outside this process and that the environment is a problem to be overcome. Recent research sees memory as the recreation of patterns in a decentralised way across the brain. The environment is an active resource which helps us to solve problems, and the body is part of the computational loop (Clark 1997). To clarify, it is not that patterns are stored in the mind: rather, they are in the environment, and our brain interacts with the environment to produce the appropriate pattern—that is, to act intelligently/competently.

This account of the way the mind works is highly controversial. While all cognitive scientists agree that the brain works through a series of immensely complex neural networks, as Pinker (2002) points out, the question is whether this 'generic network theory' can explain all human psychology. His conclusion is that it cannot: we need to link neural network theory to the innate complexity of the mind developed through natural selection.

The implications of this new research for professional and vocational education are profound. The connectionist perspective challenges the traditional view of knowledge held by most educators—that there is a distinction between knowing *that* and knowing *how*. Both forms of knowledge are better understood as part of a holistic process of pattern recognition. What it suggests is a quite different kind of mind from the one conjured up by the container metaphor. It is a mind that does not contain knowledge but is knowledgeable (Bereiter & Scardamalia 1996, Bereiter 2000). It also provides us with a framework for thinking about the perennial problem of professional education, the theory–practice gap. It suggests that the old dichotomies between thinking and doing, mind and body, are fundamentally wrong, and that as a consequence we need to rethink our assumptions about how to produce capable practitioners. The most important of these old assumptions is that acquiring propositional knowledge enables practitioners to transfer knowledge and skills over many contexts. This is not to suggest that we abandon codified knowledge but that we must rethink its connection to the world of practice and the tacit knowledge that develops through acting in and on the world.

Knowledge, learning and practice

Over recent years there has been a great deal of interest in what has been called situated learning. Lave and Wenger (1991) and Chaiklin and Lave (1993), in a number of studies of learning through apprenticeship-type situations, postulate that knowledge is built through participating in a group that already has competence and are willing to allow the learner to become, progressively, part of the core of their community. This progressive participation involves the learner developing an identity as a member of the group. Lave and Wenger's studies of formal and informal apprenticeships in a number of countries show that apprentices actually generate new knowledge rather than just follow others. They generate their own tacit knowledge, which is fused with work and with a changing identity. Learners are engaged in a process of constructing their world. Learning to do is part of learning to become and to belong (OECD 2000a). This is a social theory of learning in stark contrast to traditional accounts, which emphasise the individual learning of propositional knowledge and assume that this forms the basis of professional competence (e.g. see Stokes & Baer 1977). This has been the assumption underpinning learning transfer theory, though it needs to be said that some authors now distinguish between 'near' and 'far' transfer (Solomon & Perkins 1989; Cornford 2002), and many now confine their arguments to examples of near transfer and the need for particular activities to encourage this (e.g. Cornford & Athanasou 1995).

Situated learning theory argues, by contrast, that transfer is the knowledge developed by acting/doing in a range of contexts or communities of practice, where each time the learner creates new knowledge. This approach does not imply that the learner can learn only by observation and emulation. The work of Vygotsky (1987) and Engeström (1995) suggests it is possible to provide ways of enhancing the motivated learner in these social settings by way of scaffolding, modelling, mentoring and coaching. Engeström suggests the need to introduce contradiction—for the teacher/mentor/coach to design experiences in social settings that will lead to genuine transformation, which move learning beyond the immediate context and beyond limited intuitive understandings. For the learner it will be a process of knowledge building, of constructing and testing theories in real settings, a process that leads to genuine understanding.

This situated perspective on learning is now widely accepted by those writing in the area of knowledge management in workplaces. Zack (1999), for example, discusses the capacity of various organisations to expropriate the tacit knowledge built up by individuals and groups working in them (the community of practice), and considers this to be the fundamental driver of business success in knowledge-based industries.

Philosophical arguments

Hager (2001) outlines a philosophical argument for a new paradigm of learning by drawing on the ideas of a number of philosophers. He argues that they all support the notion that learning is based on the development of capacities that go far beyond the cognitive. A major conclusion of his recent work is that knowledge as integrated in judgements is the capacity to act in and on the world, and that the acquisition of knowledge (and this includes knowhow of various kinds as well as propositional knowledge) alters both the world and the learner who is part of the world.

He concludes that the learning of propositions (the old learning paradigm) is not irrelevant but is part of a wider process of learning, which becomes integrated/holistic through the exercise of judgements in the world. This is another way of saying that the development of competence is a holistic activity involving individuals and groups acting in and on the world in a cognitive-affective-somatic fashion.

A NEW CONCEPTION OF COMPETENCE

It seems to me that the literature in a number of fields is converging. Cognitive science, neuroscience and situated constructivism shift the focus in learning theory from the individual to individuals acting and learning in specific social contexts. The findings of these and the other disciplines I've discussed are complementary. As St Julian (2000) points out, connectionism, with its emphasis on pattern completion, parallels the real-world capacity of humans to work in the 'swamp' of everyday reality (Schön 1987), with its incomplete and even wrong data. But connectionism has problems of its own, specifically an inadequate explanation for the stability and replicability of knowledge—that is, the capacity to use knowledge beyond the immediate context. This gap is, however, filled by situated learning theory and activity theory, with its emphasis on scaffolding and modelling in the community of practice, which enable the individual to apply knowledge beyond the immediate context. The importance of the combination of the new neuroscience and cognitive sciences on the one hand and situated learning on the other is that it provides us with a way of looking at so-called 'generic/key competencies'. People need to be given the opportunity to be immersed in the world in various contexts, with some scaffolding to help them test their intuitive theories and to make judgements. None of this is to deny the role of institutions in developing and teaching propositional knowledge, but the development of key competencies requires more than that.

We need to accept that much of what makes people competent, resourceful, adroit (i.e. what makes them knowledgeable) is largely tacit, instinctive, intuitive, difficult to pin down and certainly can't be located in objects stored in the mind. Such things as number sense, taste, artistic appreciation, sensitivity, communication and creativity are not dealt with satisfactorily in educational organisations or programs. But they need to be brought into the mainstream (Bereiter 2000).

We also need to accept that learning is developed through doing, through acting in the world. Learning is a process that involves the emotions and the formation of identity through adapting to the world in which the person is situated—in the communities of practice in which we work and live. The challenge is to shift the focus of professional and vocational education, from training the individual mind, to the social settings in which the individual becomes part of the community of practice; from facts and rules stored in the brain until we need to use them, to enacting knowledge through activity; from a conception of humanity centred exclusively on the brain, to a wider conception in which humans are seen as embodied creatures embedded in the social world.

TEACHING AND LEARNING KEY COMPETENCIES

Before focusing briefly on the implications of my argument for the learning of key competencies, I will provide some empirical evidence of how teachers in the vocational sector in one country have attempted to organise student learning for these competencies.

Over a four-year period in 1993–97, the Australian government provided a great deal of money to teachers in both the general and vocational education sectors to pilot methods for teaching and learning the Australian version of the key competencies (collecting, analysing and organising information, communicating ideas and information, planning and organising activities, working with others in teams, using mathematical ideas and techniques, solving problems, using technology). There were some 80 action research projects in general and vocational education, and at the end of the trial period two meta-analyses to summarise findings in each sector were commissioned (Hager, Moy & Gonczi 1997).

The meta-analyses concluded that:

- The best examples of teaching and learning were those where teachers encouraged active independent learning in students, especially in ways that simulated later life contexts. These projects included such things as work experience programs, group projects, discovery methods in classes and development of portfolios.
- The better projects were those that integrated the key competencies in the teaching of other material, rather than attempting to teach them as stand-alone entities.
- There seemed to be more success in student outcomes when the key competencies were made explicit, even when they were integrated in other activities.
- In many instances it was not possible to separate the key competencies in the process of teaching and learning.

Educational implications

The most obvious implication is that teaching, learning and research in universities and vocational colleges should have close ties with the world of practice. This means that educational institutions must develop a broader view of both knowledge and professional practice. Although there are some similarities between all forms of knowledge, there are also significant historical differences between the knowledge traditionally valued in universities and the knowledge produced by the largely informal learning that occurs during the course of professional practice. A new professional education would need to overcome these differences. I will concentrate here on professional education in universities, as this is where the problems are starkest.

As I mentioned earlier, there have long been attempts to link universities to the professional world. These include professional placements, cooperative education arrangements and clinical/practicum/field placements. In addition, the workplace is both a learning resource and a site of learning. This is reflected in the wide use of such pedagogical tools as negotiated learning contracts and work-related projects.

But the new professional education needs to go further. It will be concerned with the workplace not merely as a site of valid knowledge production and transmission but as one that is equally valid to institutional knowledge production.

What would the learning principles for a new professional education and their implications for course design/pedagogy be? Let me present four, which are an adaptation of Hager's principles (2001):

1. Experience of professional practice is essential to the acquisition of professional competence.
2. Professional practice requires a broader range of knowledge and performance capacity than is covered by the traditional disciplines. This needs to be reflected in the desired outcomes of the courses offered.
3. Student learning progresses from dealing with clearcut problems having a single correct solution to dealing with situations in which the problem is unclear and in which there is no single correct solution. This suggests a problem-based approach for the institutional component of all professional courses. There is no place for a transmission approach to learning. This does not mean that traditional disciplinary knowledge cannot be introduced but that it should be taught in such a way that it can be applied and where theories that

people hold intuitively can be subject to rigorous testing. As Popper suggests, theories cannot be understood until they can be reinvented or reconstructed and tried out.

4. Learners must develop generic capabilities and dispositions (including the capacity for ongoing learning as the nature of their professional practice evolves and expands) that will enable them to deal with a range of complex situations, and to do so in ways congruent with a set of moral principles. These capabilities are best developed through the knowledge building undertaken during work in a community of practice. There will be a need for professional coaches to work with students in workplace settings, professionals who with the help of the university staff can design the scaffolds and contradictions that will lead to knowledge building.

So what should the balance between the university and the workplace in the provision of professional education be?

One form would be apprenticeship models for undergraduate education and postgraduate work-based learning degrees. An example of the former is the change in the UK to teacher education in which two-thirds of the degree is undertaken in a school under the supervision of professional colleagues.

In another form, called 'work-based learning' in Australia and the UK, learners design learning programs around their work responsibilities. Such degrees already exist in a number of UK universities and will be further developed through the fledgling University of Industry. At my own university we have a number of such degrees in their early stages with a couple of organisations—a large insurance company, and the State Department of Education and Training.

As Solomon (2000) points out, these learning arrangements are a three-way partnership between the work organisation, the learner and the university. The learning program is linked to the strategic goals of the organisation, while assessment and accreditation are the responsibility of the university. The learning opportunities found in such degrees are not contrived, but are real activities being undertaken in the workplace. For example, a school principal designs a quality assurance process for teaching and learning in his/her school, or an employee in the IT section of an organisation in the financial industry designs data warehouse architecture for a distribution program.

Learners undertake such projects under supervision. They also take subjects (or part-subjects) that are deemed suitable by the university and the learner. Advanced standing can be given for experience or for under-taking in-house courses. Assessments are typically based on performance, so the emergent paradigm of 'authentic assessment' is most suited to these awards.

Clearly these awards seek to build on Gibbons' mode 2 knowledge (although they can incorporate mode 1, too). These programs are specific and pragmatic on the one hand, though they also attempt to build the development of generic competencies into their design. They do this by providing learning opportunities in many contexts, in association with others, and with specific scaffolds built into the particular contexts.

It is desirable for universities to experiment with variations of these forms, across the continuum from totally institution based (although these would have to be largely problem-based to keep in step with the new theory of mind outlined earlier) through to completely workplace-based learning.

My preference is for programs where the majority of learning is undertaken in the workplace. Both practitioners and academics would design learning experiences. Such a model of professional education would require a different set of relationships between universities/professional associations and employers. Some examples of reasonably good relationships already exist: the professional year in accounting, cooperative programs and so on. But there needs to be something more—cooperation between the various parties, leading to work-based learning as a rich educative experience.

CONCLUSION

It will be obvious from the arguments presented in this chapter that I believe vocational and professional education should take place largely outside formal educational institutions, though these will still play a vital role. If we are to take seriously the development of key competencies in vocational and professional education, we need something of a revo-lution. Educators need to change their assumptions about learning, and employers and professional and industry associations need to recognise their central contribution to learning. Educational policy needs to encour-age partnerships, experimentation, and research on new pedagogies.

My argument also has important implications for lifelong learning. We need to embrace the idea of a learning society in which all social institutions are acknowledged to have a learning dimension and a respon-sibility for the growth and development of their members.

3

THE EDUCATIONAL NATURE OF FEMINIST ACTION

Nelly P. Stromquist

Feminism as a global movement emerged in response to concrete problems confronting women in their individual and collective lives. The first wave of the movement, from the mid-1800s to the beginning of the 1900s, sought basic rights for women, such as voting and education. In those days the emphasis was on gaining recognition for women as people who could make contributions to society as wives and mothers. The second wave of the movement, from the mid 1900s to the present, has been characterised by its demand for citizens' rights, independent of obligations to family. The contemporary movement seeks gender equality, but increasingly attached to it is a serious contestation of the social order and the concomitant need to redefine gender ideologies that, in setting separate notions of femininity and masculinity, constrain women.

There is no consensus on the form feminist activism should take. Groups bent on the attainment of parity seek active collaboration with the state to influence the formation of public policies. Critical feminists recognise the patriarchal forms of organisation and male supremacy that characterise many political institutions; they are less willing to see the state as a potential ally and consider, on the contrary, that resistance by women is a prerequisite for effective change. Yet other feminist groups are so concerned with the destruction of the heterosexual order that their approach is almost exclusively cultural. They prefer to work on issues such as representation, fluid identities and the questioning of binary categories, rather than on the practical issues of how current economic and social problems are addressed or alliances developed. Because of this diversity of problem definition and solution, feminist groups have not devised or advocated a particular model of public space and public discourse (Magno 2002).

Despite considerable heterogeneity, the women's movement is best understood as an attempt to introduce change from outside the centres of established political power. Its activities are carried out by persons with little power, whose legitimacy to represent others is often contested. The main source of their authority is not formal representation but resides in the attainment and transmission of new knowledge and the fostering of a new social vision. Education is a primary tool in this process. But until recently, activists and scholars paid little attention to the role of education in the women's movement.

In this chapter I will discuss educational work with poor women in Latin America through data collected from three case studies of women-led organisations: one in the Dominican Republic (CIPAF) and two in Peru (Manuela Ramos and Flora Tristan). I visited these organisations during a period of four years. These NGOs were selected because of their lengthy existence (each about 22 years), their clear institutional objectives, and their sustained performance in their selected areas of work. By focusing on NGOs that had existed for a long time I wanted to examine how feminist organisations have evolved, defined their objectives, developed strategies and, most importantly, used education as a means to carry out and attain their objectives.

The three NGOs vary in their approach to low-income women. CIPAF (Stromquist 2001) made the decision not to work in the direct provision of services to individual women; it chose, instead, to work with women's organisations by providing them with key skills and knowledge to strengthen their organisational performance and facilitate their political mobilisation. Manuela Ramos has followed a service approach, and has been constantly engaged in direct attention to individual women in aspects related to health, income generation and human rights (focusing on such issues as domestic violence). Flora Tristan also initially provided direct services to women in low-income neighbourhoods. Over time it has developed an organisational profile that seeks greater leverage on national public policies in such areas as democracy, human rights and sexual and reproductive rights, while maintaining a monitoring role of state responses to gender and democracy.

FEMINISM AND TRANSFORMATIVE ACTION

Feminism in Latin America remains true to its origins and its *raison d'être*: to assert the equal worth of women, and to struggle for equality and ultimately to promote a new social order. Reasons for this continuity can be understood first in the economic and political character of the countries, which face poverty and substantial degrees of inequality between the rich and the poor—inequalities that become greatly magnified when we look at gender issues in interaction with other social markers, such as social class, ethnicity and 'race'. Second, many of the Latin American feminists of the 1970s and 80s came from an experience with leftist political parties. This imprinted on them an enduring concern for the plight of less fortunate social classes. Third, the struggle of poor women for access to health, education, housing, work and other basic human rights is so evident that it has been a constant priority for feminist activism.

In Latin America, activists in the women's movement tend to be middle-class, usually with university education, generally in fields from the social sciences, a few from education and social work, and increasingly from such areas as medicine (to address sexual and reproductive health rights) and law (to consider the growing array of human rights that need protection). The women's movement, unlike any of the other new social movements, has not been characterised by engagement in physical confrontations with other groups, nor has it been the target of physical reprisals as has been the case with the ecological movement, the anti-war movement, indigenous-rights movements or the anti-neoliberal economic model movements.

The women's movement has relied mostly on creating anti-hegemonic consensus through non-formal education (NFE) (Stromquist 2001). At times it has relied on informal education (Foley 1999), by using its own media to convey an understanding of issues of importance to the women's movement and to raise awareness about the need for prompt collective or national government action. In a few instances, women's and feminist groups have also demonstrated against beauty contests, economic measures detrimental to the poorer sectors of society, and the existence of corrupt and authoritarian governments.

Unlike forms of collective action within indigenous movements, the women's movement seeks self-determination not in terms of territory but in terms of rights specific to women's welfare, ranging from control over their bodies (including protection against rape and domestic violence) to questions of access to economic, and social and political equality. Successful action for many women's groups increasingly means not just equal access to benefits and services offered by the state but also the creation of new services for women. For these groups, successful action means also the creation of new cultural understandings regarding roles, capabilities, and overall representations around masculinity and femininity.

In contrast with the prevailing postmodern discourse in industrialised countries, which tends to deny the centrality and validity of globalising categories such as 'society' and 'women', all three women-led NGOs in this study have taken a very concrete approach to the recognition of women as a social category and to the struggle for rights and benefits predicated on the specificity of being a woman. In general, postmodern ideas have had minimal impact on feminists in the Latin American region, in part because postmodernity has not proposed any particularly emancipatory project, although its ideas permit a complex and dynamic model for analysing social, economic and political relations.

The question of what constitutes transformative action has received considerable attention in the sociological and political literature. Some consider that transformation occurs when the state or the nature of the state has undergone substantial change. Others are inclined to see transformation as a more gradual accretion of progressive public policies and new social practices. Referring to marginalised groups, Keck and Sikkink see transformative success not in terms of how demands are processed within the politics of institutional representation but in terms of how they have destabilising effects on the 'dominant discourses and exclusionary practices' that operate in many societies. In their view, success involves 'producing new information and reframing old debates' in terms of what a particular problem means, the sites for contesting it, and the configuration of participants (1998: 11; see also Foley 1999; Mayo 1998; Schugurensky 2000).

REACHING LOW-INCOME WOMEN

As women tend to engage less in protest events, working with them implies recognising physical sites where they congregate on a regular basis or where they can be invited to attend. The place of work can be considered a suitable terrain to reach women; thus women-led NGOs have targeted women working in industrial firms and agricultural enterprises. Seeking to work with oppressed women, these NGOs have also targeted women working in domestic service as maids. Finally, they have sought to provide services to women in their marginalised communities.

Over time, women-led NGOs have learned that mixed-sex work places are difficult to reach because of opposition from or reluctance to help by male-dominated labour unions. CIPAF, for instance, found it possible to work with women agricultural workers only when they were organised in their own unions. Both Manuela Ramos and Flora Tristan sought initially to work with, among others, women in domestic service, but the dispersion of these women and the inability to secure a time at which they could meet regularly ended up producing studies about them rather than engaging them in direct political action.

The changing economic environment has also played a role in making access to women difficult. In CIPAF's Dominican Republic, the main sector of the economy is no longer agriculture but tourism. Approachable women are therefore now found not so much among rural workers but are working in hotels and seaside resorts in jobs with minimal possibilities to unionise. In the same country, free trade zones, where women work in large plants engaged mostly in garment manufacturing, also present obstacles to the organisation of women. Not only are the *maquiladora* firms very hostile to any unionisation attempts but, because of advances in production technologies, the factories now have much greater mobility than before, and are able to pick up and move across countries as well as across communities within the same country.

Feminists have also reached low-income women through mothers' clubs and the health centres. Women-led NGOs have often used mothers' clubs to provide women with feminist knowledge and information related to basic needs, but urgent economic needs in these communities have necessitated the provision of individual assistance along material lines, such as income-generation skills, micro-lending or legal services.

FEMINIST EDUCATION AND ACTION

From a feminist perspective, formal educational systems have limitations regarding their potential for transformative knowledge, as one of their key functions centres on the maintenance of social harmony and thus reinforces the status quo. In the case of education that progresses from primary to secondary levels, a predetermined curriculum casts aside knowledge that questions the status quo; moreover, students at that level are young and thus relatively unable to engage in transformative social action. In the case of higher education, professional and academic preparation often pushes aside considerations of more reflective and less instrumental knowledge. While formal education must be a target of social change, the fact is that education outside those structures regulated by credentials, exams and competitive selection currently offers the greatest possibility for the creation and transmission of transformative knowledge.

While an essential goal of the women's movement is the reduction of inequalities between men and women, this result cannot be obtained merely through demands for human rights. An important prerequisite to reaching the goal must be the women's self-identification as members of a specific group of disadvantaged persons. For this to occur, internal action (e.g. consciousness-raising and empowerment) must precede external action (e.g. pressuring the state). A limitation of human rights activism is that it is based on a juridical model of individual complaints against state agents for their denial of civic liberties. Brysk notes that this is a 'model singularly inappropriate for indigenous people's concerns; victims are often the community at large, violators include state and nonstate agents, and the violations combine denial of economic and cultural rights with more narrowly defined political coercion' (2000: 202). A similar argument can be extended to women, as the nature of gender problems permeates the entire society and the state does not emerge as a neutral adjudicator. Yet the human rights principle is key to the women's movement and a major source of global support. As Dorsey observes, 'The human rights framework is predicated on the principle that transnational linkages and global norms are essential for the protection of all human rights and could readily serve as an organizing principle upon which women's political claims could be advanced globally' (1997: 357). Women, consequently, need education, first, to find forms of personal and collective empowerment and, subsequently, to demand human rights. And the education that is most useful to them is that afforded by critical pedagogy, which is attentive to power relations and the role of conscious identity formation. Critical pedagogy plays a fundamental role in enabling women to examine taken-for-granted beliefs about the nature of their reality, the knowledge they have acquired, and the experience they have accumulated throughout the years.

The critical knowledge pursued by the women's movement is by nature comprehensive, as it must play a role in the construction of a new democratic order. Thus, it cannot be limited to a narrow set of subjects but rather must consider a wide-ranging set of personal events and understandings, as well as objective knowledge about the condition of women and men in various spheres of our social world. In consequence, the educational strategies of women-led NGOs show a careful balance between working for identity formation and pressing the state for redress. These strategies show also a powerful combination of following a predetermined curriculum and being responsive to local needs. All three NGOs treated here have a strong sense of the feminist knowledge they wish to convey to low-income women. At the same time, they have responded to requests for addressing household priorities such as access to credit, health facilities and even food.

The predetermined educational agenda of the women-led NGOs has centred on such topics as 'women and subordination' and 'feminist theory'. This content has been considered necessary for the development of women's collective identity, and for women understanding that there are problematic situations that can be transformed through collective action. CIPAF has approached the task of education by seeking agreements with individual women's groups to provide them with non-formal feminist education. According to a member of CIPAF: 'We discussed certain terms: types of courses to offer, schedules, instructional methodologies, but we did not negotiate our feminist content'. Not surprisingly, several groups rejected CIPAF's offer, but some of the most powerful women's organisations did agree to work with CIPAF. Education linked to knowledge that could be applied to political action in favour of women was not a proposal easily accepted. Several members of CIPAF recalled meeting with strong resistance to any feminist project, including those attempted by mixed-sex NGOs working along genuinely democratic lines. This rejection was observed in the reluctance of these NGOs to work on joint activities and, more concretely, in the vandalism of many of the posters that CIPAF had distributed and placed in strategic spaces.

THE ROLE OF NON-FORMAL AND POPULAR EDUCATION

As Schugurensky (2000: 516) notes, several features characterise popular education:

- a rejection of the political neutrality of adult education, recognising instead the connection between knowledge and power and between structure and agency, and the acknowledgement that adult education can play a role not only in reinforcing but also in challenging oppressive social relations;

- an explicit political commitment to work with the poor and the marginalised and to enable social movements to attain 'progressive' social and economic change;
- a participatory pedagogy that focuses on the collective, originates from the people's daily lived experience, and promotes a dialogue between popular knowledge and systematised (scientific) knowledge; and
- a constant attempt to relate education to social action, linking critical reflection to research, mobilisation, and organisational structures.

Dealing with poor women who, because of the sexual division of labour and their large share of domestic chores, family responsibilities and the community-support activities in which they engage, have little time and energy to attend educational programs, women-led NGOs have had to be very creative in designing educational interventions with high appeal, short duration and yet discernible impact. The most typical forms of intervention are *talleres* (workshops), very short and practical sets of activities (usually about three hours) around a specific subject. Other forms of non-formal education include *jornadas* (or day-long meetings around several issues) and *cursos* (regular meetings over several months). *Talleres* on such topics as domestic violence, women's right to land titles, reproductive and sexual rights, and political participation have been a means of transmitting knowledge about gender issues. These workshops have included discussion on the subordination of women, on the interplay between ideological force and material conditions, and on the intersection of gender, class, and ethnicity. They have also tackled the concrete problems of women in unions, political parties and community organisations.

The educational activities of the three NGOs have dealt with issues central to the awareness of women's problematic conditions in such areas as reproductive health, education, domestic relations, income and land tenancy—areas in which women are placed at the greatest socially constructed disadvantage vis-à-vis men. The skills provided by their courses include self-development, organisation, leadership and lobbying. Working intuitively on a dialogical education, the NFE programs conducted by the women-led NGOs have fostered the construction of articulate and democratic subjects. The power of dialogical learning, identified by Freire (1970) and Habermas (1987) as fundamental to the creation of active subjects, is evident in the educational actions of the women's NGOs.

The type of knowledge provided by these organisations through their NFE programs is not available in formal educational institutions. The women-led NGOs have thus acted to formulate new discourses, create strong feminist identities, and put pressure on key levels of government. Through their multiple and recurrent NFE activities, the women's NGOs have not only fostered among their beneficiaries the acquisition of oppositional language but provided them with a concrete understanding of the principles, process and institutions that influence economic and social life and, in particular, how these dynamics influence the conditions of women and men in their society.

Helping women with low levels of formal education has necessitated forms of teaching and learning that are innovative and flexible. NFE courses offered by the three NGOs have used materials that are colourful and descriptive enough to stimulate participation, while covering theoretical and abstract issues. For much of their work with adult women, the women-led NGOs have relied on objectives and methodologies developed by popular education. These include the constant use of group conversations or dialogues among the participants, simulation exercises, role-playing, and large-group presentations by some of the women elected by their groups. Often these sessions are preceded by physical exercises, to produce a state of relaxation. Simulation activities include, for instance, the following: 'Imagine you go up a mountain and find there an ancient and wise woman. What questions would you ask her?' Role-playing has involved women acting as judges and assessing cases of rape. Through these activities, the non-formal education courses promote the development of self-confidence and improve verbal expression. The courses also promote the ability to find positive and negative aspects in any given situation.

In approaching women with low levels of education and little time for engaging in educational activities, the women-led NGOs have contributed a number of innovations to adult education, primarily by making the sessions short and appealing. Popular education techniques, such as constant dialogue among classroom participants, experiential techniques that result in greater agency by the students, games and physical exercises, and in some cases dances and songs, have been used in the educational activities to convey knowledge and information.

The emphasis in these educational ventures has often been on rescuing lived experiences. To this end, workshop facilitators introduce a variety of playful exercises to break learners' initial reticence. Learning has tended to involve the examination of one's own life. The instructors have regularly assumed the position of facilitator—not 'teacher'—and have worked to create horizontal relations with the women they intend to assist. The styles of facilitators in dealing with others have displayed informality, simplicity, openness and the establishment of rapport. The objective of the non-formal and informal education has been to facilitate women's ability to think and reflect on their environment so that they may gain a greater measure of cognitive, psychological and political empowerment.

A former participant of the non-formal education program and today director of a women's shelter in Peru states:

> Yes. We have made progress. Now we can speak about domestic violence. My husband does not say, 'I washed the dishes'. He does it and he does not announce it. There have been definite improvements in domestic life, but there have been many breaking points too. The cost is high. But now domestic work is shared especially among young couples. The sharing of tasks within homes has changed. Alvaro Vargas Llosa said that it would be a great invention the one that would enable a man to become pregnant.

The above is particularly informative because the woman making the statement had a low level of formal education, finishing only primary school. She now recognises that washing dishes is a task that must be done without claiming special credit. She also realises that changing routines at home is not easy but that the cost is necessary, especially as new generations will profit. Finally, her reference to a political writer denotes her awareness of politics. It also reveals her ability to think that the value of experience could make others think differently. This is a reflection of the sophisticated thinking that comes from substantial reflection on and awareness of one's social reality.

Remembering her participation in the workshops offered by Flora Tristan, a woman who today is a community leader in a low-income neighbourhood states:

> To have Flora Tristan is like having your own company, a place where women helped me. I grew a lot within the organization and Flora Tristan helped me find fulfillment as a woman, as a mother, as a citizen . . . to have the power to share my social ideals with other women. The *Floras*

[members of Flora Tristan] welcomed me and helped me not to become overwhelmed by my condition. The great majority of women in Metropolitan Lima are single mothers. The courses I took used lots of paper drawings and participation, with dynamics in which, without realizing it, you become very much engaged in the workshop. [Those workshops were] not those where one talks and all the others sleep. They were very social women, very kind women.

We can see here the multidimensional nature of Flora Tristan's assistance, which in the case of this woman involved facilitating a new identity for her as a women, helping her with domestic concerns, and expanding her political horizons. The testimony by this woman leader also reveals the highly participatory nature of the workshops, one in which the participants were not 'sleeping'.

INFORMAL EDUCATION

Significant informal learning occurs through the activities women undertake as they manage their own organisations. But there are three major additional sources of informal learning: campaigns on a specific topic, demonstrations, and feminist media. There are demonstrations that centre on demands to improve one's condition (health, housing) or that are general, symbolic demonstrations seeking to awaken and reconstruct new values and identities.

All three NGOs have conducted campaigns on such issues as the decriminalisation of abortion and against domestic violence. In the case of Peru, a number of demonstrations have involved women standing for hours in front of the Supreme Court building to demand the return to democratic rule and the resignation of President Alberto Fujimori (who eventually fled the country). In both the Dominican Republic and Peru, demonstrations have taken place against the Miss Universe contest—actions that immediately secured media attention and ample coverage. In many of these manifestations, the presence of both middle-class (primarily university students) and low-income women has been evident. Participation in actions in downtown Lima by low-income women represented considerable sacrifice, coming as many did from the outskirts of Lima and spending their limited resources on bus tickets. Demonstrations using cultural symbols to promote informal learning emerge during annual celebrations on special days (particularly on 8 March to celebrate International Women's Day, on 25 November to commemorate the Day on Violence Against Women, and on 26 May to celebrate Women's Health Day). On these occasions, events in a public space using art forms such as songs, poetry, popular theatre, posters, dances and so on call attention to women's issues as well as providing a space where assertive identities as women are exhibited.

The marches create spaces for intense contact among women and a chance to express and clarify ideas and objectives. They also create opportunities for women of different levels of education and social class to come together and work towards the same objective. The design of strategies, the selection of schedules and the consideration of myriad logistical aspects concerning the marches create a rich terrain for the acquisition of knowledge, abilities and leadership skills. Marches, during which one occupies the streets, makes one's voice felt through slogans and becomes the centre of attention of passers-by, are incredibly empowering exercises; through collective and thus protected action, they provide opportunities to gain a sense of agency. In this way, without teachers, tests or a predetermined curriculum, the learning of valuable and useful skills and indelible memory is achieved.

Additional forms of informal education have occurred through the use of the NGOs' own media. In the Dominican Republic, CIPAF has made constant and widespread use of its own newspaper to transmit feminist information. Manuela Ramos and Flora Tristan, working in conjunction with other women-led NGOs, have established a feminist radio station (*Milenia Radio*) to convey programs ranging from health to political analysis.

In Peru, Flora Tristan exposed a government program that sterilised over 200 000 low-income women between 1993 and 2000, with the consent of only 10% of the women. Through protests in the newspapers, the publication of a book on the subject and the mobilisation of several feminist groups, this initiative substantially reduced the sterilisation rate. The experience, as several others in the past, produced complex learning about the functioning of the government bureaucracy, the points at which it could be pressed to react, and (especially) the power of joint action through multiple avenues of expression.

THE IMPORTANCE OF A SPECIAL SOCIAL SPACE

Access to non-formal and informal education is made possible by the existence of organisations with tangible location and infrastructure. The organisations, or *casas* as they are also called, provide spaces where women can safely practise their skills to participate in politics and make claims on the state. These spaces create areas where women can both plan and rehearse political action. Far from being ghettoes, which connotes isolation, the NGOs provide spaces where women can develop these skills away from a controlling masculine gaze, and where they can hone skills that enable them to intervene more effectively in society.

Magno (2002) concludes from her study of three feminist organis-ations in Israel that marginalised groups require special assets, particularly social networks and specialised knowledge and skills. Given their ex-clusion from formal politics, they need to create a public space in which to act on their knowledge. This combination of education and activity, which Magno calls 'political capital', then serves to fuel social change among civic organisations. Melucci corroborates the critical importance of network development, noting that empowerment is produced through a network of relationships which, in his view, 'constitute the submerged reality of the movement' (1988: 335; see also Melucci 1989).

POLITICAL AND EDUCATIONAL TRAJECTORIES

The link between the women-led NGOs in the study and economically marginalised women shows a path that has shifted from seeking to work in coordination with men (particularly those in labour unions) to women working by themselves. The experience of the three NGOs also shows a shift, from approaching clearly marginalised women such as those working in domestic service, in subsistence agriculture or for larger agri-cultural firms, to working with women who are easier to reach because they already operate within some organisation or group.

The strategy of Manuela Ramos has emphasised concrete responses to poverty. Thus, it has provided its intended beneficiaries with mini-credits to ensure their livelihood. On the other hand, it is clear that these women have been offered not only loans but also the opportunity to gain some understanding about their own condition and gender issues in general. In Peru, perhaps because urban poverty is so visible, both Manuela Ramos and Flora Tristan have supplied women with medical and legal attention. Again, these services have gone beyond helping individual women. In the case of Manuela Ramos, the provision of sexual and reproductive health services has been tied to a model of empowering women in decision making regarding sexual relations. In the case of Flora Tristan, the medical service is utilised in order to gain deeper insight into what effective sexual and reproductive health policies for women should be. Both NGOs engage in the provision of health services not only to help the women per se but also to establish legitimacy on health issues and to be able to monitor state practices in this regard. The implementation of the 1994 Cairo agreement on sexual and reproductive health is of serious concern to both organisations.

As a longstanding member of Flora Tristan affirms:

> We have gained the street, the universities, the professional organiz-
> ations, the State. There is recognition that these changes have taken place.
> Feminists who work on international issues (Vienna, Cairo, Beijing) have
> entered into themes that used to be the exclusive domain of men, such
> as human rights. We have assaulted the UN. What we accomplished in
> Beijing was a triumph of the international feminist movement. About
> 20 years ago, when we spoke about domestic violence, everybody would
> say, that is a private matter. Today, no one would say this is so. Or that
> women cannot participate in the labor force.

The preceding discussion of the gains made by women's organisations has to be balanced by a recognition of the difficulties they face. The paths traversed by the women-led NGOs show that their actions have at times been shaped by the priorities of funding agencies. Recent work by CIPAF and Manuela Ramos on questions of democracy as defined and promoted by USAID have led these NGOs to work primarily with women candidates for political office or with women who have attained political office either at the municipal level (mayors and councilwomen) or in the national government (deputies and senators). These women tend to be middle-class; work with them has been useful to prepare them to become more assertive and aware of the inequalities between women and men. On the other hand, attention to these women has meant less attention to other women, except in the case of Manuela Ramos, which won a major USAID contract to work on reproductive and sexual health with very-low-income populations. This latter activity has represented a major opportunity as well as a major challenge for Manuela Ramos. It has given the organisation the possibility to work in many remote regions of Peru. It has also come with constraining conditions on its work: it is prohibited from considering abortion in its discussions of family plan-ning and is thus prevented from considering one of the key means of women's control over their bodies.

Women organised in NGOs attempt to speak on behalf of poor and marginalised women. They also seek to speak for women in general.

This raises the issue of who is entitled to speak for the other, particularly when they have not been elected as representatives. Several voices critical of women-led NGOs have asked them directly, 'Who are you to talk on my behalf?'. This problem has been part of a debate within feminism in Latin America since 1997. A few women, particularly those who do not see themselves reflected in the priorities of women-led NGOs that do not work actively on issues of sexual orientation, have questioned the right of these NGOs to represent them. Another larger group of women who are in favour of abortion rights and wish to wait no longer have also been critical of what they call the 'NGOisation' of the women's movement, which in their view has transformed the women in the movement from 'activists' to 'experts' who have thus entered into 'clientelistic' relations with government and donor agencies, engaging in self-censorship in order not to lose their contract or grant support.

Another problem for women's organisations is the way contemporary industrial production disperses women (often through subcontracting at the home level) to prevent their unionisation. Consequently, low-income women are becoming harder to reach and organise. It is through the provision of basic services such as micro-credit, health advice and legal assistance that women-led NGOs are creating spaces to have access to low-income women.

But in the final analysis Latin American women's organisations have made considerable gains. Impacts of feminist action have translated into new legislation on family violence, rape, fathers' child support, access to land titles, training of police and judges to implement feminist laws, increase in the political representation of women via electoral quotas, incorporation of feminist ideas in educational plans (in the case of CIPAF only), formation of national alliances to work on minimum plans of action, and the creation of diffuse but highly mobilisable networks.

CONCLUSION

Two principles have characterised feminist NGO work with low-income women. First, education has been treated as political action, in the sense that it has been used to provide a critical analysis of power relations. Second, political engagement has been attempted through educational means. To make these principles a reality, the NGOs have had to engage first in knowledge production and then in knowledge dissemination. As feminist NGOs operate on the margins of formal political structures, they have harnessed NFE and informal education to their feminist project. The development of counter-hegemonic knowledge has not been without tension. The NGOs have sought to navigate a difficult terrain between prescriptive and process approaches to learning.

To work with other women in developing a coherent political strategy, it has been necessary for sections of the women's movement to consolidate themselves in the form of NGOs. The creation of formal organisations has been unavoidable in order for these women to obtain funds, develop stable institutions with well-trained staff, determine areas of strategic action, pursue objectives, assess results, and engage in organisational self-improvement as needed. Clearly, the work of these NGOs demonstrates that individual agency and organisational structure need to be combined: agency is essential to remain inspirational and to select an agenda and path of action; structure is crucial to attract donors, carry out stable actions, strategise, and learn over time.

Women's organisations perform important transformative and emancipatory functions that enable women to develop new feminist identities, become political agents, and learn to engage in collective forms of social change. From the three case studies we have treated here, it appears that women-led NGOs in Latin America continue to direct their concern towards low-income women, seeking to provide them with the information, knowledge and strategies that they need both to improve and to transform their lives. Thomas (cited in Mayo 1998) proposes the following criteria to assess whether an educational project is emancipatory in character: the presence of a language of critique, one that considers changes at the roots of the system; a view of education that differs from the conventional system; an interrogation of whose knowledge is considered legitimate, and why; efforts that call for agency; and an examination of the confluence of class, race, ethnicity and gender. One can confidently state that, by combining discussion of the concrete conditions and problems facing women, by introducing awareness of the way gender operates in society to create power asymmetries, and by fostering women's agency in various dimensions of their lives, the three women-led NGOs have indeed engaged in emancipatory education.

The prevailing view of politics has tended to see women as important beneficiaries of state action rather than as actors who can be protagonists of their own transformation, a transformation that must reach and permeate elements of the macroeconomic and cultural environment that shape gender relations (Vavrus 2002). The work of these women-led NGOs is powerful evidence that women can act and that their autonomous actions can have positive and powerful effects. These NGOs demonstrate that, while operating from the margins of the formal political arena, women's organisations are working to expand the concept of citizenship and to contest various forms of (still) gendered citizenship.

While work with low-income, marginalised women is a standard feature of many feminist NGOs, these groups are finding it increasingly difficult to reach their intended audience because of labour market conditions propelling the widespread atomisation of women workers. The NGOs do manage to utilise spaces linked to basic services that low-income women need, but the opportunities are becoming increasingly limited. Most national governments are positioning themselves to succeed in economic arenas, and that means working with individuals almost exclusively in the formal education system and reducing activities of social welfare, including health. There are international and national funds available for issues such as domestic violence, maternal care and family planning, but it is difficult to open the terms of the debate under typical contractual conditions with development agencies that may prefer narrow parameters of technical assistance.

Attention to economically marginalised women is still paramount, despite political and financial leverage by important funding agencies that seek to reduce the nature of the intervention to the solution of practical needs. Under these conditions, it is difficult for women-led NGOs to spend sufficient time in the provision of NFE courses and the creation of informal learning opportunities that raise gender consciousness and enhance the range of empowerment attributes—attributes that in the long run offer the best promise for the resolution of both practical and strategic needs.

PART II

Core Knowledge and Skills

4

UNDERSTANDING ADULT LEARNERS

Tara Fenwick & Mark Tennant

The understanding of adult learning processes has undergone dramatic changes over the past few decades. New theories informing adult learning continue to appear, existing theories get attacked or reinvented, while educators must wonder where, amid all the argument, lies the best approach for their practice. The answer of course is that there is no one best way to understand learning, just as learners and educators are each very different and constantly changing.

Thus, our explorations of adult learning here are based on three assumptions. First, no one theory of learning or of facilitating learning trumps the others. There is no generic essentialised 'adult learner' who can be described in ways that accurately and responsibly portray the myriad differences between people and the changes they experience. Indeed, ideas of adulthood vary so widely that announcing 'adult' learning as a unique and distinct category has become a dubious enterprise.

Second, learning is not a mental process occurring in a vacuum. The context of a person's life—with its unique cultural, political, physical and social dynamics—influences what learning experiences are encountered and how they are engaged. Furthermore, 'context' is not a static container in which learners float but is active and dynamic.

Third, the 'learner' is not an object separable from the 'educator' in teaching–learning situations. The positionality of the educator (whether as expert, coach, liberator, observer, arbiter, commentator, guide, decoder) affects how learners perceive, feel, behave and remember. Considerations of learning involving teachers should begin with educators' self-reflection on their own influence in that context, and on their biased perception of what is happening.

Mindful of these three considerations, we offer in this chapter various theories of adult learning grouped into four perspectives. Think of these as four different lenses for viewing learning processes. The *learning as acquisition* lens understands knowledge as a substantive thing—a skill or competency, concept, new language, habit, expertise or wisdom—that an individual obtains through learning experiences. *Learning as reflection* is a lens focusing on learners as active constructors of knowledge, creating new meanings and realities rather than ingesting pre-existing knowledge. The *practice-based community* lens of learning focuses more on people's ability to participate meaningfully in everyday activities within particular communities of practice than on their mental meanings. The lens of *learning as embodied co-emergent process* challenges people-centred notions to portray learning as emerging in the relationships that develop among all people and everything in a particular situation—people, spatial arrangements and movements, tools and objects. While appearing mutually oppositional, these four perspectives are not so clearly distinct as the categorisation implies. But even as they sometimes overlap and blur, each suggests its own definition of learning as a process of change, which is why one overarching definition here would be presumptuous. Furthermore, the four perspectives represent only one way of categorising theories of adult learning.

While each advocates a different approach, one is not necessarily better or truer than the others. In fact, just as these different perspectives arose in different circumstances, and were shaped by authors' different politics and philosophies, they each may illuminate learning processes and suggest educative responses in particular pedagogical situations. They each deserve careful reading and, where possible, follow-up through the additional resources we have suggested. It is too easy to reject an approach because it does not resonate with our personal experiences of learning and teaching. This shuts out the possibility not only of other people having very different experiences but also of opening ourselves to challenging new explanations of learning, which may demand that we step away from our personal worlds of comfortable beliefs and values. At the same time so-called traditional theories of learning are sometimes wrongly dismissed as simplistic, misdirected, or even morally reprehensible. While these allegations can be levelled at many theories, both old and new, certain historical ideas of adult learning that are maligned are also misrepresented or misunderstood. For example, psychological theories of adult development often are inaccurately portrayed as lacking attention to sociocultural contexts, an error that unfairly dismisses potentially fruitful theories.

The critical reader looks carefully at theories in terms not only of their fit with one's experience but also of their coherence of argument (in providing evidence, balance, inclusiveness, and defensible agenda, claims, ethics and exclusions) and their potential for enhancing educational practice. While we have selected theories that we believe represent responsible and productive argument, they each have their own limitations. It remains for educators to determine the utility, for their own practice and philosophy, of the perspectives presented here.

LEARNING AS AN ACQUISITIONAL PROCESS

Perhaps the most familiar to many educators, the 'acquisition' perspective examines how mental information processing occurs, how cognitive structures develop and change, and how a repertoire of new behaviours is acquired and used as practical intelligence or expertise. What is acquired is not just knowledge content but strategies or capacities to develop new knowledge or cope with unfamiliar situations. The focus is on the individual, and particularly that person's conscious, rational activities of perceiving, interpreting, categorising and storing knowledge. Schemata theorists, for example, suggest that as learners we first acquire new information, interpret it according to our previous experiences, then evaluate and remember concepts using our existing mental schemata or categories, and restructure our concepts and organising schemata as we are challenged by new experiences (Rumelhart & Norman, 1978).

What tends to be undertheorised is how social capital and situational politics influence cognition. This includes the politics of cultural recognition that influence what counts as learnable knowledge or acquisitive processes. Intuitive, emotional, embodied, spiritual or other 'non-rational' learning processes are overlooked by some acquisition theories. Nonetheless, the theories presented below each point to the importance of context, even if they tend to emphasise cognitive processing.

Historical 'intelligence' theorists such as Cattell, Sternberg and Gardner may have been limited by cultural bias, essentialism and over-focus on academic ability, but all three explained adults' cognitive development as the interaction of experience and environment with inherent capacity. Cattell (1963) suggested that adults have two domains of intelligence. Fluid intelligence includes inherited cognitive ability:

memory, abstraction skills, and the ability to perceive relationships, adapt to new situations and solve problems. Crystallised intelligence is our content-knowledge: information, judgements, and meanings constructed through learning experiences. However, the interconnections of this experiential or so-called crystallised intelligence with problem-solving, perceptual and other cognitive abilities are unclear. Sternberg (1988) argues that intelligent behaviour derives from the interaction of three dimensions: 'components', our internal mental mechanisms and processes; 'experiences' with certain tasks and situations affecting how we deal with new tasks; and 'context', or particular situations that determine what makes intelligent behaviour. This theory of 'triarchic intelligence' thus emphasises academic ability (verbal and logical-mathematical skills), practical ability and real-world contexts. Gardner's (1993) seven distinct 'multiple intelligences' also stress variance among individuals and contexts: musical intelligence, bodily-kinaesthetic intelligence, spatial visual intelligence, personal intelligence (understanding of self), interpersonal intelligence (understanding of others), linguistic intelligence and logical-mathematical intelligence.

More recently, attention has focused on 'practical intelligence' (Resnick 1987) and 'emotional intelligence' (Goleman 1998), articulating dimensions such as self-awareness and empathy. Studies in practical intelligence are typically conducted on real-life tasks in everyday situations. For example, Scribner (1984) investigated and documented the practical thinking of workers in her pioneering studies of everyday thinking in a milk factory. She found that practical thought has five distinct features: it is marked by flexibility; it incorporates the external environment into the problem-solving system; expert practical thinkers adopt effort saving as a higher-order cognitive strategy, which informs the way they work; practical thought is highly reliant on domain-specific knowledge; and practical thought reformulates and redefines problems for ease of solution. In the context of particular domains of work, practical intelligence is often referred to as expertise. Expertise research commonly compares the performance of novices and recognised experts in a particular task or domain. Obviously this raises questions about who makes these novice–expert determinations and according to what criteria, but we can reasonably accept that there may be some consensus in a domain community about the existence of a range of effective practices and participants. Classically, expertise studies examined chess players (Chase & Simon 1973); then branched to a variety of mostly vocational domains (e.g. medicine, nursing, law, bar-tending, taxi-driving and the like).

Chi et al. (1998) summarised the findings of these expertise studies. Experts appear to act faster and more efficiently; to perceive large meaningful patterns; to see and represent a problem at a deeper, more principled level than novices; to spend time analysing problems, especially when these are ill-structured; to have superior memory; and to be aware of their mistakes and the complexity of problems they face. Particularly interesting is the repeated finding that experts excel mainly in their own domains.

Like other intelligence theories, expertise theories assume that individuals can acquire both knowledge and learning capacity in particular domains ranging from academic to everyday. Also like earlier theories, expertise theories sometimes do not account satisfactorily for the socio-cultural dynamics sustaining or thwarting learning, or how people's acquired capacities decay rapidly, or why people at times cannot apply their capacities to new situations. Expertise studies do not explain how different forms of expertise develop and are recognised (or not) in particular domains, how different dimensions of individuals' lives contribute to their 'expertise', or why some individuals with lengthy experience in a domain are non-experts. Another way of conceptualising acquired learning is suggested by Nonaka and Takeuchi (1995). Rather than splitting experts from novices, they focus on the extent to which learning is more tacit (personal, embedded in action and perhaps unconscious) and more explicit (articulated, identifiable and conscious). Individuals and even groups supposedly acquire tacit knowledge through everyday experimentation or by unconsciously imitating others. When tacit is converted to explicit knowledge, they claim, it can be analysed and shared among people.

All acquisition theories have some explanatory power when examining the range of different individuals' engagements with learning opportunities. These theories maintain that some concepts and practices do exist as a 'body' or discipline of previously developed knowledge, and that a learner encounters and integrates these. They suggest links among sociological and psychological theories of human behaviour, and emphasise that learners do acquire competencies in ways that cannot be fully explained through structures such as social class, economic privilege, group affiliation and networks. Acquisition theories also raise issues about 'transfer'—translating and sharing knowledge among applications and groups. For example, expertise studies show that experts may develop procedure-bound routines that are locked into particular contexts and that blind them to the insight of relative novices. Nonaka and

Takeuchi's work suggests ways to 'convert' and move knowledge from tacit to explicit forms, and from one group to another.

However, acquisition theories tend to imply a fundamentally additive conception of learning. Their representation of knowledge as a substantive thing antedating the learning individual who ingests it is vehemently denied by critics (see below). Acquisition theory does not focus on the differential knowledge that people construct, individually and collectively, from their experiences. Nor does it dwell on how adults revisit and reconstruct these meanings, or how they often experience transformation of identities and knowledge through reflective learning processes.

LEARNING AS A REFLECTIVE PROCESS

This influential adult learning perspective casts the individual as a central actor in a drama of personal 'meaning-making'. As learners reflect on their lived experience, they actively interpret what they see and hear, emphasising aspects of greatest personal interest or familiarity, and so construct and transform their own unique knowledge. This means that in a classroom of adults listening to a presentation, each learner will most likely construct a very different understanding of what they are hearing (which may or may not approximate what the speaker thinks she/he is saying!).

Some writers associated with reflective constructivism, such as Piaget (1966), focus on the individual, alternating between *assimilation* of newly constructed concepts and *accommodation* of these constructs to new encounters. Others, like Vygotsky (1978), focus on the social interaction between the individual and the environment, showing that in the process of constructing knowledge we affect those around us as much as we are affected by them. However, all reflective learning theories share one central belief: as learners we construct, through reflection, a personal understanding of relevant structures of meaning derived from our actions in the world.

In the adult learning literature, this view is embedded in the writings of Boud and Walker (1991), Kolb (1984), Mezirow (1991), Schön (1983) and many others. For Kolb (1984), learning is a tension and conflict-filled process, oscillating between concrete emotional experiences and deliberate cognitive reflection. Although all adults are exposed to a multitude of life experiences, Kolb maintains, not everyone learns from these. Learning happens only when there is reflective thought and internal 'processing' by the learner, in a way that actively makes sense of an experience and links it to previous learning.

Schön (1983) has been a significant promoter of reflective processes to understand workplace learning. Schön's view is that adults work amid uncertainty, complexity and value conflict, often managing problems for which few existing rules learned through formal training or past experience can apply. He argues that we learn by noticing and framing problems in particular ways, then experimenting with solutions. When we encounter unique problems or situations containing some element of surprise, we are prompted to *reflect-in-action* by improvising on the spot, thinking up and refining and retesting various responses. Afterwards we *reflect-on-action*, examining what we did, how we did it, and what alternatives exist. Other writers have continued to refine Schön's ideas of reflective practice. Boud and Walker (1991), for example, emphasised the importance of an individual's 'readiness' to learn from an experience and attention to feelings in reflection.

In the everyday process of 'meaning-making' and problem solving, reflective theories explain that we learn procedural knowledge (how to do things or solve problems) and propositional knowledge (what things mean) through reflecting on experiences. But in critical reflection people question how they framed the problem in the first place. Even if no apparent problems exist, the thoughtful practitioner questions situations, asking why things are the way they are, why events unfold in the way they do. People also reflect critically to problematise their own actions, asking: Why did I do what I did? What beliefs inform my practice, and how are these beliefs helping or hindering my work?

Brookfield (1995, 2001) and Mezirow (1991, 2000) both have theorised how such critical reflection interrupts, reconstructs and thus transforms human beliefs. Brookfield (1995) suggests that when we reflect on our experience with 'skeptical questioning' and 'imaginative speculation', we refine, deepen or correct our knowledge constructions. The key is confronting and perhaps rupturing our deepest beliefs, including those dominant ideologies that we have uncritically absorbed from our cultural communities (2001).

Mezirow's (1991) theory of 'transformative learning' is based on a tri-level concept of critical reflection on experience. When adults encounter a disorienting dilemma or undesirable outcome, reflection is often triggered. Reflection on the *content* of the experience (What happened?) or *process* they employed (How did it happen?) may promote procedural learning. But when reflection challenges the very *premises* undergirding problem-solving processes (What's wrong with how I am seeing what happened and how it happened?), we move toward a *transformation* in our world views. Mezirow has continued to argue, throughout the exhaustive debates around his theory (see Taylor, 1998), that this process of vigorous critical reflection transforms our 'meaning perspectives' to become more 'inclusive, differentiating, permeable, critically reflective, and integrative of experience' (Mezirow 1991: 14).

Autobiography—a process of purposeful, critical reflection on our life stories to find meaning, weaving together many forms and occasions of our memoried experience—is championed by adult educators such as Dominicé (2000) and West (1996). Through autobiography, a person's sense of self interacting with context becomes more apparent, for the individual watches and listens to the self acting in various contexts over periods of time. In a broader sense, autobiographical reflection helps learners understand the values and models of their changing environments—social, cultural, economic, political—and their own responses to these. Dominicé calls this 'the difficult process of becoming oneself' (2000: 73), interpreting one's never-ending struggle for identity and life meaning, a process which 'helps adults develop confidence and direction for future learning'.

Critical reflection is also fundamental to popular education or the forms of learning that Allman (2001) calls revolutionary critical education. Unlike the individualistic theory of Mezirow, both are rooted in the collective. Through critical reflection combined with social action, groups develop new awareness of social inequities and oppressions they had taken for granted, and envision more just formations (see chapters 3 and 15). These approaches celebrate *praxis*—the integration of critical reflection with action—and support a shift in focus to practice.

LEARNING AS A PRACTICE-BASED COMMUNITY PROCESS

One problem with explaining adult learning as a straightforward matter of individuals reflecting carefully and even critically on their experiences is that we are embedded so thoroughly in our cultures that we may not be able to distance our thinking from our own experiences. Garrick (1999), for example, suggests that what we imagine to be our 'experience' is created by a particular discourse.[1] Discourses shape how we perceive what Schön has called 'routine' and 'non-routine' problems, how we interpret our own actions, and what knowledge we consider worthy of learning. A second problem with 'mentalist' reflective views of learning is their separation of thinking from acting. A growing shift to conceptualise learning as more relational and contextual than reflection-based is evident among situative theorists (i.e. Greeno 1997; Lave & Wenger 1991; Rogoff 1990; Wenger 1998). They argue that learning is rooted in the situation in which a person participates, not in the head of that person as intellectual concepts produced by reflection. Knowing and learning are defined as engaging in changing processes of human participation in a particular community of practice. A community of practice is any group of individuals who work together for a period (such as a sports team, a workplace department or project group, a class or club) developing particular ways of doing things and talking about things that their members come to learn. Lave and Wenger (1991) argue that individuals learn *as* they participate by interacting with the community (with its history, assumptions and cultural values, rules and patterns of relationship), the tools at hand (including objects, technology, languages and images), and the moment's activity (its purposes, norms and practical challenges). Thus, knowing is interminably inventive and entwined with doing. The objective is to become a full participant in the community of practice, not to learn *about* the practice. The community itself defines what constitutes legitimate practice.

Further in this vein, activity theory presents an 'expansive' view of learning rooted in practice (Engeström et al. 1999) that has been taken up in many recent analyses of workplace learning and innovation. Learning is distributed throughout a community, and is viewed as change in a community's joint action. The object is a problem at which activity is directed: this object shapes activity, determines the horizon of possible action, and is eventually changed into an outcome. The community's activity is shaped by its rules and cultural norms, division of labour and power, and the 'mediating artifacts' (language, tools, technologies) that it uses to pursue the object—and these in turn shape the object. Learning occurs as a cycle of questioning something in this activity system, analysing its causes, modelling a new explanation or solution, implementing this model in the system, reflecting on it and consolidating it. But unlike individualist reflection-on-experience models, activity theory views learning as the collective construction and resolution of successively evolving tensions or contradictions in a complex system. The learning process involves the system's objects, mediating artifacts, and the perspectives of participants (Engeström et al. 1999).

In workplace contexts, Gold and associates (2000) emphasise how language in a community of practice determines what is considered good and right in that community and what counts as truth and reality. This phenomenon is most evident in the community's stories. These stories are value-saturated, and function as a 'reflective infrastructure' to make sense of what is taking place. They not only provide a resource for everyday talk but also, more importantly, preserve the community from outside disturbances. Through dozens of direct and indirect exchanges with others throughout a single day, individuals adopt various positions and identities, adapt their behaviour, choose new action, and contribute to the ongoing network of meanings and collective action. The community itself learns, write Gold and Watson, by improvising new practices through these networks in response to a problem or difficulty.

A study of community learning in a prominent flute-manufacturing plant (Cook & Yanow 1993) showed that learning is as much about *preservation* of distinct practices as about innovation. As each flute was passed to the next craftsperson to work on, comments focused on the 'right feel' of the flute (for this firm) to perfect its build or correct an 'odd feel' in its workings. Thus, as novices were being initiated through practice, the community was learning to adapt to newcomers' idiosyncrasies while preserving its own identity. An individual cannot be considered separately from the configuration. Every practical judgement made amid everyday 'hot action' (Beckett & Hager 2000) is embedded in the sorts of activity and talk and one-to-one interactions that are allowed and tacitly understood in a particular community of practice.

Wildemeersch et al. (1998) suggest that individuals change by being exposed to different configurations in community relationships. As individuals interact across different communities, they bring meanings from one group to another, in turn challenging the new group's definitions of reality. There is always tension between the individual's beliefs and societal meanings. Neither is determined completely by the other, and both are always shifting through the interactions in relationships. But key to both the individual and societal learning is 'a continuing process of dialogue and co-operation with people located in other configurations . . . making unexpected connections'.

Truth claims then become problematic. Knowledge is not judged by what is 'true' and 'false' but by what is relevant in this particular situation, what is worth knowing and doing, what is convenient for whom, and what to do next (Chaiklin & Lave 1993). The emphasis is on improving one's ability to *participate meaningfully* in particular practices, and on moving to 'legitimate' or more central roles within communities. What is meaningful must be negotiated between different individuals' desires (including the desire to belong), the community's changing requirements for certain forms of participation, and contextual features accepted as constraints.

Critics of the situative view, however, have raised concern about the political, ethical and strategic effects of a community's practices. What about patterns and procedures that are unjust or dysfunctional, confounding the community's stated purposes? What about inequitable opportunities to participate in a community—how do people who are excluded or marginalised become more fully involved, and what does it mean to be on the periphery? What about traditions—how does a community break free from habitual practices that have become rigidly resistant to improvement or change? Others have wondered how the situative view accounts for power flowing through a community, delineating centres and margins, granting control to some, generating conflict among others, and maintaining hegemonic beliefs and norms of acting. Some claim that learning viewed as increasingly meaningful participation in a community of practice still separates individuals from group, humans from environment, subject from object, and body from mind (see below).

LEARNING AS AN EMBODIED CO-EMERGENT PROCESS

In search of holism, practice-based perspectives of learning have continued to evolve and draw on disciplines like complexity theory, ecology theory, cybernetics and technocultural theory. A range of rich learning theories have appeared in the past two decades that move entirely away from a rational brain-centred view of learning to an embodied ecological view, exploring how cognition, identities and environment are co-emergent.

For example, enactivist learning theorists (Maturana & Varela 1987; Varela, Thompson & Rosch 1991) maintain that the systems represented by person and context are inseparable, and that change or cognition occurs from emerging systems affected by the intentional tinkering of one with the other. Humans are completely interconnected with the systems in which they act. Maturana and Varela (1987) have represented the unfolding of this interconnection as a series of 'structural couplings'. When two systems coincide, the 'perturbations' of one system excite responses in the structural dynamics of the other. The resultant 'coupling' creates a new transcendent unity of action and identities that could not have been achieved independently by either participant. Educators might understand this phenomenon through the example of conversation. As each person contributes, changing the conversational dynamic, other participants are changed, the relational space and governing rules among them change, and the looping-back changes the contributor. This is 'mutual specification' (Varela et al. 1991), the fundamental dynamic of systems constantly engaging in joint action and interaction. As actors are influenced by symbols and actions in which they participate, they adapt and learn. As they do so, their behaviours and thus their effects on the systems connected with them change. With each change these complex systems shift, changing their patterns of interaction and the individual identities of all actors enmeshed in them. Thus environment and learner emerge together in the process of cognition, although this is a false dichotomy, as there is no context separate from any particular system such as an individual actor.

Ecological learning theory also considers knowledge to be embedded in conduct and constantly enacted as we move through the world. Davis, Sumara and Luce-Kapler (2000) argue against the notion of 'tacit knowledge' (implying that it exists within independent cognitive agents, and drives their actions), explaining that particular actions unfold in circumstances that evoke them. For example, a 'choreography of movement' can be seen among any group of people working together. In fact, argue Davis and Sumara, we often find ourselves quickly swept up in collective patterns of behaviour and expectation when we join a community, even patterns we might consciously disparage. Often this joint action overwhelms our attempts to control it through critical reflection. The problem lies not in 'false ideology' or underdeveloped critical abilities but in a misleading conceptualisation of the learning *figure* separated from the contextual *ground*. Ecological theory draws attention to the 'background', and examines myriad fluctuations, subtle interactions, intuitions, and the series of consequences emerging from any single action. The focus of learning here is not on the components of experience (which other perspectives might describe in fragmented terms: person, experience, tools, community, activity) but on the *relationships* binding them together in complex systems.

Incorporating principles of complex adaptive systems, this ecological perspective recognises the systems in which people live and learn, whether at micro-levels such as immune systems or at macro-levels such as weather patterns, a forest or the stock market. Studies have shown that these systems—not just the human beings whose behaviours are embedded in them—remember, forget, recognise, hypothesise, err, adapt and thus learn (Davis et al. 2000). A system is continually inventive and self-modifying, adapting to changes within it and around it through interactions at micro-levels whose effects form patterns all by themselves.

The outcome of all these dynamic interactions of a system's parts is unpredictable. The key to a healthy system—able to adapt creatively to changing conditions—is cooperative diversity among its parts. A human body, for example, relies on highly specialised subsystems that not only each respond to different circumstances and different needs but have also learned to cohabitate and communicate with one another. Thus learning is the continuous improvisation of alternate actions and responses to changing situations, undertaken by the system's parts. More sudden transformation can occur in response to a major shock to the system, throwing it into disequilibrium. Computer-generated images of systems undergoing disequilibrium show that they go through a phase of swinging between extremes, before self-organising gradually into a new pattern or identity that can continue cohabiting with and adapting to the other systems in its environment. After the episode, the system resumes its continuous improvisation, although now more resilient and more flexible, to learn its way through any anomalies it encounters.

Learning is then defined as 'a process through which one becomes capable of more sophisticated, more flexible, more creative action' (Davis et al. 2000: 73). Learning processes are not limited to human individuals and communities, although human beings do function as whole systems that learn, adapt, organise and transform themselves as distinct identities. But human beings also are part of larger systems that learn, adapt, organise and transform themselves as distinct identities. As parts of these continuously learning larger systems, humans themselves bear characteristics of larger patterns, larger identities—a little like the single fern leaf resembling the whole fern plant. The difference is that humans participate in many complex learning systems at once.

Actor-network theory (ANT), while not a learning theory, is beginning to appear in adult education research, explaining how relationships work in a learning system. As described by writers like Latour (1993), any changes we might describe as learning new ideas, innovations, changes in behaviour, transformation, emerge through networks of actors. Actors are entities (both humans and non-humans) that have become mobilised by a particular network into acting out some kind of work to maintain the network's integrity. This work links actors together, through intermediaries (texts, products, services, money), in a process of translation. Each entity becomes an actor by translating its will into another actor through an intermediary, such as a student translating a teacher into a disciplinarian through a particular set of behaviours. Each entity also belongs to other networks in which it is called on to act differently, taking on different shapes and capacities. A blackboard, for example, is a technology that embeds both networks that produced it and networks that have established its possible uses and constraints. In any classroom actor network the blackboard can be ignored, manipulated in various ways, or ascribed different forms of power. Thus, no actor has an essential self outside a given network: nothing is given in the order of things, actors perform themselves into existence. Like most contemporary theories, ANT is continually being revised as it responds to its challengers (Law & Hassard 1999).

Critics of systems-based learning theories point out that humans seem to become dehumanised and anonymous with all this emphasis on objects, machines, action, networks and systems. Furthermore, a complex system can continuously learn and adapt itself very effectively for oppressive, destructive, even evil purposes. So how can individual parts of the system, such as humans in a certain social system, learn in ways that may change the system's direction to more generative, democratic, healthy directions? Here is where we can begin to explore ways for adult educators to insert themselves productively and ethically into continuously adaptive learning systems.

ENGAGING WITH THEORIES OF ADULT LEARNING

Michael Collins (1991: 47) suggests that we approach the theory–practice relationship in a non-dogmatic way.

> Adult educators, along with other professionals, often suggest that competent performance is a matter of familiarizing oneself with theories and, then, of putting these acquired theories into practice as relevant occasions arise. This does not seem to represent the case in any of the roles, professional or otherwise, we perform in our everyday world. 'Putting theory into practice', as the problem is often characterised, carries with it the presumption that a particular theoretical model can faithfully represent a particular order of reality. This deterministic notion, questioned even in the natural sciences, is not at all appropriate for the human sciences, which focus on the problem of human performance (competence) and provide much of the knowledge base for the helping professions. Though an understanding of theoretical constructions is important to any serious vocational endeavour, it is more efficacious to think in terms of engaging thoughtfully with theory and, then, putting *ourselves* into practice rather than putting theory into practice.

What are the implications of making this subtle shift from 'theory into practice' to 'ourselves into practice'? Most importantly, the emphasis moves from knowledge being contained within formal theory to knowledge being created from practice. The implication is that theory can inform practice and that practice can inform theory. It is not a matter of asking whether theory, in the light of practice, is confirmed or disconfirmed. Instead the question is whether theory helps to illuminate practice, whether it improves our potential as reflective practitioners and helps us interpret and understand our practice: does it provide us with a discourse for analysing practice?

Collins' view is a particular way of looking at the relationship between theory and practice, and, just as different learning theories can be categorised (as we have done above), so too can different ways of relating theory to practice. In this regard practitioners can be differentiated in terms of how they see their practitioner knowledge: is it primarily disciplinary knowledge, applied/instrumental knowledge, or situated knowledge? These positions constitute different lenses through which to see the relationship between theory and practice. They also have implications for the way in which competing learning theories are analysed, the way the 'subject' of adult learning is portrayed, and the way the educator's role is configured. These three perspectives and their implications are outlined below.

Disciplinary perspective

By disciplinary perspective we mean the adoption of the view that there is a body of adult learning knowledge to be mastered, that there are agreed practices and conventions for the generation of knowledge in adult learning, and that the knowledge produced is generalisable and even universal. This perspective is compatible with the liberal humanist tradition, which informs much of the adult learning literature.

Competing theories

Typically the apparent contradiction between adult learning as a foundation discipline and the existence of competing theories is addressed by acknowledging that it is not as if one theory is 'right' and the others 'wrong'. Diverse theories are not viewed as competing, but as each offering a different and valuable perspective on learning. Alternatively or additionally one can appeal to Kuhn's analysis of the progress of science, whereby in the development of any discipline there is a period wherein different theoretical paradigms compete for ascendancy. Accordingly, the pursuit of a theory of adult learning should not be abandoned simply because it has not yet 'got it right'.

The main task for the educator from a disciplinary perspective is to understand different theoretical positions and associated empirical findings. While critique is important, it is mainly conceptual and empirical, limited to the framework of disciplined inquiry. That is, it looks at whether the concepts employed were mutually exclusive and exhaustive, and whether the experimental or statistical manipulations adhered to sound procedures and processes.

The subject of adult learning

The 'subject' of adult learning is portrayed, implicitly or explicitly, as the essential self, and the project of research is to search for the truth about this subject (its motivation, learning styles, cognitive strategies, developmental trajectories etc.). This subject of adult learning fits nicely with the liberal humanist tradition, where education is said to lead to a greater awareness of self through cultivating an identity which is independent, rational, autonomous and coherent, and which has a sense of social responsibility.

Theory–practice relationship

A disciplinary perspective separates academic from practical knowledge. While knowledge may be applied in various ways to work, community and family life, any such application is seen as the practitioner's concern. After all, goes the reasoning, the academy cannot anticipate in advance all the possible applications of such general knowledge. Issues of application are thus sidestepped, except perhaps for a few analogies with everyday experience.

Applied/ instrumental perspective

From this perspective, the principal question posed is: How can adult learning knowledge be used?

Competing theories

The question of 'use' with respect to competing theories is typically framed as: How does adopting a particular theory affect my practice?

Once this question is posed there is a slippage from the pursuit of 'truth' to the pursuit of utility, with a corresponding realisation that 'getting it right' (i.e. getting the theory right) is largely based on assumptions about the person that are clearly social and cultural. This of course is recognisable as a social constructivist position. From this position the problem of competing paradigms remains but is cast differently: the various theories are not seen as competing to find the 'truth', rather they are competing ideologies about the person. To the extent that theories have material effects on how we see ourselves and others, they are important from a political rather than scientific point of view. The main task for the educator then becomes critiquing each theory from a political and ethical point of view: what practices are promoted by the paradigm, and whose interests do these practices serve? The choice of a paradigm is a matter of which one best reflects the politics of one's educational stance.

An alternative adoption of the instrumental perspective is that of the eclectic educator, one who does not wish to commit to a particular theoretical paradigm. Such a practitioner recognises that different theories produce different insights and promote different practices, and as a practitioner such insights and practices simply add to one's repertoire of educational interventions and understandings.

The subject of adult learning

An instrumental perspective sees adult learning as producing a competent and efficacious person, one who has mastered the knowledge and acquired the skills to act in the world with confidence. His or her competence resides in continual learning, professional formation and personal development. With regard to personal development, the aim is to produce a critical subject, one manifestation of which is the critically reflective practitioner who is capable of demystifying and, where appropriate, challenging and problematising existing practices.

Theory–practice relationship

One issue immediately becomes apparent when posing a question about 'usefulness': it concerns the difficulties associated with the status of adult learning knowledge. It is simply not the kind of knowledge that can be applied with any degree of certainty. Even if the research findings were accepted as legitimate there remain issues about where really useful knowledge is to be found. For example, it is not at all clear that knowing something general about how adults learn is more useful than, say, a detailed knowledge of a particular group of adult learners.

The focus on use/application begins the process of undermining the disciplinary status of adult learning theory. First, the search for 'grand theory'—and in a general sense the 'truth'—is abandoned, or at least rendered irrelevant, in favour of a thoroughgoing pragmatic approach to 'findings'. Second, the importance is recognised of contextual, practical, 'working knowledge' which sits alongside knowledge produced in the academy. This recognition disrupts the conventional theory-to-practice relationship characterising the disciplinary perspective. The practitioner emphasis shifts from putting theory *into* practice, to engaging with theory and then putting *oneself* into practice (as in Collins 1991).

The situated perspective

This perspective views educators' knowledge as primarily derived from their situated practice.

Competing theories

The task for the educator is not to judge different theories according to their truth, practical application or ideological position; rather it is to understand competing theories as stories that are made possible through particular historical, cultural and political conditions. They are not the only stories available, and one's experiences can be read differently— indeed, multiple readings are encouraged. Furthermore, theoretical 'stories' do not have a privileged position over other kinds of stories. The distinction between theory and practice largely disappears.

The subject of adult learning

Replacing the 'essential' or 'efficacious' self is the 'relational' self, in which the self cannot be seen as separate from the particular relationship in which one is engaged. The educational emphasis is not on unearthing who one is as a learner or on getting one's identity 'right' but rather on inventing, modulating and multiplying one's relationships as a learner. In exploring new ways of relating to others, a multiplicity of self-accounts or narratives is invited, a particular account coming into play in a particular relationship. This idea of self-narration changing according to the relationship in which one is engaged illustrates a shift in focus, from individual selves coming together to form a relationship to one where the relationship takes centre stage, with selves being realised principally as a byproduct of relatedness.

Theory–practice relationship

Situated knowledge implies knowledge that is continually in process. In many ways the theory–practice relationship is dissolved as practitioners are invited to theorise practice. Knowledge is thus seen as thoroughly situated.

CONCLUSION

In this chapter we have outlined four lenses through which to understand adult learning. We argued at the outset that a single unified 'theory' of adult learning is neither desirable or possible, that learning cannot be construed as a solely mental process existing within the mind of an individual, and that in a teaching–learning context any consideration of the learner must necessarily involve an understanding of the role of the teacher. Moreover, we argued that educators need to critically reflect on their position with respect to different theoretical perspectives. The final section thus examines ways in which educators can approach the variety of learning theories available. It will be clear to the reader that there is an entanglement between perspectives for understanding adult learning and perspectives for engaging with theories of adult learning. It should also be clear that we advocate the adoption of multiple perspectives, and that closure on any single perspective reduces rather than enhances the possibilities of adult learning.

5

TEACHING ADULTS

Tom Nesbit, Linda Leach
& Griff Foley

Great teachers think strategically and act with commitment. When we watch such teachers we can see, and admire, their grasp of teaching technique. But these teachers have more than skill: they also think and act at a number of levels. Such teachers have a deep understanding of themselves and their students, and of the organisational contexts in which they work. They 'think on their feet', and take a long-term view of their work. Their work is underpinned by a passionate commitment to particular values.

This chapter offers some insight into what makes great teaching for adults. It is structured in five parts. The first presents several studies and theories that we have found especially useful in thinking about teaching. The second examines insights into teaching drawn from some broader psychological and social theories. The third considers the implications of such research by examining more closely particular principles and methods of teaching adults. The fourth considers several teaching contexts and sites, and the conclusion offers some examples of those we hold to be great teachers.

RESEARCH ON TEACHING

Teaching has been a subject of discussion since Plato and of systematic research for over 100 years. This research has produced countless books, articles, conference papers and guides for practice. For adult educators there are a number of problems with teaching research:

- Most of it examines the teaching of children and youth in classrooms, and so does not reflect either the diversity of student ages and backgrounds or the rich array of social contexts and classroom settings that are found in adult education.
- Teaching is such a complex activity that it is difficult to devise reliable and valid ways of researching it.
- There is so much research on teaching that it is difficult for the practitioner to get access to it, or to know what is useful or valid.
- It is easy to be blinded by the ordinariness and familiarity of classrooms and classroom behaviour.
- Most teaching research has, until lately, been structured around quite narrow notions of 'teacher effectiveness'.
- Research tends to focus on one aspect of teaching, and rarely establishes links between various phenomena and different levels of analysis.

In general, researchers have tended to focus on the 'what' and the 'how' of teaching. Yet research on teaching can help us examine how day-to-day classroom interactions reflect social structures and ideologies. To understand *why* teachers work as they do, we must look at the main trends in teaching research.

Teacher effectiveness

Teachers, administrators and policy makers want to know what works in teaching. So the focus on 'teacher effectiveness', or what teachers can do to better help their students to learn, is understandable. The assumption is that differences in teacher skills (e.g. clarity of presentation, structuring of lessons, verbal fluency) and qualities (e.g. enthusiasm, warmth, confidence) will affect student learning. Thus, researchers have attempted to identify which teacher behaviours generate better student learning so that others can be systematically trained in these behaviours. The preferred form of such training in most teacher education programs is 'micro-teaching': that is, laboratory practice of particular teaching techniques such as introducing or concluding a lesson or questioning students, and supervised practice in real classrooms (Shulman 1986).

However, teacher effectiveness research has ambiguous results. Comprehensive surveys of teaching and educational opportunity (Brundage & Mackeracher 1980; Coleman et al. 1966) concluded that research on teacher effectiveness showed only that 'most teaching behaviour is unrelated to learner outcomes'. Leading teaching researchers

Biddle and Dunkin (1987: 121) have argued that 'most studies of teaching effects provide little evidence that the effect in question was produced by teaching and not some other causative factor'. Yet teachers and students know that there *is* a relationship between the way teachers teach and what students learn. But teaching and learning are such complex and context-specific activities that teacher effectiveness research can offer only the most general conclusion. Consider these apparently contradictory findings:

- Class size and student achievement are, 'on average', negatively correlated (Biddle & Dunkin 1987).
- 'Lecturing is at least as effective as other methods at presenting information and providing explanations' (Brown 1987).
- Effective teachers are those who do the most teaching (Barr & Dreeben 1978).

Canadian adult educator Daniel Pratt (1981) concluded that an effective presenter of knowledge (measured by student satisfaction, and increase in student knowledge and understanding) was one who was precise and clear in her/his presentations, and alive and moving (Pratt used the more scientific-sounding term 'high teacher animation') (see Figure 5.1).

Teacher effectiveness research thus suggests that thorough preparation and careful structuring of sessions helps precision and clarity in presentation and that the more time spent with each student, the more lively and engaging teachers are, the more effective teaching will be. However, the effectiveness paradigm omits so much: it says nothing about the content of teaching, about how teachers and students make sense of their work, or about the ways teaching and learning are affected by social and cultural factors.

Teaching functions

Usefully, teacher effectiveness research has documented some of what teachers actually do. Teachers do not just present information but perform a number of roles or functions. For example, Ira Shor (1980), who teaches working-class students at the City University of New York, says that in his classroom work he fills the following nine roles:

- convenor
- facilitator
- advocate (of missing perspectives)

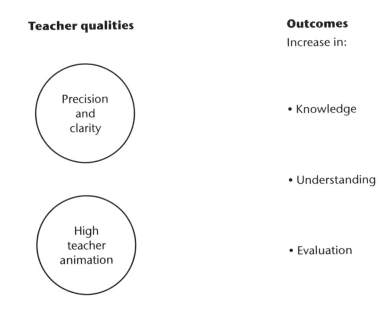

Teacher qualities

Precision
and
clarity

High
teacher
animation

Outcomes
Increase in:

• Knowledge

• Understanding

• Evaluation

Figure 5.1: The effective presenter

- adversary (of oppressive behaviour)
- lecturer
- recorder
- mediator
- clearing house
- librarian.

John Heron, who trains adult educators and other professionals in England, has developed the notion of teaching functions in an interesting way. Heron (1989, 1993) argues that there are only six 'authentic interventions' that a teacher can make. Three of these interventions Heron calls 'authoritative', because they involve the practitioner in trying to directly influence the individual or group. The other three interventions are 'facilitative', or indirect (see Table 5.1). For Heron, a skilled practitioner is one who can move from one intervention to another as required. Interestingly, research into teaching functions shows that 'indirect teaching' (student work organised by teachers) contributes more to students' learning than direct (didactic) teaching (Shulman 1986).

Styles	Category	Descriptions
Authoritative	Prescribe	Advise, judge, criticise, evaluate, direct, demand, demonstrate
	Inform	Be didactic, instruct/inform, interpret
	Confront	Challenge, feedback, question directly, expose
Facilitative	Be cathartic	Release tension in
	Catalyse	Elicit information, encourage
	Support	Approve, confirm, validate

Table 5.1: Heron's six-category intervention analysis

Teachers' beliefs and values

Believing that teachers intentionally choose what to do, some researchers are interested in the meanings and interpretations that teachers make of their own actions. Within adult education this approach is best represented in the work of Pratt, who believes that teachers come to their practice with a set of values, 'a perspective, a set of interrelated beliefs and intentions which give meaning and justification for our actions' (Pratt & Associates 1998: 33). Using extensive empirical data collected in a number of countries, Pratt has identified how rarely teachers examine their own values, and has developed a 'Teaching Perspectives Inventory' (TPI). This on-line instrument collects information on five elements of the learning/teaching process—teacher, learners, content, context, ideals— and the relationships between them. Pratt and his colleagues have used these data to identify five distinct teaching perspectives: transmission, which focuses on delivering content; apprenticeship, which models ways of working and being; developmental, which cultivates ways of thinking; nurturing, which facilitates personal agency; and social reform, which seeks to create a better society. Although every teacher holds at least some part of every perspective, one (or at most two) tends to dominate in individual teachers. When teachers describe their approaches to teaching and examine their own TPI profiles, they can identify their dominant perspectives and use them as a tool for reflection on the underlying assumptions and values that guide their work. For Pratt, understanding your perspective on teaching helps you become a more effective teacher.

Social dynamics of classrooms and schools

Teachers, of course, do not work in a vacuum but in specific locations and social contexts. Dissatisfaction with one-dimensional studies of teacher–student interaction led, in the 1970s, to research that tried to capture more completely the dynamics of teaching and learning, particularly by looking at how the dynamics of teachers' and learners' thinking are institutionally situated. Many of these studies (see Shulman 1986) show that students see education as a matter of completing set work and achieving grades, rather than as the attainment of understanding. Although the first research in this area examined children rather than adults, it is useful to highlight a study of the first eight days of classroom life for a group of black kindergarten children in 1960s Harlem (Rist 1970). Noting how the deeper dynamics of institution-alised education often reproduce relationships of exploitation and oppression, Rist showed how within a few days the black, university-educated teacher had streamed the children according to their racial and class characteristics, and had them reproducing, or failing to reproduce, the roles of white middle-class families. In a similar study, Paul Willis (1978) spent a year with a group of northern English teenagers in their final year of high school. The coherent working-class culture of these 'lads' so successfully resisted the attempted imposition by the school of an academic and achievement-oriented middle-class culture that the boys all did badly scholastically and wound up in low-skilled, low-paid jobs.

These studies argue that education reproduces existing social, economic and cultural relationships. Education may focus on such things as productive work, respect for age and the primacy of maintaining good relationships among people in communities. But Bowles and Gintis (1976) maintained that the authoritarian, teacher-dominated approach to education also produces something else: obedient and passive workers who expect to be disciplined from without. Even more student-centred approaches to teaching can domesticate students, by getting them to internalise norms like the importance of working without supervision, behaving predictably, knowing what is expected without having to be told, and so forth (Keddie 1971; Sharp & Green 1975). These studies, although they have been criticised for being overdeterministic (Sarup 1978), suggest that educational institutions socialise students in ways of thinking and acting that help maintain capitalism, patriarchy and other oppressive social arrangements (Spender & Sarah 1980; Belenky et al. 1986). Subsequent work has explored more subtly the dynamics of reproduction and shown them to be complex, contradictory and open to resistance (or 'contestation') and change (for a discussion of this literature, see Nesbit 1998).

Contexts of teaching

During the last decades of the 20th century, teaching research shifted towards more contextual explorations of the 'cultures of teaching' (Pratt & Nesbit 2000).

Such studies utilised anthropological, autobiographical, ethnographic and sociological research methods. They also used analytical tools to help explain how local behaviours and processes, and the purposes, reasons and motives behind them, might be linked to wider structural issues and influences. One body of research in this area is that of 'frame factor theory' (Lundgren 1981; Nesbit 1998), which analyses how teaching processes are chosen, developed, enabled and constrained by certain 'frames', themselves the product of larger social structures. Because any society and the educational system it promotes are inextricably linked, cultural, political, economic and social structures influence educational processes. They do not directly determine classroom behaviours and interactions but act more as causal influences through mediating frame factors. Examples of frames on teaching include where it is located and its particular physical setting, the curriculum or required content and the textbooks used, and a number of institutional influences such as the size of the class or the time available for teaching.

Such sociocultural or critical perspectives to understanding teaching can also highlight political and cultural issues, such as the supposed impartiality of much curricula or debates about what forms of authority, knowledge and regulation are legitimised and transmitted (Apple 1990; Cervero, Wilson & Associates 2001). For instance, much recent literature draws attention to the educational concerns and interests of the less privileged. Scholars such as Walters (1997), Haig-Brown (1995), hooks (1994), Tisdell (1995) and Grace (1996) explore, respectively, how such factors as class, race, gender or sexual orientation affect teaching. They question how systems of privilege and oppression are played out in learning environments, whose interests are being served in various approaches to teaching, and how constructions of teacher identity affect those who teach in various situations and communities.

BEYOND PRACTICALITIES: CONCEPTUAL INFLUENCES

Teaching is such a practical activity that educators often resist theories that come from anywhere but a practical classroom context. In the 1960s and 70s, dissatisfaction with teacher effectiveness research led adult educators to focus on their own experiences of encouraging learning. This opened a number of distinctive theoretical strands, both psychological and sociological, which have heavily influenced ideas about the teaching of adults.

Cognitive conceptual approaches

People, constantly confronted with a mass of stimuli, impose cognitive frameworks that help them make sense of the world (Mayer 1981). This has significant implications for teaching. It means that learners are active: they do not passively absorb information but process or *construct* it in their own ways. Teachers therefore need to know more about how students think and learn. Research must attend carefully not only to teaching but to learning as well.

Constructivist views of learning are very influential in adult education. Psychological or radical constructivists (e.g. Von Glaserfeld 1995) build on Piaget's ideas to argue that we develop our knowledge and understanding largely as individuals. Further, they argue that learning is an internal, cognitive process. Social constructivists (e.g. Gergen 2001; Prawat 1996) draw on the work of Vygotsky (1978, 1987), and maintain that learning is more than what takes place within our minds. They argue that learning is fundamentally a social process: we learn through our interactions with others. Social constructivists hold that culture and context affect the ways in which we interpret our worlds and therefore the knowledge we construct.

Apart from the work of US progressive educators (notably John Dewey) and Russian cognitive psychologists (notably Lev Vygotsky) in the 1920s and 30s (see Kolb 1984; Youngman 1986), constructivist interpretations were overwhelmed by behaviourist psychology until the 1950s, when the development of computers revived interest in how people process information and there was a surge of research in cognitive psychology.

Another interesting cognitive development theorist is William Perry (1970). Through interviews with Harvard undergraduates, he showed that they moved through nine 'epistemological positions', or 'ways of knowing'. He found that students moved from seeing knowledge as something that is handed down to them by authorities to seeing knowledge as relative (everyone has the right to their own opinion), to seeing that knowledge is constructed by people in particular social contexts, in accordance with particular values (see also Belenky et al. 1986).

Ausubel (1963, 1968) and others (e.g. Entwistle 1984; Marton et al. 1984) have examined the relationship between learning context (the way knowledge is presented to learners) and learning strategy (the way learners learn). They distinguish between 'reception learning', in which learners absorb what they are taught, and 'discovery learning', in which learners are able to inductively build up their own understanding. Either of these types of learning can be meaningful or rote. Meaningful learning occurs when learners are able to relate new knowledge to their existing cognitive frameworks. When learners cannot do this they must learn by rote. Whether meaningful or rote learning occurs depends both on how knowledge is presented to students and on the sorts of learning strategies used by students (Candy 1991; Entwistle 1984; Gibbs 1996).

A general understanding of such concepts as learning style, epistemological position, discovery and reception learning, and meaningful and rote learning, can help us become more sensitive to how our students learn. At a more systematic level, understanding the ways learners think enables educators to help students develop *learning strategies*, ways of understanding and acting on their learning. For example, by asking open-ended rather than closed questions, a teacher can give learners opportunities to develop a meaningful rather than a surface or reproductive orientation to learning. Again, by encouraging the use of 'mind maps' (Buzan 1978) or 'concept maps' (Novak & Gowin 1984), adult educators can encourage students to understand that they can develop their own ways of grasping and using knowledge.

Humanistic psychology

Other profound conceptual influences on teaching adults are drawn from humanistic psychology. The roots of this psychology lie in the existential philosophy of writers like Kierkegaard and Buber, who maintained that individuals, while free to choose which course of action they will take, are also responsible for their actions. This philosophy contrasted with the determinism of behaviourist and Freudian psychology, and much of sociology (Kovel 1987; Youngman 1986). It flowered in the optimistic atmosphere of the postwar United States, where alternative therapies dedicated to the development of 'human potential' emerged, ranging from the Gestalt psychology of Fritz Perls to the body work of Patricia Rolfe (Rowan 1976).

Humanistic psychology made a great impact on education, particularly through the work of the therapist and educator Carl Rogers. His notions of 'meaningful learning' and 'facilitation' turned conventional wisdom about teaching and learning on its head, and encouraged a shift from direct teaching to teaching learners how to learn. Rogers saw therapy and education as ways of emancipating people. He distinguished between meaningless, oppressive and alienating learning, which, he maintained, constituted the bulk of the formal education curriculum, and 'significant, meaningful, experiential learning', which was self-initiated and involved the whole person (Rogers 1969). The dilemma for the humanistic educator, as Rogers saw it, was to devise alternative ways of working within an education system characterised by 'a prescribed curriculum, similar assignments for all students, lecturing as the only mode of instruction, standards by which all students are externally evaluated, and instructor-chosen grades as the measure of learning', all of which precluded meaningful learning (Rogers 1969). Rogers' critique of conventional education and his concept of facilitation have been a dominant influence in adult education for the past 30 years, so that most adult educators now see themselves as facilitators of learning rather than as didacts. Also, his educational theory helped generate a whole literature on experience-based learning.

Rogers' critique of the dominant 'telling' mode of teaching was one strand in a radical analysis of education that developed in the late 1960s and early 70s. Notable among the critics were Paulo Freire, who contrasted 'banking' and liberatory education, Ivan Illich and Paul Goodman, with their ideas of replacing oppressive institutionalised education with voluntary learning networks, and John Holt, with his practical ideas for more creative and participatory classroom teaching. The accounts of the difficult and inspiring work in 'liberatory classrooms' of Kohl, Kozol, Henry, Serle and others, and Postman and Weingartner's devastatingly funny critique of conventional education, are covered in a survey of radical educational writing (Wright 1990).

Critical pedagogy

'Critical pedagogy' developed out of the 'social dynamics' writing discussed above, but rejects the determinism of that work. Critical pedagogy also finds fault with both the teacher effectiveness and humanistic approaches to teaching because of their failure to tackle social and ethical issues.

The main theoretical tenets of critical pedagogy, and their implications for the practice of teaching, can be summarised as follows:

- Critical pedagogy is concerned with the ways in which 'meaning is produced, mediated, legitimated and challenged' (McLaren 1988) in formal and informal educational settings.
- Critical pedagogy places teaching and learning firmly in their social context. Particular attention is paid to the interaction of teaching and class, gender and race.
- Critical pedagogy focuses on relations of domination, on the ways in which, in capitalist society, culture, ideology and power intersect and control people in such sites as the workplace (through the hierarchical management of work), the marketplace (through consumerism, facilitated by advertising) and educational institutions (through teaching methods, overt and hidden curricula, teacher ideologies etc.).
- Critical pedagogy seeks to help students see through and challenge dominant (or 'hegemonic') meanings and practices. It also seeks to identify, celebrate, critique and build on popular and subordinate cultures, and a common democratic culture.
- This inductive and democratic pedagogy works from students' experience, but moves beyond it to expose the dynamics of everyday social reality, and to offer learners choices for action.
- With critical pedagogy, the mode of teaching is dialogical. The teacher reflects the students' experiences back to them in ways that enable them to analyse and discuss them critically, and then to consider ways in which they might change their lives.
- The critical teacher both supports and challenges her/his students. The teacher, as Belenky et al. (1986: 217–18) point out, can be seen as a midwife:

Midwife teachers are the opposite of banker teachers. While the bankers deposit knowledge in the learner's head, the midwives draw it out. They assist the students in giving birth to their own ideas, in making their own tacit knowledge explicit and elaborating it. They support their students' thinking, but they do not do the students' thinking for them or expect the students to think as they do.

There are some detailed accounts of critical teaching with adults: for example, Shor's (1980, 1985, 1992, 1996) analyses of his New York University English classes, Lovett's (1975) discussion of his community development work in Liverpool, England, Wallerstein's (1983) account of teaching English to immigrants in California, Stromquist's (1997) work with the emancipatory literacy program MOVA in Brazil, and Newman's (1993) account of his experiences in Australian trade union education.

Feminist pedagogies

The development of feminist scholarship was one of the most significant intellectual developments of the 20th century, an aspect of the 'second wave' of feminism that emerged in the 1960s and which has been concerned with 'enlarging the concept of politics to include the personal, the cultural and the ideological' (Marshment 1997: 125). From the 1960s onwards in many countries women's studies courses were established in adult and higher education, often developing from informal consciousness-raising efforts in women's groups. After these courses were established, important pedagogical issues had to be confronted. Primary among these was the relationship of teacher and student. Women wanted to move away from the dominant hierarchical-pedagogical relationship that involved teachers in transmitting their knowledge to students and then assessing whether the students had absorbed the teaching.

Feminist educators challenged hierarchical teacher–student relationships and experimented with alternative practices such as joint essays and presentations, team teaching, autobiographical writing and collective marking (see Robinson 1997 for further reading on these innovations). Feminist educators sought to build 'safe spaces' in which women students could analyse their experiences and find their 'authentic voices'. As they did this, teachers and students had to work through difficult issues. How can one reconcile a desire to work in women-centred, cooperative and nurturing ways in male-dominated, hierarchical, rationalising, certifying institutions? How does one work in classrooms with differences among women by class, race, sexuality, ability and age? Women's struggles with these issues have produced a large body of literature (e.g. see Bhavani 1997; Maher & Tetreault 1994; Thompson 1997).

WHAT TEACHERS DO

The above conceptual approaches have each significantly influenced the practice of adult education. We now explore some results of their application—the principles that guide work with adult learners, the concept of self-directed learning, and the use of critical reflection and discussion methods.

Adult teaching and learning principles

In general, adult educators tend to follow several key principles in their work. These are based partly on evidence of what constitutes effective and satisfying learning and teaching, but they are just as much statements of the value positions of particular adult educators. There are various versions of adult learning principles. Probably the most extensive is Brundage and Mackeracher's 1980 survey of literature on teaching, learning and program development, in which they identify 36 learning principles and discuss the implications of each for teaching and program planning. In his own comprehensive survey, Brookfield (1986) discusses six 'principles of effective practice in facilitating learning'. These six principles (voluntary participation, mutual respect, collaborative spirit, action and reflection, critical reflection, and self-direction), while greatly influenced by the concepts of humanistic and cognitive psychology, move beyond them and demonstrate an awareness of the importance of social context, and human agency, in adult education.

Self-directed learning

The idea of learning being facilitated rather than taught has been linked to the notion that adults should and do direct their own learning rather than having it directed by teachers. It is now accepted that the bulk of adult learning is informal and self-directed. There is a long tradition of autonomous adult learning, stretching back to working-class autodidacts and beyond (Johnson 1979). American data from the 1970s suggest that more than two-thirds of total adult learning efforts are self-directed (Brookfield 1986). Research conducted by Canadian adult educator Alan Tough (1979) revealed that adults spent around 700 hours each year on systematic learning activities planned and conducted by the adults themselves.

There is a large literature on the theory and practice of self-directed learning (see Candy 1991 for a comprehensive review; Leach 2000; Brookfield 1984). For many adult educators the most interesting question about self-directed learning is: How can teachers devise ways of giving students greater control over their learning? To do this is much harder than it may at first appear. The structure and culture of both educational institutions and work organisations (which are in turn shaped by broader social and cultural forces) tend to reproduce rather than alter social relations. The challenge for the educator interested in promoting self-directed learning is how to create spaces in which it can develop, within largely hostile environments. Studies of self-directed learning in adult education and training (see Foley 1992) show that essential to its success are:

- teachers' ability to understand learning and teaching from the learners' perspective;
- teachers providing clear procedures and support to enable learners to move from teacher-directed to self-directed learning;
- teachers and students developing honest interpersonal relationships, allowing all issues to be discussed and acted on;
- development of a 'learning–teaching dialectic', enabling learners to direct their learning while at the same time being challenged and extended, rather than indulged, by their teachers;
- teachers having a deep understanding of the structure, culture and dynamics of the organisations in which they work.

Critical reflection

One subfield of adult education—professional development—has developed a strong interest in the concept of reflection. Donald Schön, his colleague Chris Argyris and others have identified how professionals face many messy problems and contexts in their practice. Rather than try to apply rules drawn from formal theory, Argyris and Schön (1974) argue that practitioners flexibly and intuitively draw on their knowledge of practice (or their informal theories—see chapter 1).

The notion of reflection is often linked to the idea of practitioners as action researchers who plan, act, observe and reflect on their practice and plan, act, observe and reflect again, in a continuing spiral. Heron (1989) and others (Schön 1987) advocate practitioners' learning to 'monitor' their 'interventions' and expand their repertoire of interventions. As professionals act, they should strive to be continually aware of the impact of their actions. This, such theorists maintain, can be achieved by asking oneself questions like:

- What happened?
- What does it mean?
- What can I do?

Reflection can also be a retrospective process, in which practitioners return to the experience, attend to their own and others' feelings about the experience, and re-evaluate the experience. (For some examples of extended reflection on practice, see Boud & Griffin 1987.)

This approach to examining practice is proving to be of great use to adult educators. It enables us to look at our practice as something that is continually in process and can be acted on. Our teaching, then, becomes something that we are continually examining and learning from, and is no longer seen as a bundle of skills to be 'mastered'.

A distinction needs to be made between, on the one hand, reflection and the associated concepts of 'action learning' and 'action science' as they are used in human resource development and professional development and, on the other hand, reflection as it is used in critical pedagogy. The former emphasis, generally referred to as 'reflection-on-action', tries to work out how people make meaning in situations and devise strategies for acting on them. It is concerned with effectiveness and 'manageable change' within existing institutions, rather than with radical institutional or social change. It is often coupled with 'problem-based' learning (see chapter 16).

Critical reflection, conversely, has as its aim the identifying and challenging of people's assumptions to foster radical social change, in democratic and sometimes revolutionary directions. Work such as that of Brookfield (1987: 2000) on critical thinking goes part-way in the direction of critical reflection, concerned as it is with encouraging people to:

- analyse the assumptions underlying their 'traditional beliefs, values, behaviours and social structures';
- be aware that these assumptions are 'historically and culturally specific';
- explore 'alternatives to the current ways of thinking and living'; and
- be skeptical of claims to universality.

Brookfield also considers the political implications of teaching people to think critically. In doing so he considers the possible revolutionary outcomes of such work, but stops short of articulating a strategy for linking education to movements for radical social change.

Discussion methods

A common thread in the various forms of critical pedagogy is the use of discussion. Facilitation, self-directed learning, andragogy and adult learning principles all focus on the importance of developing a teaching and learning process that supports and encourages adult learners. This humanistic-based tradition in adult education has, however, been criticised for its lack of interest in the content of education and its consequent naiveté about the social and ethical outcomes of education. An examination of the discussion group tradition in adult education helps us to see that in teaching and learning both content and process are important.

In a sustained body of work on discussion as an educational method, Brookfield (1985, 1990; Brookfield & Preskill 1999) points out that for many adult educators, discussion is seen as the 'education method par excellence'. Two features are generally seen to be central to the concept of discussion in adult education: 'purposeful conversation . . . about a topic of mutual interest', and a notion of equal participation, a roughly equal sharing of conversational time. The goals of discussion are both cognitive and affective: the development of participants' analytical capacities, their enhanced appreciation of the complexities of issues, their increased identification with subject matter, and their higher tolerance of opposing viewpoints. Drawing on studies of discussion groups in action, Brookfield emphasises that, particularly in our competitive and individualistic culture, the attainment of these goals is problematic. As he notes, discussion groups can often become 'an arena of psychodynamic struggle', in which 'students will be alternately defensive and aggressive'. Brookfield argues that meaningful and productive discussion is more likely to take place if the following four conditions prevail:

- the discussion topic is stimulating;
- the group leader is well versed in both group dynamics and the topic under discussion;
- group members possess reasonably developed reasoning and communication skills; and
- group members have devised and agreed on 'an appropriate moral culture' for group discussion.

For Brookfield, this last condition is crucial. It 'means that the group must spend some time agreeing upon a set of procedural rules concerning the manner in which equity of participation is to be realised'. These procedural rules will in turn be based on ethical principles identified as essential to the functioning of discussion groups—reasonableness (openness to others' arguments and perspectives), peaceableness and orderliness, truthfulness, freedom, equality, and respect for persons.

There are other lively accounts of discussion groups in adult education. One of the most interesting of these is Lovett's (1975) account of the operation of discussion groups in community centres, a mothers' club and a pub in a working-class area in Liverpool, England. Lovett's analysis distinguishes between what he calls 'social group work' and educational discussion. The goal of the former is social and therapeutic; the goal of the latter is to 'develop understanding, to help people make up their minds about a variety of issues, to assess evidence, to formulate conclusions'. It intends to extend the learners' 'understanding, cognitive ability and linguistic resources'.

SITES OF TEACHING

These ways of understanding teaching have stimulated a resurgence of interest in the intersections of learning and teaching in four specific contexts or sites of adult education practice: vocational education and workplace literacy, distance education, higher education, and social movements. Distance education and workplace learning are dealt with more fully elsewhere in this book; here we focus on teaching in higher education and social movements. In both cases, recent developments draw heavily on teaching approaches generated by the critical, feminist and other radical influences discussed above.

Higher education

Universities in many countries are increasingly demanding improvements in the quality of higher education teaching. The development of such concepts as 'lifelong learning' and 'learning society' have encouraged universities and other institutions of further and higher education to become more responsive to public needs and to be more entrepreneurial in attracting adult and 'non-traditional' learners (Jarvis 2002). Indeed, one of the most noticeable changes in higher education in the past generation has been the emergence of adult learners as a major constituency. Such students tend to be far more demanding and vocal than their younger counterparts. Consequently, perceptions of the quality of university provision have become crucial, and universities are becoming more interested in teaching.

We regard this as a welcome development, not least because it extends the principles of adult education into new spheres of practice. For many years, adult education research has shown that adults learn best when they are actively engaged in learning experiences and when the curriculum builds on their life experiences and interests. Despite this, dominant approaches to teaching in higher education have favoured traditional lectures and other didactic methods. According to a recent US report, 'many current higher education practices are ill adapted to the needs of . . . adult learners. They pose barriers to participation which include a lack of flexibility in . . . academic content [and] modes of instruction' (Commission for a Nation of Lifelong Learners 1997: 3).

To address these concerns, one study sought to identify exactly what existing institutional practices were most effective for adult learners in North American colleges and universities (Council for Adult and Ex-periential Learning 1999). The study suggested that universities create a learner-centred environment. It also recommended that teaching/learn-ing should involve learners in collaborative learning experiences centred around their lives and work, including helping them to identify and meet their own learning goals. The report recommends that the teaching/learning process be redesigned to be personalised, active, collaborative, experiential, and to build on the theories, philosophies and best practices of adult learning.

This is a radical departure for most higher education institutions and offers significant hope to critical adult educators. It assumes that adult learners themselves can create knowledge and that, as activists and intel-lectuals, they will be eager to connect their new understandings with the skills and knowledge necessary to change their lives and work. If students can be encouraged to relate readings and in-class activities to their own and fellow students' daily situations and practices, they can become moti-vated to select assignments and projects that enhance their academic skills and understanding. Embedding this pedagogical approach firmly in every educational activity recognises that as work is the sphere in which the experience of problems is most acute, then it also becomes the best social location for collective intellectual and personal action (see also chapter 2).

Critical scholars in a variety of disciplines are now examining how the practices and contexts of university teaching are embedded within systems of power and domination, and how disciplines and disciplinary knowledge shape teaching and learning. For them, teaching itself is a critical component in the pursuit of emancipation and progressive social change. Such scholars are beginning to question and challenge epistemological and disciplinary boundaries. For example, Barnett (1997), Kumar (1997), Margolis (2001), several of the chapters in Cervero, Wilson and Associates' (2001) exploration of power in adult education, and Thompson's (2000) examination of the politics and practice of widening participation in higher education, all highlight the intersections of critical pedagogy, educational institutions and the public sphere. These essays, by leading scholars in adult education, literary and cultural studies, queer studies, ethnic studies, and working-class history and literature, discuss pedagogies that are informed by a concern to democratise knowledge-making and learning and to promote lasting change within our institutions of adult and higher education.

Social movements

The concepts of critical reflection and critical pedagogy are attractive to educators with an interest in social justice and radical social change. But there are many barriers to the implementation of these ideas, such as the isolation in which many educators have to work, the individualistic and competitive nature of institutionalised education, and the messages of the dominant culture transmitted through the mass media, the family, and most education. It is interesting then, and heartening, to find teachers who manage, despite all the constraints, to teach critically. It is also stimulating, and sometimes inspiring, to explore the theory of critical pedagogy, which takes us into such areas as radical and feminist theories, and highlights the optimistic notion of popular education.

Popular education emerged from 19th and 20th century peoples' struggles and mass movements. Its methods are those of critical pedagogy, with an emphasis on working from the learner's experience, locating that experience in a broader social context and devising collective strategies for change (Arnold & Burke 1984). There are several detailed accounts of popular education. One of these relates to the work of Myles Horton, who founded the Highlander Folk School, a residential college in Tennessee which for more than 70 years has provided education for trade unionists, civil rights workers and environmental activists. Horton and his colleagues appear to have developed a genuinely democratic way of working with adult learners. Their starting point is a deep respect for learners and their life experience (Horton, Kohl & Kohl 1990). The historian of Highlander, Frank Adams (1975), writes of the 'one axiom that never changes at Highlander: learn from the people; start their education where they are'. Horton himself put it like this: 'Our job is to help them understand that if they can analyse their experiences and build on those experiences and maybe transfer those experiences even, then they have a power they are comfortable with' (Moyers 1981).

When they come to Highlander, learners have experience but lack techniques for analysing it. The educators teach the learners how to develop these techniques (Moyers 1981):

> One of the things we have to do . . . is to learn how to relate our experience to theirs and you do that by analogy, you do that by storytelling. You don't get off and say: 'Look, here are some facts we're going to dump on you.' We say: 'Oh, you might consider this. Now this happened to somebody kinda like you in a different situation.' So we get them to do the same thing, with each other—get peer teaching going.

This sort of education develops genuine dialogue, in which each party listens to, and learns from, the other. This is grounded and difficult educational work. Some of the difficulties (and gains) in this sort of work, and the unresolvable tensions that arise in it, are explored with great honesty and sensitivity by David Head in his account of his work with doss-house dwellers at Kingsway Day Centre in London in the 1970s. Head begins by confronting educators with an unpalatable fact about their work: 'Education is invasion'. We educators, Head notes, like to believe that our 'interventions' are 'friendly invasions'. But our work inevitably carries with it 'overtones of occupation, cultural imposition . . . the territory of the learners is occupied by change-bringing forces' (Head 1977: 127).

Head then outlines the intricate dynamics of educational work with fragile and wounded learners, learners who will flee at the first hint of condescension. In the course of his account, he affirms the truths about democratic teaching discovered by the Highlander educators: 'If we are to avoid the worse aspects of invasion', he writes, 'our aim must be to begin where people are and discover with them where it is worth going' (Head 1977: 135). This involves educators struggling with learners to build a relationship that is based on a notion of solidarity rather than on 'helping'.

For an adult educator to work with learners 'in solidarity' means to support and provide resources for learners, to challenge and extend them, but never to patronise or try to control them. It means educators using their power to create educational situations in which learners can exercise power (Gore 1992). This is the most useful meaning of the much abused and co-opted notion of 'empowerment'. Despite popular misconceptions, empowerment is neither something that educators can do to or for learners, nor is it an abandonment of power by the educator.

What distinguishes critical teaching in social movements is its focus on and use of power. Both Head and Horton, in their different ways, see their learners as being oppressed; both direct their educational efforts to helping learners act collectively on their oppression. Both have asked, and loudly answered, the question posed by the old union song 'Whose side are you on?'. Significantly, both have, in Amilcar Cabral's (1974) vivid sense, committed 'class suicide': they have decided that they want no part in maintaining an oppressive social order and have turned their backs on the power that accrues to the already privileged. And in making that step they have developed a democratic approach to teaching. Instead of making pronouncements about what they can do, they have learned to ask 'What can we do, with you?'.

CONCLUSION

Considering previous research and different perspectives and approaches to teaching is important. Yet good teachers usually become great by teaching a lot themselves—and then by reflecting on what they do and why they do it. Read some of the biographies of great teachers to see this critical reflection at work. Some teaching autobiographies and biographies we have found stimulating and inspiring include the excellent educational biography of Myles Horton (Adams 1975). Horton's autobiography, *The Long Haul* (Horton, Kohl & Kohl 1990), was published just before he died in 1990, as was *We Make the Road by Walking*, a collection of his conversations on education and social change with Paulo Freire (Bell, Gaventa & Peters 1990). This latter book offers stories and reflections that reveal the passion, politics and hope that permeated both men's teaching and made them two of the 20th century's most influential adult educators. There is also a two-hour videotaped interview with Horton, in which he talks at length about his approach to education (Moyers 1981).

Also interesting are Jane Thompson's (1983) account of her work with women in Southampton, Mike Newman's (1979, 1993, 1994, 1999) lively accounts of his experiences in community, labour and higher education, David Head's (1977, 1978) analyses of his work with homeless and working-class people in London during the same period, bell hooks' (1994) evocation of education as the 'practice of freedom', and the biographical dialogues with critical educators collected in Torres (1998). For all of these authors, teaching students to explore and challenge racial, gender and class boundaries is one of a teacher's most important goals.

Accounts of the work of educators like Horton and Head, the recollections and polemics of the radical educators of the 1960s and 70s, and of teachers like Paulo Freire, Maxine Greene, A.S. Neill, Parker Palmer and Sylvia Ashton-Warner, confirm that great teachers are those who bring honesty, compassion, humour and passion to their work. In teaching, as with any other human activity, the sum is greater than its parts. While it is useful to analyse what, say, Myles Horton does, and to examine the theory behind his practice, Myles Horton, the teacher and the human being, is more than technique and theory. This is an optimistic realisation, and one of its implications is that while we can learn a lot from studying other teachers, we should not try to model ourselves on them—we should be ourselves. We should also recognise that though each of us has to develop our own way of understanding teaching, we will never fully understand it. All we can do is try to develop a fuller and more sensitive awareness of what happens when people teach. Indeed, Palmer (1998) argues that we can only teach who we are, that we need to identify 'the teacher within' and then to teach with authenticity and integrity from that identity.

6

PROGRAM DEVELOPMENT IN ADULT EDUCATION AND TRAINING

Thomas Sork & Mike Newman

Learning is a mysterious process, and deciding on, designing and then conducting a program for a group of adults requires imagination, flexibility and willingness to take risks. Some adult education and training theorists have attempted to tie the process down by developing sets of guidelines or lists of steps to follow, but in doing so they deny the artistry and magic of the process. Program development in adult education is much more like the production of a piece of theatre in which, if everything goes well, ideas, people and resources coalesce. A lot of hard work and clear thinking is needed. There are some accepted and proven ways of doing things, but there are very few absolute rules.

In this chapter we explore how adult educators and trainers might play a part in managing and directing this process. We look at examples of educational programs, and define the term 'program'. We look at how programs come into being, at the various players in the design and implementation of a program, and at the contexts in which the development of a program can take place. We then discuss a number of approaches to program development, identifying key theorists, discussing the strengths and weaknesses of various models, and examining how the various theories of program development have changed in emphasis over the years.

But before delving too deeply into the topic of program development, we need to explore something that is curious—and slightly disturbing—about this literature. When one looks at the origins of most of the writing and research done in this area, it is obvious that scholars in North America have dominated—some might even say colonised—this corner of the field. This is curious because the development of programs is a central activity of educators and trainers worldwide, yet one has to work hard to find substantive writing from outside North America. And when one looks closely at whose work is most often referenced, it is apparent that (with a few notable exceptions) they are Anglo/white and male. Sork (2000), among others, has noted this characteristic of the literature, and encourages readers to keep this in mind as they assess planning frameworks and models with such narrow origins.

The dominance of North American white males in this area of scholarship is also disturbing because this literature continues to privilege what Schön (1983) calls the technical-rational tradition in professional practice. In Schön's words, practice based on the technical-rational tradition is characterised by 'instrumental problem-solving made rigorous by the application of scientific theory and technique' (1981: 21). Wilson and Cervero (1997) discuss this dominance in adult education planning literature and highlight the need to break free from the conceptual and theoretical shackles that have constrained the way we understand the process of developing programs. Instrumental problem solving—the technical domain of planning—has an important role, but thinking about program development *only* in these terms excludes other processes and metaphors that might better capture its complexity and creative potential. We wonder, too, why so few women have contributed to scholarship in this area. It may well be the case that technical-rationality is not an inviting tradition for women, who may be more concerned with the creative, intuitive and relational aspects of planning. Newman (2000: 59), writing from outside North America, distances himself from the technical-rational tradition by asserting that 'program development is an art, not a science'. On reflection, though, it may be more accurate to say that program development can be thought of as *either* an art or a science, but might more productively be considered a bit of both, as Malcolm Knowles (1970: 38) notes.

PROGRAM DEFINED

Definitions are difficult. In adult education the word 'program' has a wide range of applications. It can denote a single educational or training event, a formal course, a collection or set of courses, an individual learning project, a workshop, a colloquium, a conference, or a public education campaign.

Educational programs may be difficult to define but they have a number of common features. People have come together—physically or virtually—for a purpose; and, for some at least, that purpose is to learn. What these people are doing has an order and sequence. And what they are doing has a time limit to it, in that the program has a discernible beginning and end (Brookfield 1986: 204). In short, we are talking about learning that has been consciously entered into and consciously organised, as opposed to all that other learning we engage in incidentally, unconsciously or unintentionally as we go about our lives. It is the feature of being consciously organised that distinguishes 'programs' from other events in which learning occurs.

PROGRAM DEVELOPMENT

Adult education programs come into being in many different ways. Some grow out of an idea: the coordinator of a community adult education centre, after a conversation with her teenage son about his new interest in science fiction, tries a course on the subject. Some programs might be designed around a particular person with a particular interest, skill or background: a university department of French, hosting a writer from France who is researching a novel he wants to set in Australia, prevails on the writer to conduct a series of public seminars on current intellectual debates in France. Some programs grow out of a local issue: a local politician, looking for ways of defusing a confrontation between the environmentalists and loggers in her town sets up a meeting with several expert speakers, followed by discussions and reports on possible ways of diversifying the local economy.

Some programs grow out of fads or fashions: researching family histories becomes a popular pastime, and the continuing education department of a university runs a course on genealogy. Some reflect social changes: a neighbourhood house organises meetings examining the struggle for women's equality. And some are in response to a crisis: following the brutal bashing of a gay man in a particular part of a large city, a number of organisations and local authorities organise a range of meetings, activities, and the making of a video aimed at combating prejudice against gay men and lesbians.

Some programs grow out of the nature or mission of the centre or organisation sponsoring them: the Family Planning Association provides courses on human sexuality. Some respond to the need of an organisation to continue, grow or renew itself: a trade union provides training for its organisers in the procedures for recruiting new members. Some programs come about because of government decisions and regulatory changes: jobs are analysed in terms of competencies, and training for those jobs is reorganised in competency-based modules consistent with the government's training reform priorities.

Some programs are set up to meet needs or respond to interests or demands: adult education and community centres run courses on communication skills, assertiveness and personal growth to meet people's individual needs; a local public library runs a program of films and lectures to meet an interest in another country generated by increased trade links and the arrival of immigrants from that country; following bitter industrial action in an isolated, single-industry town, a labour union demands that the management pay for a series of meetings to be conducted by educators and counsellors aimed at bringing the community back together.

In essence each program has its own story, and the program developer—the educator or trainer—enters the story at some point, often after it has started; plays a major part in writing the story for a while by designing and coordinating the program itself; and then at some stage eases out of the story, leaving others to take it on. So the adult educators and counsellors who were invited to enter the single-industry town and run those meetings entered a story that was well underway. They learned about the dispute and the tensions in the town both during the dispute and in its aftermath, then designed and conducted a number of meetings bringing together strikers, strike-breakers and representatives of management in roughly equal numbers, letting them talk out the events they had been through, express their feelings and learn from each other. At the end of an intensive week of meetings, the educators left and the townspeople carried on with the process of dealing with, and one hopes healing, their community's wounds.

It is the process through which organised learning experiences come into being that is the focus of this chapter. We are calling this 'program development', but it is also commonly referred to as 'program planning'.

The players

Learning programs can involve a number of players. There will be the learners, of course, and facilitators, teachers, tutors, counsellors or

99

trainers. There are likely to be administrators, organisers, managers or supporters of some kind. And there are likely to be organisations, governments or authorities that house, finance or sponsor the program in some way.

There may be occasions when there is only one player—the learner. In this case an individual adult engages in a program of learning independently, identifying what she or he wants to learn, and deciding how to go about learning it. Examples might be a young single person improving her or his cooking skills, someone choosing and then developing the necessary skills to effectively use a personal computer, or a parent who thinks his or her teenage children may come into contact with drugs getting information about the use and abuse of drugs. The learner may use community facilities such as libraries, museums and other public bodies, bookshops, the mass media, the Internet, friends and experts she or he makes contact with. The learner may also use existing programs, such as short courses, learning kits, educational video or web-based programs. But in selecting and using all these resources, the learner develops an individually designed learning program and is answerable to no-one but her- or himself. One of the major researchers into adults conducting their own learning, Alan Tough (1979), indicates that adults spend hundreds of hours a year engaged in learning projects that they have planned themselves.

There will also be occasions when there are two players in a learning program—the learner and the tutor. The learner is likely to have approached the tutor (to learn piano, or to be put through a personal fitness program, for example), so is seeking the tutor's knowledge or skill. But as the learner has engaged the tutor, she or he will be constantly judging whether what the tutor is providing is worth going on with.

We might describe most individualised learning and one-to-one learning as belonging to the informal arena of education and training. In most formal contexts, however, there will be three distinct players— the learner, the teacher or trainer, and an organisation controlling, requiring or providing the program.

Often in this case it is the organisation or wider political and economic forces that set the policy and the parameters, allowing only so much room for the educator and the learners to vary the design. Governments, for example, can control educational programs through selective funding and assessment frameworks. A trainer working within the human resources division of a company will know that the training program she or he designs must ultimately contribute to the efficiency and productivity of the company. The trainer may provide a course that encourages the personal growth of the participants but will need to justify the course in terms of its benefit to the organisation.

A course in a further education college may come about as a result of the college's consultations with local industry, may have to meet the requirements laid down by an industry training board, and may have to conform to a competency-based format and standards laid down by a state, provincial or national committee for training curriculum and a competency standards body.

In each of these cases the educator responsible for delivering the educational program will be constrained in the way she or he can design the learning. Part of the educator's skill will be to operate creatively within those constraints. Policy may be set, and so may the educational program's broad objectives. The format may in part also be prescribed, in that it must relate to an occupation that has been analysed in terms of competencies. However, the educator may have more control over the design and delivery of sections of the program, and in the encounter with the participants there will inevitably be adjustments and renegotiation of the curriculum relating to the individual and collective needs of those participants.

The context

Program development takes place within a context, and so the educator must take notice of, adjust to, react to, or make use of that context. The contexts are many, and most are interrelated. They are political, economic, social, organisational, aesthetic, moral, spiritual and historical. In some cases, the context severely limits the choices available to the educator, while in other cases the context presents a rich variety of possibilities. It is important to understand that the context is dynamic, can be acted on by the educator, and is a key factor in the development of programs. For many years, the context seemed to be a taken-for-granted aspect of program development. Some theorists mentioned the context, but it was usually described as a 'given' that the educator had to be aware of but had little hope of altering. More recently, context has been regarded as a combination of material conditions and socially constructed understandings. Some of these understandings and conditions may be difficult to change, but others will be malleable in the hands of a skilful educator.

PROGRAM DEVELOPMENT MODELS

There are a number of writers on adult education and training who have tried to detail the complex process of devising, designing and implementing an educational program and who have developed models or frameworks to either guide this process or to help us understand its dynamics. Some of these models can be overly mechanistic, unrealistic, or simply too complex, but many also contain excellent ideas for practitioners. We discuss several of the most important models below, identifying noteworthy similarities and differences.

Four major influences

Some teaching programs are structured on a body of knowledge. The liberal tradition in adult education draws on the 19th century university practice of dividing knowledge into disciplines. A course therefore would be defined by an academic discipline, taught by an expert in that discipline, and its structure would be based on the given wisdom among scholars about how that discipline was normally organised when taught. The process would be seen as transferring a body of knowledge in an orderly way from the expert to the students, and at the same time as gradually initiating the students into the critical and research processes associated with that discipline. In the adult education context there might be some negotiation about the curriculum with the students—Albert Mainsbridge (1920), who founded the Workers' Educational Association in Britain in 1904, encouraged the practice of the teacher discussing the curriculum of a course at the first meeting—but the image of this kind of adult education is still that of the lecturer addressing a body of students, the lecturer active and the students attentive but essentially passive recipients. As the teacher possesses the knowledge to be taught, he or she possesses the authority. He or she designs the course according to the dictates of the subject and the traditions of the discipline within which that subject falls.

Some teaching programs are structured around the transfer of a skill. As the United States began asserting itself towards the end of the 19th century and into the 20th as the dominant industrial nation, North Americans were influential in developing industrial work structures and the kind of training that might go with it. Frederick Winslow Taylor developed his concepts of scientific management in the 1890s, breaking skills down into their component actions, developing new kinds of supervision and decision structures, setting standards for work, and developing forms of bonuses and piece rates. His ideas helped develop the production lines in time for the factories of World War I and for the industries after the war. Taylor himself believed his ideas would benefit both workers and management, but they did lay the basis for the oppressive work conditions in, say, parts of the automobile industry in the 1920s and 30s. In this period, agricultural workers were walking away from farms that were turning into dustbowls, and looking for work in the cities. They might have had no mechanical or industrial knowledge at all, but they could be taught a single action and placed on a production line. Training was reduced to an absolute minimum. As there was no need for them to know what happened further up or further down the line, in its extreme form this kind of induction into a factory was a form of training in a number of predetermined and prescribed actions without reference to any knowledge at all.

Of course we have depicted an extreme example of this kind of reductionist training, but an emphasis on actions rather than knowledge (behaviour rather than cognition) could be given a kind of respectability in contexts beyond the factory floor by reference to behavioural psychology, with its interest in stimulus and response and its emphasis on observable behaviours and measurable outcomes.

Some educators sought to wrest control of learning from the authority of the subject, the dehumanising influences of some kinds of industrial training and the reductionist nature of some behavioural training. John Dewey (Cross-Durrant 1987) was one of the most prominent of these, and was responsible in his writings and teaching during the first four decades of the 20th century for shifting some of the attention away from outcomes or bodies of knowledge and back to the learner as a person with feelings, interests, needs and preoccupations and in whom learning is a phenomenon of lifelong growth. In the 1920s, 30s and 40s in the USA, Eduard Lindeman (Brookfield 1987) argued for adult education to be an act of free will, emphasised discussion as a method, and articulated a vision of a democratic society informed and safeguarded by networks of neighbourhood discussion groups.

These four influences—the liberal tradition's emphasis on knowledge and the subject, the Taylorist or behaviouralist emphasis on performance and outcome, Dewey's focus on the learner as a person, and Lindeman's emphasis on society and community—are all to be seen in the first, and in many ways most influential, program development model we want to examine.

Conventional models

In 1949 Ralph Tyler published his small but influential *Basic Principles of Curriculum and Instruction*. The book is in four major chapters, and these chapters in effect outline a four-stage model for planning an educational program:

1. deciding on educational purposes;
2. selecting learning experiences to achieve those purposes;
3. organising the learning experiences for effective instruction; and
4. evaluating the effectiveness of the learning experiences.

The model is simple but not simplistic. Tyler's steps are couched in the form of questions to be studied, and he structures his book around explanations of procedures by which the questions can be answered. He argues that the answers arrived at will vary according to the people, the subjects and the institutional context; thus, while providing a quite tightly structured framework within which to design educational programs, he nonetheless allows for considerable flexibility in the actual programs that might come into being (Tyler 1949: 2). Although his book was written for public school educators, its influence was felt in all sectors of education, including adult education.

Tyler calls his first chapter 'What educational purposes should the school seek to attain?', and proposes that the source of educational objectives should be the learners themselves, contemporary life outside the school, the institution's and educator's philosophies, and subject-matter specialists. From the outset, therefore, Tyler is arguing that we should take account of people, society and the intellectual climate, as well as the experts in the subject, in deciding on our educational purposes and setting course objectives.

Tyler's second chapter is entitled 'How can learning experiences be selected which are likely to be useful in attaining these objectives?'. There he makes the point that it is the experience the learner goes through that counts. The trainer may provide information, instruction and exercises and in effect create a complex environment for the participants, but it is in the participants' interaction with that environment that learning takes place. Tyler states categorically that it is what the learners do that they learn, not what the teacher does (1949: 63). From this principle flow a number of others—that the participants must be given an opportunity to practise the kind of behaviour implied by the objective, that the practice should be satisfying, and that it be appropriate to the participants' present 'attainments' and 'predispositions'.

In the third chapter, entitled 'How can learning experiences be organised for effective instruction?', Tyler develops this theme of relevance to the learner when he warns us against designing programs or courses according to the apparent 'logic' of a subject. He draws a distinction between logical organisation, which he describes as 'the relationship of curriculum elements as viewed by an expert in the field', and psychological organisation, which he describes as 'the relationship as it may appear to the learner' (1949: 97). He warns, for example, against automatically organising history courses chronologically. This may seem 'logical' but may not be the best way for a learner to come to grips with the meaning of history. The learner might actually see the relevance of historical analysis better by starting with an examination of the current state of affairs and then tracking back in various ways.

If we follow Tyler's reasoning, we release ourselves from the tyranny of the academic subject and can look for other ways of organising learning. Tyler suggests several ways of structuring a program. These include using a chronological order, the increasing application of a process or principle, expanding the breadth and range of an activity, starting with description followed by analysis, providing information followed by intellectual principles, and presenting a unified world view. However, he argues that whatever form the organisation of learning might take, three criteria should be met—continuity, sequence, and integration. *Continuity*, Tyler says, is achieved by the reiteration of major elements in the curriculum. If a skill, principle or concept is taught, then the course should provide 'recurring and continuing opportunity' for the skill, principle or concept to be practised, applied or dealt with 'again and again'. But continuity—simple reiteration—is not enough. A program of learning should have *sequence* as well: each experience should lead the learner to a higher level of study and understanding. In Tyler's third criterion, *integration*, elements of learning should be organised in a way that allows the learner to develop a unified view, to integrate what has been learned into her or his behaviour as a whole.

In his fourth chapter, 'How can the effectiveness of learning experiences be evaluated?', Tyler argues that our purpose in education is to bring about a change in the behaviours of our participants and that to evaluate a learning program we need to 'appraise the behaviour' of our participants at an early point in the training, at a later point, and some time after the training has been completed.

It is in discussing evaluation that Tyler clearly demonstrates that he is still drawing on behaviourist ideas. Objectives, in a sense, frame his model, being both the starting and finishing points, and those objectives are to be expressed in terms of change in the learners' behaviours. Evaluation is achieved by observing those changed behaviours and checking them against the program's stated objectives. Despite his emphasis on the learner, his challenge to the authority of the subject and the subject specialists, and his argument that the program designer should take account of 'contemporary life', Tyler restricts his model by locking it into objectives. Once the objectives are set, and with evaluation relying on meeting those objectives, the educators and learners will be less likely to explore, take risks, go off on tangents, pursue their own interests and engage in kinds of learning that might take them into unexplored territory.

Inevitably some of Tyler's examples are dated, but his ideas are still current, and many of the curriculum design models at present in use, particularly in institution-based adult education and training, could be said to be 'Tylerian'. It has to be noted, however, that Tyler's model differs in one significant way from many of these later models. Tyler discusses concepts of need, but understanding need is subsumed within the process of defining educational purposes, and his model does not, as many later models do, include the assessment of needs as a clearly articulated and significant first step in the process of developing a learning program.

Cyril Houle, in his book *The Design of Education* (1996), expands Tyler's model and interprets it into a specifically *adult* educational form. Houle envisages adult learning as taking place in such places as 'the factory, the community, the labor union' as well as more conventional educational settings, and he argues that educational responses in 'natural settings' will need to be many-faceted.

For example, a safety specialist acting as a change agent may reduce the highway accident rate by better law enforcement, improved engineering and more effective education. She/he may apply this third remedy in many ways: mass campaigns to inform drivers of the rules of the road, stringent training programs for those who want drivers' licences, instruction of engineers on appropriate standards of highway construction and of law enforcement officers on how to carry out their duties, and special courses required of habitual breakers of traffic laws (Houle 1996: 21).

This leads Houle to argue that there will be different categories of program, and these differences will be defined by which players hold the authority and control over the program and for whom the program is intended, rather than by the subject matter or methods used.

Having located his discussion in these adult or 'natural' settings, Houle outlines a *planning framework* of 'decision points and components'. The components of his framework are:

1. A possible educational activity is identified.
2. A decision is made to proceed.
3. Objectives are identified and refined.
4. A suitable format is designed.
5. The format is fitted into larger patterns of life.
6. The plan is put into effect.
7. The results are measured and appraised.

Houle presents his model as a number of decisions to make rather than steps to follow, and accompanies each decision point or component in the model with detailed discussion and examples.

It is Malcolm Knowles that places the concept of need firmly in a program development model for adult education and training. Knowles' book, entitled *The Modern Practice of Adult Education* (1970, 1980), has been hugely influential, particularly in North American adult education. Knowles' model involves the following steps:

1. *Establishing an organisational climate*. Here he discusses ways of establishing an educative environment within an organisation that is built on a democratic philosophy and a recognition of the need for change and growth. This he describes as 'creating a climate conducive to learning', and he argues that such a climate should be expressed in the formal policy of the organisation.
2. *Establishing a structure*. Here he discusses ways of creating the right kind of committees or other structures to support and promote adult education within the organisation.
3. *Assessing needs and interests*. Here he examines different kinds of needs and interests that individuals, organisations and communities might have, and then outlines a number of ways of identifying them.
4. *Translating needs into program objectives*. Here he discusses how the needs that have been assessed should be screened through three filters—the purposes of the institution, feasibility, and the interests of the clientele.
5. *Designing a program*. Here he discusses various principles of program and course design, and processes for selecting different formats for learning.

6. *Operating the program.* Here he discusses the practicalities of implementing and managing a program, including recruitment of teachers, promotion, recruitment of participants, and management of finance and facilities.
7. *Evaluating the program.* Here he discusses purposes and methods of evaluation, and the uses to which the findings can be put.

Knowles' book is filled with useful guidelines, practical hints, case studies and examples. His particular contributions are an emphasis on establishing a climate and structure conducive to adult learning, the highlighting of the concept of need, and his attempts to reconcile the needs of the individual with those of the organisation.

In *Developing Programs in Adult Education,* Edgar Boone, Dale Safrit and Jo Jones (2002) propose a model based on a 'systems approach' that is made up of three major subprocesses, each of which is guided by a number of assumptions, is contingent on several organisational concepts, and is made up of a number of 'processual tasks'. Boone et al. describe this as 'a conceptual model', and present program development as a dense and complex set of activities informed by values and beliefs.

The three major subprocesses are: planning, design and implementation, and evaluation and accountability. Under *planning* there is a whole section made up of five tasks, all concerned with understanding and developing commitment to the organisation and to its renewal. In *design and implementation* there are four tasks aimed at linking the organisation to its publics. Under *evaluation and accountability* there is a task concerned with using evaluation findings for organisational renewal.

This model appears to be based on the assumption that one of the major reasons for conducting educational programs is the development and renewal of the organisation. It may be a model that is designed for a formally constituted adult education provider, but it is also a model that can be used to develop and promote any organisation. Boone et al. provide a bridge, then, between the Tylerian models of the 1950s, 60s and 70s with their interest, in part at least, in individual learners and their needs and interests, and those human resource development and industrial training models developed in the 1980s and into the 90s that are concerned with the training of functions and the promotion of organisational interests.

The human resource development models that emerged during the 1980s and 90s are largely Tylerian, but with certain significant differences.

108

Those concerned with training, supporting and developing executives and middle managers use processes influenced by Knowles' model, as his model allows for mixing the personal development of the individual with the requirements of the organisation and society. This is evidenced by the number of human resource developers and trainers who contributed to a book edited by Knowles (*Andragogy in Action*, 1984) and, as stated in the preface of the book, did so as a tribute to him for his influence on their work. However, often when human resource development (HRD) models are elaborated—as, for example, by Nadler and Nadler (1994)—it becomes clear that the overriding purpose is to further the interests of the organisation.

Leonard and Zeace Nadler's 'Critical Events Model' consists of a sequence of events linked by evaluation and feedback. The eight events are:

1. Identify the needs of the organisation.
2. Specify job performance.
3. Identify learner needs.
4. Determine objectives.
5. Build curriculum.
6. Select instructional strategies.
7. Obtain instructional resources.
8. Conduct training.

They make the following comments when describing the process of identifying the needs of the organisation (1994: 34):

> Problems arise within groups (the total organisation or parts of it) and with individuals (employees and external customers). The needs of individuals and the organisation do not have to be in conflict, though such a conflict sometimes exists. Generally, the needs of both the individual and the organisation have to be identified. However, because HRD is provided by the organisation, it is necessary to first look at the organisational needs. This can be done without demeaning or ignoring individuals.

Nadler and Nadler are quite clear about beginning the design process by identifying organisational needs. This HRD perspective privileges organisational needs over individual needs, which has provoked criticism that people should not be thought of primarily as instruments of production, especially when that leads to training programs that ignore the potential of workers to learn new capabilities that may be unrelated to the immediate requirements of the job or beyond the current goals of the organisation. But Nadler and Nadler try to counter this criticism by distinguishing between training, which focuses on current job requirements, and education, which focuses on learning beyond the current job. Although we don't find this distinction very convincing as a practical matter, it does indicate that Nadler and Nadler recognise the importance of developing programs that help adults grow beyond immediate job requirements.

Laurie Field, in *Skilling Australia* (1990), applies a Tylerian model to the world of industrial training. He draws his examples from the training of hairdressers, road tanker drivers, draftspeople, bank clerks, car mechanics, chemical workers, telecommunications technicians, retail industry workers and workers in the food industry. His model consists of the following stages:

1. *Investigate skills and training issues*. Here he discusses how the trainer might enter a workplace, carry out an exploratory study, and then use different kinds of research to understand the workplace and identify the problems and issues that can be addressed through training.
2. *Analyse competencies for a job*. Here he discusses the concept of skill and offers a schema for describing occupations and jobs and then developing comprehensive lists of competencies necessary to perform those jobs.
3. *State performance objectives*. Here he discusses how to write performance objectives that state the activity, the conditions under which the activity must be performed and the standards that must be achieved for each competency identified.
4. *Structure a training program*. Here he examines different ways of building a sequence into a training program, and the different ways skills training can be provided. These include off-site training in a college, in-house training, simulator training (often using computer models) and on-the-job training.
5. *Deliver the training*. Field then provides a number of chapters looking at different methods of delivering training—on the design and use of job aids such as reference guides, user manuals and computer aids; on-the-job training; the use of computers in training; and modularised training. He also devotes a chapter to the processes involved in explaining and demonstrating a task.

6. *Supervise practice*. At several stages in the book Field discusses the processes of transferring skills learnt to the actual job. Here he examines ways of providing the learner with structured and supervised practice in the skills learnt.

7. *Assess skills*. Here he discusses ways of testing learners' competence, and of assessing the change in their skills and knowledge as a result of the training.

As even this brief summary indicates, Field's model is concerned with getting people to *perform* more skilfully to make the organisation more efficient and more productive. He argues that organisations can and should be changed to increase efficiency, and that there should be moves towards a 'more co-operative, participative relationship between workers and management' (1990: 8). But there seems to be little room in the model for providing opportunities in training to enable people to think and behave differently and therefore significantly to alter the goals and structures in the organisation.

Rosemary Caffarella (2002), one of the few women who have written extensively on program planning, has developed an 'interactive model' that avoids some of the major weaknesses of many frameworks grounded in the Tylerian/technical-rational tradition. Her model consists of the following 12 components, which she has derived from her own earlier work and the work of other writers:

1. discerning the context;
2. building a solid base of support;
3. identifying program needs;
4. sorting and prioritising program ideas;
5. developing program objectives;
6. designing instructional plans;
7. devising transfer-of-learning plans;
8. formulating evaluation plans;
9. making recommendations and communicating results;
10. selecting formats, schedules, and staff needs;
11. preparing budgets and marketing plans;
12. coordinating facilities and on-site events.

The model is 'interactive' in the sense that: 'it has no real beginnings or endings. Rather, persons responsible for planning programs for adults are encouraged to use the relevant parts of the model in any order and combination based on the planning situation' (2002: 21). This departure from the stepwise approach of many earlier models is an attempt to make the model more flexible, but it retains many of the features of those from the technical-rational tradition. One especially noteworthy addition that Caffarella has made is transfer-of-learning plans. Few models seem concerned about what happens to learning 'after the applause' (Ottoson 1997), but Caffarella gives this neglected aspect of planning suitable emphasis by pointing out things that planners can do while designing the program to increase the likelihood that what is learned will be applied. There are growing expectations for accountability for the application of learning beyond the confines of programs, so developing a plan for promoting application back in the 'natural environments' of the participants—their workplaces, their homes, their communities—requires more systematic attention. Another noteworthy feature of Caffarella's treatment of planning is that she explicitly discusses ethics. She joins a small but growing number of scholars who recognise that regardless of whether you think of program development as an art or a science, it is rife with ethical choices and the occasional ethical dilemma (Brockett & Hiemstra 1998).

Thus far we have introduced models that have clear roots in the technical-rational tradition as defined earlier by Schön, even though some—like Caffarella's—are very sophisticated elaborations of Tyler's framework. Now we turn our attention to two ways of thinking about program development that depart substantially from the Tylerian frame and invite educators to reconsider the way they engage in the work of planning.

Beyond the conventional

In 1994, Ronald Cervero and Arthur Wilson introduced adult educators to a fundamentally new way of thinking about program development. They claimed that planning programs in adult education was best understood as a process of negotiating interests among stakeholders connected by complex power relations. This way of thinking about planning was heavily influenced by Forester (1989, 1993), whose work in community planning emphasises the central importance of power relations. Cervero and Wilson define power as 'the capacity to act, distributed to people by virtue of the enduring social relationships in which they participate' (1996: 29). They note quite correctly that this capacity to act is not equally distributed among a group of planning actors, so that most planning situations are characterised by asymmetrical power relations. In order to be effective, planners must be able to 'read' the power relations in a planning situation and then employ various tactics to ensure that all stakeholders have equal (or as equal as possible) opportunities to influence the design of the program—a process they refer to as 'substantively democratic planning'.

Unlike most authors, Cervero and Wilson use case studies of actual planning situations to illustrate the application of their framework. Numerous research studies have been published that employ their framework as an analytical tool, and other scholars have presented case studies of planning using their framework to describe what is happening (Cervero & Wilson 1996). In one respect, this interest in the role of power in educational planning is nothing new. More than 30 years ago, Freire (1970) sensitised adult educators to the major power imbalances that exist in society and described an approach to literacy education that encouraged learners to empower themselves in the face of economic and other forms of oppression. What is new in Cervero and Wilson's work is the way they have used the concepts of power, interests and negotiation to reframe our understanding of planning. They have encouraged us to place the technical aspects of planning in the background and to foreground power and the process through which interests are negotiated as programs are developed. Like Caffarella, Cervero and Wilson also speak explicitly about the ethical choices that planners make—about who is invited to 'sit' at the metaphorical planning table, whose interests are heard and incorporated into the design of the program and, ultimately, who benefits from the program.

What Cervero and Wilson do not provide is a blueprint or set of instructions for how to plan when the focus is on negotiating power and interests. This may make their framework less attractive to some practitioners because it does not provide the kind of specific guidance in completing planning tasks that, for example, Boone et al.'s conceptual model and Caffarella's interactive model do. Another limitation of Cervero and Wilson's framework is that it seems to classify everything that happens in planning as 'negotiation', when other concepts (e.g. mediation, manipulation) might be better labels to describe what is happening (Sork 1996). Negotiating interests is certainly a central part of many program development efforts, but to fully understand the complexities of the process may require a richer set of descriptive concepts. But, even with these limitations, their framework is valuable because it shifts our attention from the techniques of planning emphasised by models grounded in the technical-rational tradition to the role of power in planning and how an understanding of power dynamics can lead to more democratic planning practice.

Building on the work of Cervero and Wilson, Yang (1999) has developed a self-assessment instrument that allows planners to determine the kinds of power and influence tactics they use when they encounter various types of planning situations. Through research with various groups of adult education practitioners, he has identified seven power and influence tactics (1999: 144):

1. *Reasoning*. The planner uses persuasion, logic, or actual evidence with the co-planner in order to gain influence over the planning process.
2. *Consulting*. The planner seeks input and ideas from the co-planner in order to gain influence over the planning process.
3. *Appealing*. The planner appeals to the emotions, predispositions, or values of the co-planner in order to gain influence over the planning process.
4. *Networking*. The planner seeks to obtain the support of other people who are important to the co-planner in order to gain influence over the planning process.
5. *Bargaining*. The planner offers to exchange things the co-planner values (or refers to past exchanges) in return for influence over the planning process.
6. *Pressuring*. The planner makes direct demands of or threats to the co-planner in order to gain influence over the planning process.
7. *Counteracting*. The planner takes wilful action (or wilfully refuses to take action) that nullifies efforts of the co-planner, in order to gain influence over the planning process.

Yang's view is that practitioners select tactics they believe will serve their interests in specific planning situations, but we are not convinced either that all adult educators are capable of employing the full range of tactics he suggests or that all of these tactics are morally equivalent. Some practitioners may, for example, refuse to employ certain of these tactics because they would be considered incompatible with the person's professional philosophy or working style. But having this list of tactics does suggest alternative processes that may help us achieve important aims, and should cause us to reflect on the kind of planners we are, what tools we have available in our professional skill set, and how we apply these skills to achieve the ends we believe are important.

A final planning framework to be discussed here is the 'question-based approach' proposed by Sork (2000). Rather than provide instructions on how to carry out various planning tasks, Sork provides a structure for generating important planning questions. He argues that far too much energy has been devoted to developing ever more sophisticated models that include all possible planning tasks. The problem with these models is that they can never hope to include all the relevant tasks or present all the possible techniques that planners might employ to complete those tasks. Such models always oversimplify the complexities of planning and suggest a sequence or order to planning that is never seen in day-to-day practice. What he provides instead is a general structure for generating important planning questions that are particular to a specific project. He claims that every planning situation is unique, and therefore each requires a unique approach. He identifies six basic elements of program planning that are similar to those found in models from the technical-rational tradition. These represent clusters of related planning tasks and serve primarily as a way to organise our thinking about the work that needs to be done (and the questions that need to be asked):

1. Analyse context and learner community.
2. Justify and focus planning.
3. Clarify intentions.
4. Prepare instructional plan.
5. Prepare administrative plan.
6. Develop summative evaluation plan.

He avoids suggesting that such processes as needs assessment, developing instructional objectives, developing marketing plans and so on are necessary for every program. Instead, he views these as tools that may be used to answer specific planning questions. And he does illustrate how his question-based approach can be used to determine, for example, whether a needs assessment is the best approach to use and, if so, how a question-based approach can be used to design a needs assessment (Sork 2001). He also identifies three domains of planning: the technical, the social-political, and the ethical. These domains intersect with the six elements of planning to produce a three-dimensional framework. To illustrate this, let's consider the first element, 'analysing the planning context and learner community'. Sork suggests that for this element there are potentially important technical, social-political and ethical questions that may need to be addressed, although he allows that some questions may address more than one domain. He warns that it would be misleading to generate a single set of questions and to assume they would apply to all programs.

Technical questions are primarily concerned with the 'how to' of planning. Examples of technical questions for this element are:

- How do we identify important players and what is the best way to involve them in planning?
- What do we need to know about the learners for whom this program is being designed and how can we best obtain this information?
- How can we determine the amount of funding available for the program?

Social-political questions concern 'the human dynamics of planning including the interests involved, the power relationships at play, and what they mean for planning' (2001: 185). Examples of social-political questions are:

- Why are we having so much trouble involving an Aboriginal repre- sentative in planning and how can we involve them?
- What are the key interests of the players and how can we surface these?
- How can we overcome the animosity that exists between labour and management so we can productively involve both in this program?

From these examples we can see that there is also a how-to dimension to social-political questions, but the primary focus is on understanding and responding to power and interests as these are described by Cervero and Wilson.

Ethical questions concern how we should act in relation to others to behave consistently with the moral framework that guides our practice. Examples include:

- What must we do to make sure this program is accessible to the disabled and unemployed in our learner community?
- Is it justifiable to require all workers to participate in this program even though some may already have the knowledge?
- How can we develop this program so it is consistent with the 'ethic of care' included in the organisation's mission statement?

Sork's framework requires planners to first think about the key questions that need answering, then to determine the best ways to answer them.

This approach is so different from conventional planning models that it may be very difficult to adopt. In fact, Sork himself says that he is 'under no illusions about the ease with which a transition can be made to a question-based approach. It is more demanding than conventional approaches so to become widely adopted, it will have to be considered worth the additional effort' (2001: 187). It may be the kind of approach that is better suited to experienced than to novice program developers.

CONCLUSION

We have tried in this chapter to illustrate how thinking about program development has evolved during the past 50 years, to show how certain ways of thinking have come to dominate this corner of the field, and to offer some new perspectives that depart from conventional thinking. The literature of adult education and training contains many ideas and models for those developing programs to draw inspiration from and to follow, but there are no hard and fast rules. The educator must approach the design of learning as a creative endeavour. And as the learners are adults, and the learning takes place in social and organisational contexts which the learners may be able to change, there will be times when the design of an educational program will become a political endeavour as well.

PART III

Social Context,
Policy and Research

7

HISTORIES OF ADULT EDUCATION

Bob Boughton, Lucy Taksa
& Mike Welton

As I write this introduction in March 2003, on the eve of the Third Gulf War, the old saw is very much in my mind: 'Those who fail to learn from history are doomed to repeat its mistakes'. The three contributors to this chapter endorse this sentiment.

Mike Welton begins the chapter by exploring the connections between history and myth. He reminds us that historians must be critical of their own assumptions. He then acts on this by critically examining the central emancipatory story of Canadian adult education, the Antigonish movement, of which he is a major historian. Welton argues that adult educators have invested Antigonish with too much emancipatory hope, and have turned it into a disabling myth. He concludes by urging adult educators to keep hoping, and working, for a better world, but to 'dream closer to the ground'. He calls for 'much deeper reflection on the historical forces that subvert the attempts of ordinary people to realise their potential'.

In the second contribution, Bob Boughton also calls for a more critical approach to adult education history. He argues that in Australia and elsewhere a liberal history of adult education has dominated, one that sees adult education evolving towards today's 'highly professionalised and depoliticised field of practice'. Boughton shows how this liberal story has repressed other histories of adult education and learning. He outlines a further Australian adult education history—a workers' history—and refers to two others: an indigenous history and a women's history. In doing this he shows that the repression of these popular adult education histories has divided and undermined popular movements by preventing them from learning from their experience. He concludes by calling for the development of 'learning movements', 'which study and learn about the world as they work to change it'.

Lucy Taksa's contribution reconstructs a particular 'lost history', the struggle over the direction of adult education in New South Wales, Australia, between the two world wars of the 20th century. Taksa traces the transplanting of the British Workers' Educational Association to Australia. She argues that the WEA, dominated by 'middle class liberals, saw education as the means for achieving individual improvement and social peace'. But this desire challenged the labour movement's demand for more radical and emancipatory social change. So Australian workers turned away from the WEA and established their own formal and informal educational structures. While these were often short-lived, they provided an independent working-class education aimed at achieving, as a union educator put it in 1924, 'a revolutionary change in existing economic and social institutions and conditions'.

SURROUNDED BY OUR STORIES: LEARNING LESSONS FROM HISTORY

The poetics of history

As a young student of anthropology at the University of British Columbia (UBC), I studied North West Coast Aboriginal cultures and marvelled at the way peoples like the Haida, Kwakiutl and Tsimshian invented stories (we called them myths) about where they came from, who they were, and what it meant to live on the earth among the killer whales and a plenitude of sea life. Many stories were about the origins of things and intricate tales of that uncanny trickster the Raven, which taught the people lessons about the subtleties of power and moral intention. These stories were embodied in the awesome totem poles, fabulous creatures piled one on another, each deeply meaningful for the people of that place and time. Many whites sensed they were in the presence of something sacred when they first sighted those poles standing guard over villages tucked into isolated bays along the rugged northwest coast of British Columbia.

It is easy for the Western anthropologist to think that we, in the West, are rather narratively thin. Aboriginal peoples may have their storytellers—where are ours? But it is obvious that we, too, are surrounded by our stories. We fill our children's lives with storybooks. And even if we don't, the popular culture (television, film, video games) does it for us. Scripts are everywhere, teaching lots of conflicting things. The colossal impact of *Star Wars* (and now *Lord of the Rings*) certainly lends support to Joseph Campbell's claim (1973) that human beings cannot live without myths. Down deep, we all love the romantic narrative (where the hero triumphs in the end, the protagonist is vanquished, the world is made right).

Any story we tell is an imaginative invention. That's what I am calling the poetics of a story. Stories are fabricated, and those living in post-traditional societies distinguish fabulous tales and legends (like ghost stories) from stories about people and events that actually happened (history). We know that truths can be contained within myths, but we can separate myth from history. But even when we move on to the ground of stories about what actually happened, contemporary historians inform us, there is usually 'something added' to the 'objective events'. History has a poetics, and the facts in themselves do not magically tell the one best story. The historian is a fabricator, who uses the language at hand, with its vast stock of rhetorical devices and metaphors and tricks, to craft an appealing and persuasive narrative.

There are many ways of telling a story, of plotting the facts. Romance, comedy, tragedy and satire are the historian's main choices of plot structure. There are different ways of interpreting facts, and different values worth affirming. But history, unlike myth or legend, does keep scraping to find the facts of the situation. How many died at the battle of the Somme or Gallipoli? How many people participated in the study clubs? What ethnic groups were they from? The historian's biggest challenge lies in being self-critical of his/her assumptions and those stories told by the actors themselves.

Our goal as historians is to tell the truth about events and people, but we know that we can never get it right finally (truthfulness about history always places the historical narrative in dialogical tension with myths—or outright lies—about the past). Though it is difficult to establish the rightness of a version of any story, be it of one's own life or that of others, three criteria can help us in this task: coherence, believability, and empirical adequacy. New data surfacing from the archives can always throw a monkey wrench into someone's story, someone who might be censoring something for one reason or another. Power and interest always tend to creep into narrative construction; critique has the task of filtering it out.

Storytelling is also a political act. Those with power, who triumph over others (usually militarily), celebrate their victories with stories of their triumph and glory. Canadian and Australian historians, for instance, have often told the story of the evolution of their respective nations such that the experience of the 'first nations' people living on the land are repressed and marginalised. We call these stories court histories. The stories add glory to the actors who triumphed. They also wilfully distort and repress others' experiences and accounts. Stories, then, have agendas behind them. Essentially, we tell stories to affirm our identities and justify our beliefs and actions in the world. But the danger is that our desire to live in an orderly, predictable and meaningful world will lead us to deceive ourselves. Stories may sweep dirt under the carpet, or into some dark corner of our consciousness. Our desire for things to end well does not mean that they will.

The Antigonish movement as the master narrative of Canadian adult education history

I have been studying this movement for many years, and recently completed a book on the movement's primary leader, Moses M. Coady (Welton 2001). The Antigonish movement is a superb example of all the issues we have been naming so far. In fact, Moses Coady and the Antigonish movement have been so deeply mythologised in both St Francis Xavier University's and the Canadian adult education movement's stories about itself that it is difficult to penetrate the 'something added' to the 'reality beneath'. Antigonish glows with a soft halo, and Canadian adult educators (professors and students alike) have spun the movement's story in such a way as to accentuate the importance of adult education to social and economic life.

The Antigonish movement is literally awash in myth. From the early to late 1930s, for an evanescent moment, this movement for a people's economy caught the imagination of the world. Journalists, liberal-minded religious leaders, papal authorities, eastern seaboard intellectuals, professors, social reformers, wild-eyed dreamers, cooperative leaders and innocent youth came to witness the 'modern miracle'—fishers, farmers and miners taking control of their economic destinies through the creation of producer and consumer cooperatives and people's banks. Those who came and saw a modern miracle were adding something to the empirical reality laid out before their eyes. Hard minds and doubting hearts simply melted as tourists of the cooperative revolution witnessed the rustic lobster factories, credit unions and co-op stores spring up in communities with previously unremarkable histories. Today Antigonish is a rather ordinary, small rural town. But it glowed with a radiant light in the 1930s and 40s. In the 1930s and 40s, the Antigonish movement was transformed into an imaginative space into which people could project their social fantasies and desires. These tourists of the cooperative revolution saw what they wanted to. Spiritually dislocated and bewildered by the scale and scope of change in the post-World War I era, many Christians desperately wanted Moses Coady to be their modern Moses, who could fashion a non-violent alternative to fascism and communism. They wanted someone to lead them out of the Egypt of oppression into the promised land of cooperation.

Like poets and ancient storytellers, Coady fabricated a mythical redemptive narrative for his audiences. In the unpublished version of his account of the Antigonish movement, *Masters of Their Own Destiny,* Coady spun the myth of the Maritimes' golden age of wood, wind and sail into an appealing prophetic story. This narrative, of the fall from the golden age into an age of decline, framed the thinking of Coady and other Extension intellectuals. Like the prophets of old, Coady proclaimed that the end of one world, the age of mercantilism, opened the way for the reception of a new one. The people, living in the exile of a fallen world, could become 'holy', moving into another reality. And their memory of the golden age, a time of self-reliance and mastery, could keep alive the possibility of a rejuvenated world in new historical circumstances.

History counters myth-making

But historians are not satisfied with mythical narratives. Contemporary economic historian Julian Gwyn (Excessive Expectations: Maritime commerce and the economic development of Nova Scotia, 1740–1870 [1998]) has convincingly disputed one piece of Coady's mythical history of Nova Scotia and the Maritimes. Gwyn denies outright the existence of any 'golden age' for Nova Scotia. The common people of the earth had never, anywhere, exercised control over their destinies. But Coady imagined that his people, humble Nova Scotians, could acquire the necessary knowledge to understand the workings of the economy and polity and the requisite skills to run the economy. This audacious image of largely uneducated, simple, unsophisticated primary producers (on farm and at sea) running their own economic affairs turned out, in the end, to be mainly a beautiful fairytale, one with an unhappy ending. Coady's chosen vessel of economic redemption never achieved the critical mass that might have, perhaps, achieved some of the things Coady's heart desired. Certainly, people in the little communities were awakened to take action in their communities, lives were changed, hope made a brief comeback.

Those who came to see the modern miracle in the late 1930s and left praising the study club movement among previously illiterate and semi-literate fishers could not anticipate that just two years later the study club movement would be effectively over, severely curtailed by the outbreak of World War II. Nor could they have looked down the historical road and imagined the way the modernist impulse to bigness and technological efficiency would gradually crush Coady's dream of a vital in-shore fishery. Today, at the beginning of a new millennium, Coady's dream of establishing the permanent cooperative kingdom has proved to be an illusion. The Atlantic Canadian fishery is in acute crisis, our forests and environment are mismanaged, our coal and steel industries have almost vanished, our dependency mentality is still in place, our governance systems are lamentable and undemocratic, our vision of a just learning society is dismal.

What can we learn from history?

The hard reality is that the incredible energy expended by so many noble souls in Extension and the communities did not transform Nova Scotian economic structures (or social and political life) in any deep or lasting way. Moses Coady tried desperately to counter fascism and communism by offering the common people an alternative, the co-operative blueprint that he believed had the divine stamp. But Coady, like other big dreamers of the early 20th century, was caught up in a redemptive narrative that failed to deliver what he had promised.

The 20th century plainly teaches us that few of us have much control over our destinies at all. Let's not stop dreaming, but let's dream close to the ground. It may well be time for a new, more modest re-storying of our work as adult educators. It may also be time for much deeper reflection on those forces at work in history constantly subverting the desires of the ordinary people for opportunities to actually realise their potential. We cannot escape the storying process. But some of the stories and old traditions we cling to may not be up to the task of confronting the puzzles of living in our turbulent age of globalism, where the old unjust structures are unwilling to leave and the new ones hesitant to come.

BURIED HISTORIES

Hidden history

Teaching 'contact history' in Central Australia in an indigenous college in the 1990s, I used to invite students to locate themselves and their families within the timelines of Australia's 'grander' historical narratives. The students' own parents and grandparents, for example, had stories their parents had told them of meeting the first white explorers to enter the district in the 1860s and 70s. Parents, uncles, mothers and aunts had been the stockworkers illegally paid below-award wages on pastoral leases, missions and government settlements until the late 1960s, then were pushed off their country when they tried to claim their rights (Hardy 1968). Many of their parents and some of their co-students were members of the 'stolen generations', removed from their families to institutions and white foster homes 'for their own good' (Australian HREOC 1997). I also learned that many stories remain repressed, within families as well as in the broader histories taught in schools and universities. Painful stories are often not told to younger generations, for fear of inflicting on them the same trauma they brought at the time. On the 'other side of the frontier', people in power are loath to acknowledge the extent to which their wealth and influence was built on inflicting that trauma. Official local 'histories' throughout Australia tell little of the dispossession and virtual slave labour of local indigenous populations that accompanied the growth of their modern economies and social structures. The politics of memory and forgetting thus hangs heavily over settler societies like the USA, Australia and Canada, as it does over any 'advanced' country whose economic and social wealth is in part a stolen legacy from the past.

As adult educators, we need to locate ourselves in this 'grander' history. In Australia, while adult educators point proudly to the profession's involvement with the civil rights movement of the 1960s, they have been less willing to acknowledge that the incarceration of indigenous peoples on settlements and missions, and their use as slave labour, had an educational justification: they were 'in training', it was said—which the mainstream 'official' profession challenged only when a political movement for indigenous rights, built by different kinds of 'educators', attained a force that could not be ignored (Boughton 2001). Contemporary adult education programs rarely teach us how to view our profession's history so critically; but those who follow this path soon discover that the field was not always as cohesive or bland as the modern 'profession' and the institutions that issue its credentials now appear to be.

Who killed radical adult education?

To understand why, we need a story. Once upon a time, in the far-off lands of northern Europe, education was a very scarce commodity. Even to read the Bible could mark you as potentially subversive, a threat to the established order ruled by church and state. Some of those who considered such restrictions a shocking imposition and the principal support of tyranny can be found in the Australian convict records of the 1790s. In those days, Scottish Jacobins with the temerity to distribute Tom Paine's Rights of Man were hauled before wealthy magistrates, men who owned the land worked by the peasants to whom the Jacobins were teaching democratic theory. They were promptly 'transported' south to the Antipodes, where Irish republicans with similarly dangerous views were soon joining them (Hughes 1987: 175–6):

> Transportation was an important feature of the machinery of English state repression . . . [It] got rid of the dissenter without making him a hero on the scaffold. He slipped off the map into a distant limbo, where his voice fell dead at his feet. There was nothing for his ideas to engage, if he were an intellectual; no machines to break or ricks to burn if a labourer. He could preach sedition to the thieves or the cockatoos, or to the wind. Nobody would care.

Repression, however, is never so complete, and these early radical educators sowed the seeds of ideas that informed the popular movements, strengthened in the 1850s by a new wave of Chartist exiles, people schooled in the tradition of 'really useful knowledge' (Johnson 1988; Thompson 1995), who joined the nascent labour movement and the movement for an independent republic. While they lost the battle for the republic, they won the eight-hour day decades before their European counterparts, and slowly set about building an organised trade union movement which was, by the 1880s, studying the texts of the great European socialist thinkers, including Mark and Engels—the 'proletarian science' which for the next 50 years formed the core curriculum of working-class autodidacts throughout the world (Connell & Irving 1980; Macintyre 1980). Sometimes they met in the Mechanics Institutes and Schools of Arts, educational institutions that local elites established for their labourers' betterment (Whiting 1994). Mostly they formed their own study circles, and discussed ideas in meetings and the popular press of their trade unions and the myriad small political parties and social progress organisations that formed around this time.

This early educational movement, despite its vitality, was deeply flawed, but another century and a lot of bitter debate would pass before its problems were recognised as such. With the benefit of hindsight, and thanks to that debate, historians now point to the exclusionary nature of this early movement, dominated by the white men who stood at the apex of the 'aristocracy of labour'. Nineteenth century feminists mounted a partial critique, but they also did not extend the human rights they demanded for themselves to the non-white peoples of the region. It was a fatal lesson not to learn, it turned out. The lack of learning embodied in the popular movement's failure to comprehend the universality of human rights was the reverse side of its lack of understanding of the global nature of its enemies. This left it unprepared for the assault on its progress launched in the 1890s by 'capital', which in those days had no qualms calling itself by its real name and self-consciously opposing itself to 'labour'. A little over a century ago, the Australian labour movement met its match as police smashed its picket lines, gaoled its leaders, and destroyed much of its growing organisation in the great strikes of the 1890s, themselves an echo of similar developments in Europe somewhat earlier and an effect of growing challenges from other European powers and a nascent United States to Britain's dominance of the capitalist world economy. The (white-male-led) workers' paradise the Australian union movement planned to build came hard up against the second wave of globalisation to crash onto these shores, colonisation itself having been the first.

Once again, learning came to the rescue, as Australian workers engaged in a new flurry of political and educational activity, scrambling to learn how to exercise more effectively their newly won extended franchise against men (as they invariably were) who had enjoyed the fruits of office for generations. In a virtual golden age of radical adult education, street meetings, public forums, study circles, plays, poetry, lectures, pamphlets and the 'popular press' multiplied in Australian cities and towns, as the 'army of labour' (military metaphors were popular) imbibed every revolutionary doctrine of the time. A learning society in action, but without the profession or the bureaucracy now considered to be its essential ingredient! The records they left behind are breath-taking in their extent and the depth and wisdom of their vision. If ever people studied how to build a better world, they did it in their thousands then, before the Australian Commonwealth had even been born and decades before an English bishop arrived to help Australian universities establish a 'workers' education association.

Stories of these times and the frenzied educational activity that char-acterised the period from the 1890s to the period immediately after the end of World War I are found in a growing body of work by social and labour historians (e.g. Damousi 1994; Burgmann 1995; Freisen & Taksa 1996). This popular educational tradition lives on today in the edu-cational work of social movements which like their forebears in these early democratic movements know that education and agitation put together become powerful catalysts of social change. In such ferment we can discern not just radical but revolutionary learning, as people discover that the future can be made differently from the past, and study how to get there. This is Mezirow's (1991) perspective transformation, but on a societal rather than an individual scale.

Studying adult education at university in the early 1990s, I knew almost none of this. The history taught then, based on the so-called classic *The Great Tradition* (Whitelock 1974), suffered from a major fault identified in a seminal article on adult educational historiography (Welton 1993). When Whitelock looked back on the past, he saw a natural, gradual evolution towards the institutions which to me offered little sense of vital and effective social engagement—university adult education departments, the Workers' Educational Association in some states, and the myriad small and underfunded community education centres that battled on at the margins. Welton's work inspired me to go in search of other traditions, as did UK and US adult educational his-torians who had similarly begun excavating their own country's records (e.g. Johnson 1988). In the process, we were all discovering that the dominance of a highly professionalised and depoliticised field of prac-tice was anything but natural. Rather, it was an outcome of a long and bitter struggle fought over what would count as real education. The victors had written a history that made their victory seem like the only possible outcome, through a simple definitional device. What the now 'officially sanctioned' institutions did was education; what social movements did was 'only' propaganda—or, worse still, 'indoctrination' (Boughton 1996, 1999).

Revisionist history research is a collective effort, in its infancy in Australian adult education. In the first edition of this book, Roger Morris signalled the need for Whitelock's hegemonic 'liberal' tradition to make way for other stories, other traditions (Foley & Morris 1995). More recent work continues the investigation (e.g. Merlyn 2001; Rushbrook & Brown 2001), but the plot is still unfolding. So whose stories, whose histories, shall we tell and write? In our classrooms, learning circles and workplace meetings, everyone has a story. If these are shared, they will begin to describe a history. Connect this history to other peoples 'histories' and popular education begins, producing and reproducing new and previously marginalised knowledge about who we are and how our societies came to be. We learn, as all good adult learners and adult teachers are taught, from our experiences. We invite you here to think of these not as the experiences of the individualised, classless, genderless, 'race-less' and 'de-historicised' adult learner the profession subsequently invented (Welton 1987), but as the experiences of the social movements of which every learner is ultimately a part, and which have a deal of unfinished, transformative learning to pursue.

The English Marxist scholar Perry Anderson reminds us that conscious programs in history 'aimed at creating or remodelling whole social structures' are relatively recent phenomena: in the 19th century, the modern labour movement gave birth to the idea that 'collective projects of social transformation . . . [could be] married to *systematic efforts to understand the processes of past and present*, to produce a pre-meditated future' (Anderson 1980: 20, my emphasis). While remaining skeptical of 'master narratives', we can still hang on to this possibility, identifying with 'learning movements' which study and learn about the world as they work to change it. Such movements require a vision of the world they seek to make (a 'pre-meditated future'), but know little of the detail or how to get there, beyond what it is possible to know in the historically specific circumstances of their time. We cannot simply jump over history to a world of ideal discourse; we have to get our hands dirty, living it, acting on it, changing things and learning as we go, with history as our collective learning journal. This is the wisdom in the title of Freire and Horton's 'talking book' on radical adult education: 'We make the road by walking' (Horton & Freire 1990).

UNCOVERING A HISTORY OF ACTIVE LEARNING

In 1983, when I was in my mid-20s, I researched the social protest that accompanied the New South Wales general strike of 1917 (Taksa 1983). The choice of this subject was influenced by many factors, but perhaps the most important was my early life as a migrant growing up in Australia, a country I knew little about because the history I learnt at school focused on Britain. My parents could provide little help. While they could recount many stories about Soviet and Polish history, they had no way of learning about Australia's past; the evening classes they attended after work provided only 'useful knowledge' in the form of basic English language skills and information on accepted cultural norms. From such learning experiences we gained the impression that Australian had a very limited history and no tradition of resistance compared to Eastern Europe. Only later, during my adolescence, was this perception challenged by the local protest against involvement in the Vietnam War. It was in this context that I was acquainted with earlier examples of public resistance, particularly against conscription. At university, I determined to find out more.

In studying the 1917 general strike I discovered a history of working-class protest that was predicated on a tradition of active learning in the workplace and outside it, on the streets, in parks, trades halls and labour colleges. At such informal sites of education I found Australian workers who had resisted the knowledge and cultural aspirations that were offered to them under the rubric of adult education. The 1917 strike occurred when a modified version of F.W. Taylor's system of manage-ment was introduced into Sydney's railway and tramway workshops. Known as scientific management, Taylor's ideas influenced not only the organisation of work but also educational reforms in the USA and Australia. Because he promoted formal training in technical colleges and universities, his ideas helped to spread the managerial and profes-sionisation ethos that has come to dominate our lives (Taksa 1992, 1993, 1995).

Before 1917, workers in NSW had already learned from their Ameri-can counterparts that Taylor's system threatened not only their working conditions but also their traditional means of acquiring knowledge from each other through observation and word of mouth in the workplace. But the workplace provided only one source of adult learning: others included trade union journals and mass meetings in places like the Sydney Domain. The knowledge obtained through all these mediums led workers to oppose Taylor's system in 1917 and inspired them to learn more about the world around them (Johnson 1988; Taksa 1983, 1991, 1994a, 1994b). Such learning provided a stark contrast to the approach adopted by formal institutions of adult education, which treated workers as passive subjects. It is precisely this treatment that has been repro-duced in the annals of adult education. By looking closely at how workers responded to the institutions of adult education we can uncover a lost history—the history of struggle between middle-class professionals and workers' representatives and between competing cultural ideals, aspirations and knowledge.

A contested terrain

Adult education became a contested terrain from the early decades of the 19th century because British workers resisted middle-class efforts to provide them with 'useful knowledge', preferring instead to pursue the opportunity for 'free inquiry' offered by workingmen's societies and socialist clubs. At the centre of this contest was a conflict between cultural aspirations and ideologies. While middle-class liberals saw education as the means for achieving individual improvement and social peace, for workers and their representatives it offered the possibility for social transformation and even emancipation. This battleground was not constrained by national and geographic boundaries. It accompanied the spread of British models of adult education to Australia's distant shores.

Arguably the most important model was the Workers' Educational Association (WEA). Formed in England in 1903, it arrived in Australia in 1913. But unlike its parent the Australian branch was unable to maintain an enduring bond with the labour movement, mainly because its offer to address specific working-class interests was quickly subordinated to the principle of non-partisanship adopted from the English Association's constitution. This principle reflected a middle-class desire to make the WEA a 'common meeting ground for all' (WEA 1914). In practice, it challenged the labour movement's desire for social change. The battle lines were drawn during World War I, when the WEA's middle-class members began to use its forums to preach the benefits of scientific management, 'efficiency' and social harmony. As they had done during the late 19th century, workers responded by relying on their own efforts and organisations for educational opportunities (Spence 1909; Patmore 1985; Taksa 1992).

Labour movement involvement

For both middle-class professionals and labour movement officials, the WEA provided a mechanism for reaching workers. It was attractive to union officials because it offered them an opportunity to influence workers' education (Mainsbridge 1920; Whitelock 1974). Indeed, the NSW Labor Council helped establish the WEA, and a large number of unions joined immediately, believing that the WEA would fulfil their aspirations (Barcan 1988; Friesen & Taksa 1996). Despite early opposition to the WEA from socialists like Luke Jones, who had been involved in the Plebs League in England, workers also joined the WEA because it seemed to whet their interest in what we might now call trade union training. By 1913, they made up the majority of students in New South Wales and Queensland. Women employed in Sydney's larger factories were also drawn to the classes held for them at the Trades Hall in 1914 (Friesen & Taksa 1996).

Yet the WEA did not succeed in being 'truly representative of working class opinion on educational questions'. When its non-partisanship affronted such cardinal labour movement principles as the 'closed shop', unions began to defect and tutorial classes in highly industrialised towns were suspended (WEA 1914–16; Stewart 1947; Whitelock 1974). Such deep-seated differences became even more pronounced when the WEA's leading missionaries united to prosecute the war by pursuing 'national efficiency' and supporting conscription.

The struggle for efficiency

In 1914 the WEA's leading Australian missionary, Meredith Atkinson, began advocating 'scientific education', one of F.W. Taylor's four principles of scientific management. A year later he used the WEA's conference on 'Trade Unionism in Australia' to spread this view to 188 delegates, of whom 55 represented trade unions. This was a tactical blunder. In response to this and Atkinson's links to conscription, 18 labour organisations disaffiliated and the WEA branch in the south-coast industrial town of Wollongong collapsed. Similar developments occurred in Queensland and South Australia. Wartime imperatives drove a wedge between labour and the WEA that was never effectively removed (Atkinson 1915; Whitelock 1974; Rowse 1978; Taksa 1993).

By 1917 members of the Victorian Socialist Party had launched their own labour college, and in 1919 others were established in Queensland and NSW. Although these were short-lived, they did represent an attempt to counter the WEA's ideological onslaught. At a conference on 'The Working Class and Education' organised by the Victorian college in 1918, speakers stressed that the WEA's claim to impartiality was untrue and that the labour college 'was a recognition of the necessity of workers to organise in the educational as they had done in the industrial and political fields'. The express goal of the Sydney college was to put 'into practice the principles which the industrial labour movement stands for—control on the job' (Rowse 1978; Earsman 1920).

By contrast, middle-class professionals wanted the WEA to help create a 'highly educated democracy'. At one WEA conference in 1919 they disparaged workers for drawing conclusions about economic subjects from labour newspapers and public meetings; these media appealed to 'class and party interests', 'poisoned the popular mind' and prevented social integration (Atkinson 1915; WEA 1919). Numerous WEA publications advocated political education to overcome the 'scientifically false' gospel of 'class hatred' preached on 'every street corner in Australia'. In his textbook for WEA students, Meredith Atkinson stressed that the cultivation of 'class hatred' was a disqualification for 'true citizenship' (Atkinson 1919; Mayo 1919).

Labour leaders responded immediately to such attacks. At a public memorial for Luke Jones in 1919, Percy Brookfield MP argued that the 'producers of this country, and every country, are the only decent citizens there are' (Police Reports 1919). By the early 1920s unions also began publishing educational literature for a wider working-class audience. In 1923 the printers' union published articles in its paper on education 'from the working-class viewpoint'. These were subsequently produced as a book. As its author put it, independent working-class education represented 'a partisan effort to improve the position of that class' and to achieve 'a revolutionary change in existing economic and social institutions and conditions'. It challenged the 'bogus education' offered by the 'outpatients departments of the Universities' (Eldridge 1924). This view was shared by other workers. As the WEA admitted, 'we are not getting the proportion of wage workers we would like to get, and it will be a long time before we do' (WEA 1919).

During the 1920s and 30s the Communist Party of Australia (CPA) became involved in delivering education from a working-class point of view. Its Trade Union Leagues provided 'training classes in Marxism'. Admittedly these attracted few workers. But the Party did reach unionists through the Militant Minority Movement, which established important links with the Miners' Federation, the Waterside Workers' Union and the Australian Railways Union in 1928. By 1931 it had gained control over the latter's newly formed Educational and Organisational Committee. Also during the early 1930s, the Party's regular newspapers, *Workers' Weekly*, *Workers' Voice* and *Red Star*, reached a combined circulation of almost 30 000, while those of its front organisations reached around 60 000 per week in NSW. At the same time, unions and rank-and-file shop committees provided study classes at the workplace and in union offices. These focused on history, economics and political affairs, and also taught practical skills like public speaking. Summer school camps were also held for unionists and their wives (Davidson 1969; *The Railway Union Gazette* 1926; *The Railroad* 1931, 1934, 1938).

These activities ran parallel to similar ones organised by the WEA, which were attended by some workers. But this only inspired more opposition. In May 1940, May Brodney used the pages of the Engineering Union's journal to attack the WEA's summer school and to call for a labour college in NSW that would provide 'instruction with a working-class bias'. This was a necessary corrective to the WEA's support for 'vested interests' and employers 'in spite of a formal attitude of impartiality'. Accordingly, she concluded that 'as long as this association continues the W.E.A. will be rejected by the workers' (Brodney 1940).

May Brodney's efforts, like those of many labour activists, have been omitted from the official chronicles of adult education. Far from being passive subjects, workers and unionists preferred to rely on their own learning and educational networks and organisations.

8

ECONOMICS, POLITICS AND ADULT EDUCATION

Shirley Walters, Carmel Borg, Peter Mayo & Griff Foley

'Political economy' does what it implies: it explores relationships between economics and politics. In discussion and writings about adult education these links are rarely analysed. Most of the time, the 'shaping context' of adult education is treated in a simplistic and deterministic way. The mantra of neoliberal economics is endlessly repeated: adult education must help economies become lean, mean and internationally competitive. This of course is no analysis at all but a justification for a set of policies and practices, which benefit some people and disadvantage others.

Griff Foley begins this chapter by arguing that neoliberal economics has led national economies into an unwinnable competition, the burden of which falls on working people. Peter Mayo and Carmel Borg then show how the neoliberal economic discourse has shaped European lifelong learning policy. Mayo and Borg emphasise that adult educators can contest the dominant human capital educational discourse and promote a more humanist and emancipatory conception of lifelong learning. In the final section, Shirley Walters discusses the potential of the Learning Cape Festival in South Africa to do this.

THE POLITICAL ECONOMY OF CAPITALISM

Economic crisis and restructuring

The liberal US scholar Lester Thurow argues that although capitalism is the dominant modern economic system, it is in profound crisis. Indicators of the crisis include slowing growth in output and job creation, declining real wages, and sudden and severe recessions. He maintains that the long-established international division of labour—between the older industrialised countries (the 'first world') and the countries that supply raw materials—has broken down. The comparative advantages held by the older industrialised countries, the result of accumulating capital through plunder, colonisation, trade and manufacturing, no longer hold. Raw materials suppliers, too, have lost comparative advantage. New products absorb fewer raw materials, less labour and more technology. 'Today', Thurow maintains, 'knowledge and skills now stand alone as the only source of comparative advantage'. There is now a 'new industrial divide' (a term coined by Piore & Sabel 1984) between high-technology and low-technology industries (Thurow 1996: 65–8).

In this new global economy, comparative advantage depends on the capacity of nations and corporations to effectively exploit new technologies and human capital. Governments and individuals come under ever-greater pressure to develop workers' skills. Business relocates to the third world to take advantage of low-cost, often well-educated labour; new technologies enable the conception of work in one country and its execution in another. Within corporations new organisational forms emerge, pushing decision making as far down the hierarchy as possible, to take advantage of workers' knowledge and skills. Work organisations also 'downsize', shedding large numbers of workers and cutting out layers of management in an effort to become more productive and competitive (1996: 26–9, 66–9, 76–82).

Costs of change

Thurow identifies two major costs of change:

1. A massive cultural change as 'human values are for the first time . . . shaped by a profit-maximizing electronic media', which communicate in emotional rather than rational ways that appear more real than reality itself, managing to persuade people, for example, of the need for radical rises in expenditure on police and prisons in an era of falling murder rates. The mass media also promote instant gratification and individualism, and work against collective sacrifice and investment in the future—the latter ironically, Thurow notes, the very values on which capitalism was originally built (1996: 82–6).
2. A massive increase in inequality. This manifests itself in a number of ways:

(a) Accelerating inequality. In the USA the distribution of income remained relatively stable from 1945 until 1968, when 'suddenly in 1968, inequality started to rise' and continued to do so. During the 1980s all of the gains in male earnings went to the wealthiest 20% of the population. By the early 1990s the top 1% of the population controlled about 40% of US wealth, double what it had held in the mid-1970s and similar to what it had been in the 1920s before the introduction of progressive taxation (1996: 20–2).

(b) Falling real wages. In the USA, the real wages of men began to fall in 1973 and by the early 1990s were falling for 'all ages, industries, occupations and every educational group'. The decreases became larger the further down the income scale one went. By the end of 1994 real wages were at the same level as they had been in the late 1950s and were still falling (1996: 22–5).

(c) Growth in unemployment and the 'working poor'. Over the past 30 years all of the older industrialised countries have experienced significant rises in either unemployment or low-wage jobs. Which of these trends a country experiences depends on government policy. The USA and Britain have opted for a low-wage strategy and have massively expanded their workforces, mostly in low-wage, low-skill service sector jobs. The USA has created an unemployed and underemployed 'contingent workforce' of temporary workers and self-employed 'independent contractors' or 'consultants' (1996: 1, 165).

In contrast, most Western European countries have opted to maintain higher real wages and government-funded social security, the cost of which has been an unemployment rate double that of the USA (10.8% compared with 5.4% in March 1995). By the mid-1990s, German manufacturing labour costs were two-thirds higher than those of the USA, and German companies like Mercedes and BMW were moving factories to the southern states of the USA. Thurow argues that in the face of such mobility of capital, Western Europe will be forced to abandon its system of wage-fixing and social welfare, which adds, for example, 40% to the cost of labour in France. Nor, he argues, does the Japanese style of 'communitarian capitalism', with lifetime employment and government support of business, offer a way out. With at least 10% of Japanese workers having little work to do, lifetime employment is in reality a disguised form of unemployment relief for workers who would be pushed out of the labour market in a more open economy. The Japanese model worked well enough during the postwar boom, but in tighter times it has become an almost profitless capitalism (1996: 1–2, 34–9, 322).

Thurow raises the spectre of a low-wage, low-social-welfare strategy inexorably spreading as country after country scrambles to compete in the global market. As we will see, the US economic historian Robert Brenner shows that this is a competition with few winners.

The economics of global turbulence

In a 1998 paper, Brenner analysed the long downturn in the world economy that began in the early 1970s, continued through the 1990s and continues into the new millennium. This downturn has been characterised by low rates of growth in output, productivity, profitability, investment and real wages, together with accelerating social inequality and high rates of unemployment and poverty (Brenner 1998: 2–7ff). This combination of factors constitutes an ongoing economic and political crisis, the indicators of which include (1998: 3–7):

- In the advanced capitalist economies, average rates of growth of output, investment, labour productivity and real wages for 1973–98 were one third to one half those for 1950–73, while the average unemployment rate more than doubled.
- In the USA between 1973 and 1996 the growth in productivity for the economy as a whole fell to its lowest level in the country's history.
- There was a 'generalised fall and long-term failure of recovery of profitability in manufacturing' in the 1970–90 period.
- While there was some recovery in the profitability of the US economy in the 1990s, it is unclear how solid the recovery is or how long it will last. This apparent recovery was built on:
  —'a repression of wages without precedent during the last century, and perhaps since the [1860–65] Civil War', real hourly wages falling 12% from their peak in 1970–90, and not rising at all in 1990–96;
  —a massive reduction of the primary (permanent, unionised) labour force and a sharp rise in the secondary (temporary, casualised) labour force; and
  —a sharp reduction in social welfare expenditure, which is reflected in an accelerating incidence of poverty and ill-health.

In short, Brenner argues, the global economy has been in a long and seemingly intractable downturn since 1973, and the recent tentative economic recovery of the USA has been won 'at the direct expense of its main economic rivals and especially its working class' (1998: 3). This long decline, Brenner maintains, is not attributable to supply-side factors (the high cost of labour and the welfare state) but rather to 'the unplanned, uncoordinated and competitive nature of capitalist production', which generates overproduction and a declining rate of profit (1998: 8, 24–6).

An unwinnable competition

Brenner argues that this extended and continuing economic crisis is being driven by 'a specific historical pattern of uneven development and international competition' (1998: 35). After World War II, trade grew rapidly, 'but it began everywhere from very low levels'. By the early 1960s the bulk of production in the US economy, the world's largest, was still for its domestic market. In this environment, the more efficient Japanese and German producers could grow and take an increasing share of world trade without affecting US firms.

But, quite suddenly, the situation changed. In the late 1950s trade barriers were radically reduced, generating an increase in world trade in the early 1960s. Lower-cost, lower price exports from Japan drove prices down, at the same time reducing the market share and profits of firms based in the older industrialised countries, such as the USA and Britain. This set off 'a process of over-investment leading to over-capacity and over-production' as manufacturers in older and newer industrialised countries scrambled for market share. The resulting sharp decline in the profitability of its manufacturing industry led the USA to devalue its dollar, first in 1973, then again in the mid-1980s and in the early 1990s. These devaluations, together with massive new investment, and the massive labour shedding and sharp reductions in real wages discussed by Thurow, increased the competitiveness of US firms. But the US competitive edge did not last long, because Japanese and German firms stayed in the global competition for markets and were then joined in the 1980s by the newly industrialised Asian countries. So competition for markets kept intensifying and, with it, overcapacity, overproduction and a declining rate of profit (Brenner 1998: 36–8).

Brenner argues that the long-running economic turbulence or crisis is ultimately attributable to the logic of capitalism. In capitalism, individuals and firms seek to maximise their profits. When new, more efficient parties enter the competition for profits, older players do not readily withdraw. Instead, even if their rate of profit declines substantially, they continue to produce. Ultimately, of course, some firms close down as costs outweigh profits. But many remain, creating a spiral of overinvestment, overcapacity, overproduction and falling profits. Various attempts are made to break the spiral—lowering the cost of labour, making labour more productive through the introduction of new technologies and new ways of organising work, controlling competition through regional trade blocs and global trade agreements. Some of these measures succeed for a while. But once the war is over the logic reasserts itself and the pattern of overproduction and declining rate of profit re-emerges (1998: 24).

Like Thurow, Brenner maintains that in the current crisis, as in earlier ones, the burden of finding a way out falls on workers. Both writers provide detailed statistics, some of which have been quoted above, to show that after the generalised fall in profitability that began in the mid-1960s, in the older industrialised countries both real wages and the social wage stagnated, and in the case of the USA declined 'sharply, virtually instantaneously, and ever increasingly' (Brenner 1998: 140). Both writers also note that this decline was deliberately induced. Over the past 25 years government and business have sought to make their economies and enterprises more productive and internationally competitive, primarily by reducing the cost of labour and increasing its flexibility. They have sought to achieve this through a range of measures, such as reducing expenditure on social infrastructure and services, reducing the primary (full-time, permanent) workforce and expanding the secondary (part-time, casual, contracting) workforce, outsourcing work to cheaper domestic and international suppliers, linking education more closely to production ('vocationalising' it), and reorganising work.

The character and logic of capitalism

Adult education is determined by capitalism. Recognising this is fundamental to acting effectively, no matter what one's politics and values. Capitalism is a system of creative destruction. Its will to profit generates an unwinnable competition among producers, which generates periodic crises, the burden of which falls on workers. Each crisis creates demands for production to be reorganised, so enterprises and nations can perform better in the competition for profit. At the same time the nature of the crisis and the system of production that generates it remain hidden from view, masked by ideologies that direct attention elsewhere—for example, towards alleged deficiencies in education provision, teachers or students, or the inadequacies of workers, or the way work is organised, all of which may be significant but are not determining. Adult educators need to understand how the characteristics and logic of the capitalist political economy shape their work.

THE EUROPEAN UNION: MEMORANDUM ON LIFELONG LEARNING

The importance of educators understanding political economy is demonstrated by contemporary European discussion and policy making on 'lifelong learning'.

Lifelong learning is an all-embracing concept incorporating the various stages of a person's education. The concept, as adopted by UNESCO (Tuijnman & Boström 2002) in the late 1960s and 70s, had a 'scientific-humanist' ring to it and accommodated both liberal and radical positions. People like Ettore Gelpi (1985), who headed UNESCO's Lifelong Education Unit, used the concept of 'lifelong education' and its related notion of the 'education-centred society' (Suchodolski 1976:64) to provide an expansive view of human beings in a context characterised by an ever-growing consumerism and media power.

This 'old' literature anticipated a more recent critical conceptualisation of lifelong learning (e.g. see Williamson 1998; Martin 2001), which counters the neoliberal tendency to see human beings in two-dimensional terms as producers and consumers. This literature critiques the 'new vocationalism' in education and its tendency to turn social problems into individual problems—to turn, for example, an economy's failure to produce jobs into a 'skills crisis' caused by education's 'failure' to produce skilled workers (Marshall 1997: 59).

Despite the humanist theory underpinning it, the concept of lifelong education can too readily serve the interests of capitalist reorganisation. For instance, much of the lifelong education literature was unaware of learning's collective dimension. Instead, it advocated a problematic concept of 'self-directed' learning (see Cropley & Dave 1978: 21). An individualised notion of self-directed learning is central to the OECD's and the European Union's (EU) conception of lifelong learning. While UNESCO provided a broad and humanist use of the concept, the OECD reduced it to little more than 'human capital theory'—'albeit laced', in the words of John Field (2001), 'with a few dashes of social democracy'.

An important discursive shift occurred in this process. With the notion of self-directed learning (as opposed to any notion of collectively directed learning) being given prominence, the emphasis was no longer on structures and institutions but on the individual lying at the centre of the educational process, who was conceived of as having the potential to take charge of his/her own learning (Tuijnman & Boström 2002: 102–3). The preferred term was no longer 'lifelong education' but 'lifelong learning', as 'education' placed the emphasis on structures and, by implication, onus on the state to ensure that these structures were in place for people to receive the kind of education to which they were entitled.

But both the OECD and the EU have managed to turn 'lifelong learning' into a policy goal, something UNESCO failed to accomplish with 'lifelong education' (Field 1998; Brine 1999; Murphy 1997). In the EU, lifelong learning was to be a central feature of the development of the 'knowledge economy' (Dale & Robertson 2002: 28; CEC 2001; Wain 2003). The major EU preoccupation was the need to pool the educational resources of European nations, to render them competitive in the face of transnational corporations' ability to derive the benefits of economies of scale through the expansion of international capital mobility (Murphy 1997: 363). Concern with capitalist restructuring was evident throughout the EU's 1994 White Paper on competitiveness (CEC 1994), which constituted the 'linchpin of post-1994 economic, social, education and training policy' (Brine 1999: 83). Lifelong learning was to be a feature of this policy (CEC 2001: 3; Field 2002: 4; Waddington 2002: 160).

Eight months after the formulation of its strategy to develop the world's best 'knowledge economy', the European Commission issued a 'Memorandum on Lifelong Learning' (CEC 2000). The Memorandum is an important source of reference for the Leonardo program (vocational education that includes vocational adult education) and the Grundtvig action (the adult education action) within the Socrates program. It also includes such initiatives as the most recent learning region initiative, more accurately the 'Regional Networks for Life-Long Learning' (R3L) pilot initiative, which is intended to provide a local and regional dimension to lifelong learning (CEC 2002). (Another learning region initiative is described in the case study from South Africa.)

The Memorandum defines lifelong learning as 'all purposeful learning activity, undertaken on an ongoing basis with the aim of improving knowledge, skills and competence' (CEC 2000: 3). The definition was formulated within the context of the European Employment Strategy (CEC 2000). The connection between lifelong learning and employment led to the voicing of strong objections during the consultation process, resulting in a change in definition that brought the social dimension element into reckoning. Like all institutions, the EU is not a monolithic entity and offers spaces wherein the hegemonic ideas it espouses can be challenged and modified through a policy-making process—a virtual 'policy soup' (Richardson 2001: 18) that allows lobbyists the opportunity of exploring different venues ('venue shopping') to try to place ideas on the agenda. The venues include the Commission itself, the European Parliament, the Council of Ministers and the costly European Court of Justice (Mazey & Richardson 2001).

Nonetheless, the lifelong learning 'policy soup' has a predominant ingredient, neoliberalism, as can be seen in the EU document *National Actions to Implement Lifelong Learning in Europe* (Cedefop/Eurydice 2001). This provides an overview of action undertaken to promote lifelong learning in accord with the six key messages underlying the EU's Memorandum. (For a fuller discussion, see Borg & Mayo 2002.)

The first key message concerns the acquisition of 'new basic skills'. In the summary of the Cedefop/Eurydice document, which leads to the detailed exposition of projects concerning these new basic skills, the authors state (2001: 15):

> The structures underlying education are changing as entire curricula are reconsidered. Whole sections of systems, if not systems themselves, are undergoing thorough reform. The result of gradually more integrated approaches is that arrangements for guidance, support and identification of skills needed by the labour market, in cooperation with the social partners, are highly significant aspects of curricular provision.

The strong link between education provision and the labour market is very evident in a number of European projects described in the Cedefop/Eurydice document. The Career-Space project, for instance, launched by seven major ICT (information and communication technology) companies in Europe and supported by the European Commission, seeks to explore new ways of addressing the perceived skills gaps generated by the 'knowledge society'. The project attempts to provide a framework for education and training institutions that defines skills and competences required by the ICT industry in Europe. While the cutting edge of the high-tech sector constitutes the main concern of the Career-Space project, the aim is to redefine the needs at all levels in all industry sectors, as 'computers and ICT specialists are needed across the broad spectrum of industries and services today' (2001: 17). In April 2001, the European Commission's 'New Strategy on Building New European Labour Markets by 2005' set up a high-level skills and mobility taskforce to 'identify the main drivers and characteristics of the new European labour market, with a particular focus on skills, lifelong learning and mobility' (2001: 17).

The European Computer Driving Licence (ECDL), launched in August 1996 and now an ICT benchmark in many countries, transcends the need for enhancing knowledge and competence in the use of personal computers and common computer applications within Europe and the rest of the world. The ECDL provides a basic qualification that will enhance 'the productivity of employees who use computers in their work, enabling better returns from investments in IT' (2001: 17).

The common thread that weaves through European discussion and action on ICT is the attempt by private enterprise to construct, once again, a 'skills crisis' rather than a 'jobs crisis'. This perceived gap, an aspect of the persistent call on the education community to render its operations more relevant, is forcing public institutions to redefine their educational priorities. The net result of this European hysteria around ICT skills is an increase in public financing of private needs in an area of human resources that is crucial to latter-day capitalism. Private and public interests, concerns and agendas are slowly becoming one. The following passage, meshing the discourses of neoliberal economics and lifelong learning, illustrates how public institutions are willing to accommodate industry's needs (2001: 18):

> A number of Member States have completely overhauled their VET systems and replaced them with competence-based systems. Such core curricula often try to find the right mix between general education subjects, generic skills, and specific or technical skills for a particular occupation or job. This is seen as part of the provision of a wide foundation for lifelong learning in initial education and training, in particular, a broad skills base on which to develop one's career and employability.

At this point, the discussion on what constitutes basic skills becomes crucial. In the context of post-secondary, particularly vocational education, apart from the highly diffused area of ICT, which is closely associated with moves towards the 'information society' and the needs of a 'knowledge economy', the document indicates that two curriculum models have been proposed in Europe. One model, promoting basic, generic and core skills (2001: 31), is characteristic of English-speaking countries, although it is seen, albeit to a lesser degree, in a number of

146

other countries (Denmark, Netherlands, Germany, Finland). The skills promoted within this approach are (2001: 31):

> the general elementary and/or cognitive competences required for a whole series of jobs, indeed all jobs: mathematics, reading, writing, problem-solving, social, communication and interpersonal competences. They are entry skills to gainful work and employment as well as skills necessary for social participation (citizenship).

The other approach, said to promote transferable (key) competences and broad professional competence (Denmark, Germany, Italy, Austria), is based on (2001: 31):

> a collection of competences transcending divisions of labour and traditional occupational profiles. The competences cited are social and communication competences, and strategic efficiency, in particular problem-solving competences, organisational competences and leadership.

Both approaches assume that the skills required for success in the market economy are the same skills necessary for active citizenship. This is in keeping with the narrow definition of citizenship favoured by those whom the British sociologist Bill Williamson (1998) calls the 'new utopians' (managers, technocrats, IT specialists). Williamson argues that their vision is gaining prominence, despite its not having any 'humane centre', being a 'systems view of the world' which, 'in its unintended outcomes, is corroding the whole social fabric of modern society' (1998: 91). The Cedefop/Eurydice document, echoing the 'new utopian vision', suggests that the educated citizen is one who can easily transfer a set of skills from the economic to the social sphere. This is a recurring feature of the other strategies outlined in the document (Borg & Mayo 2002).

The EU Memorandum on Lifelong Learning and the projects that drew inspiration from it show the extent of dilution that has occurred with respect to the once more expansive concept of lifelong education as propounded by the group of writers whose main ideas were discussed earlier. Some of their humanistic considerations, together with those of other writers, were co-opted in the service of a document seeking to provide a humanistic facade to what is, in effect, a neoliberal-inspired set of guidelines. These guidelines are intended to sharpen member countries' competitive edge in a globalising economy. The original concept of lifelong education has been appropriated by capitalism and narrowed in the process, a situation that is true also of many other potentially oppositional discourses. Such appropriations are a feature of capitalism's dynamic nature. Adult educators ought to be made aware of the extent of the dilution so that they can reclaim the finer, more humanistic and in certain cases radical aspects of the 'old' lifelong education discourse, and join the struggle[1] for the development of an alternative and emancipatory conception of lifelong learning, one that emphasises the collective dimension of learning and conceives of the learner/citizen as a social actor (Martin, 2001).

The EU policy and programs discussed here allow space for the development of alternative and emancipatory conceptions of lifelong learning. It would be a mistake to conceive of institutions in monolithic terms, and this very much applies to the EU. No hegemonic arrangement is ever complete: it has constantly to be negotiated and renegotiated. It is within this process of renegotiation that opportunities to appropriate the dominant discourse, for transformative ends, can arise. Quite instructive in this regard is the following case study from South Africa. It focuses on the learning region, a concept which, as we have shown with respect to the EU, is being given prominence in the contemporary lifelong learning discourse.

THE LEARNING CAPE FESTIVAL

The 2002 Learning Cape Festival in South Africa was bookended by National Woman's Day (9 August) at one end and International Literacy Day (8 September) at the other. It kicked off with the recognition of the well-known human rights activist Emeritus Archbishop Tutu as an outstanding lifelong learner and teacher.

During one hectic month over 500 learning events were held, which included schoolchildren, early childhood educators, adult educators, civil servants from a range of departments, adult literacy learners, community workers, businesspeople, vocational educators, trade unionists, journalists and university staff. The learning events occurred across a wide range of institutions and geographical areas in the Western Cape Province. The Festival was a part of a broader strategy towards socioeconomic development that highlights the importance of building a culture of lifelong learning.

Participants in the Learning Cape Festival brought different economic and political analyses to the event. The approach I as Chair of the Steering Committee encouraged foregrounded the deep historical, political and material causes of limited education and training opportunities for working-class, poor, black women and rural citizens. Therefore, emphasis was placed not only on individual access to learning opportunities but also on the importance of learning in social contexts. The Festival strove to operate outside narrow party political frameworks, but there was recognition of the deeply political nature of the work at hand.

Background

The 'Learning Cape' is one of four pillars discussed in the Western Cape Provincial Administration's White Paper on the 'knowledge economy' (PAWC 2001). The White Paper argues the case for an intimate relationship between economic development and learning, but it also recognises that economic development will not occur without greater equity and serious poverty alleviation. The Western Cape is the second-wealthiest province in South Africa, which is a middle-income country. On one hand, certain parts of the economy (e.g. tourism, services for film, media, IT, and the fruit and wine industry) are fairly buoyant. On the other, 65% of people earn below $US 200 per month, there is 24% unemployment, 30% of adults are 'illiterate', 75% of preschoolers do not have access to early childhood development opportunities, and the number of TB and HIV/AIDS-infected people is growing rapidly. The disparity between rich and poor is one of the most extreme in the world.

Attempts to develop learning cities and regions as part of an economic development strategy are becoming increasingly common in high-income countries (Hofmaier 1999; Longworth 1999). A 'learning region' takes lifelong learning to be central to developing a knowledge economy, which can be defined as 'an economy in which applied information is used in all sectors to improve productivity and seek competitive advantage through innovation' (SAUVCA 2001). The development of a learning region generally involves concentrating effort on high-end economic research and development and rapidly increasing participation rates in higher education. The question for adult educators in Cape Town, concerned with social transformation towards equity and social justice, is whether this is the sort of learning and development that they wish to encourage. The dilemma facing educators is captured in a University of Western Cape discussion paper (DLL 2001):

> The challenge for the Western Cape is to strike the balance in terms of resources between the external focus of promoting the region

competitively in terms of the global knowledge economy and getting things 'right at home' where the focus is on poverty alleviation and employment creation. There is growing evidence that unless things are 'right at home' it is likely that the attempts to compete globally will merely privilege the few and serve to cause greater differentiation in our society.

The paper goes on to propose that the concept of the Learning Cape be built through developing pilot projects; creating awareness of the importance of learning to personal, social and economic development; encouraging collaborative engagement within and across sectors through partnerships, networking, and the creation of clusters of innovation to fast-track economic development. The paper suggests that an annual Learning Cape Festival could contribute to the development of this concept and strategy.

The proposal for a festival was canvassed by the provincial Department of Economic Development and Tourism among people in higher education, civil society, trade unions, business, local government, libraries, and the Department of Education. A Steering Committee was set up to run it. Starting the Festival on National Woman's Day and ending it on International Literacy Day aimed to ensure that the most marginalised citizens would be prominent in designing the Festival.

Outcomes

I will not attempt to do justice here to the depth, breadth and texture of the month's activities but will discuss some pockets of intense engagement to illustrate how the Festival promoted transformative learning.

The way in which one working-class township used the Festival highlighted the festival's strategic potential. Manenberg and Tambo Village are very poor, gang-dominated, residential areas. Two community workers involved in an urban renewal process decided to use the Festival as a way of furthering the achievements of the Clean Green and Safe Smart campaigns, where residents had come together to undertake sustainable community projects to improve their quality of life. Russell Dudley, one of the community workers, reported that in this conflict-ridden area the month-long Festival was fully supported, and was one of the only 'spaces' in the community to be free of conflict. Everyone could agree on the importance of building a lifelong learning culture. The Festival initiated and profiled programs on adult literacy, early childhood development, health, science (in partnership with higher education), small business skills development, sports and recreation, and second-chance learning. These programs attempted to link learning to discussion and action on community and economic development. While detailed assessments of the learning outcomes of the Festival have not yet been done, it demonstrated the meaning of lifelong learning in action. It encouraged residents to engage in learning for personal development. It drew residents into debates on what development should or could mean for them in their area. It mobilised resources for local citizens by bringing outside agencies into the area. It raised the profile of education and economic development projects, and it drew people into work-related skills programs. It publicised local citizen actions in Manenberg and Tambo Village to the broader Cape Town community.

Higher Education Institutions (HEIs) also got involved. I and a group of adult educators with long histories in progressive social movements gave leadership in the five HEIs and organised a Higher Education and Regional Development Public Debate and Symposium. This was the first time that HEIs had engaged civil society, labour, business and government in debate on provincial economic and social development. The initiative has laid the groundwork for closer collaboration between the Department of Economic Development and higher education. It has also facilitated cooperation among the five HEIs, which generally compete with one another. It has publicised the imperative for HEIs to be proactively involved in social and economic development.

At the University of Western Cape, one of the 55 Festival learning activities was a 'Recognition of Prior Learning in the Workplace' symposium, which brought together 70 RPL specialists from HEIs, workplaces, trade unions and vocational training providers. Collaboration between students and staff produced a photo exhibit, 'Lives of Learning', which was on public display for the month and which graphically depicted the difficult daily lives of older, working students. An important outcome was the public media attention obtained for the challenges faced by adult learners and the importance of recognising the different knowledges they bring to higher education. Another event, co-hosted with women's NGOs, was entitled 'Too Scared to Learn: The effects of violence and abuse on women's and girls' learning'. This brought together school teachers, counsellors, adult educators and early childhood educators from poor, working-class areas, from government, from education institutions, who shared experiences of the impact on learning of violence and abuse. The popular education methodologies of Jenny Horsman (1999), a Canadian educator, inspired local activists. In a society where abuse of children and women is so widespread, the emphasis on 'healing' rather than 'violence' was significant for participants seeking ways to obtain justice for children and women.

A network of civil society organisations, the Adult Learners' Forum, hosted an event which entertained and recognised 1000 ABE learners from adult learning centres. Adults who cannot read and write are largely invisible in South African society. This event brought their problems to the fore through the media. It also affirmed and encouraged their active involvement in learning. In addition, a network of libraries throughout the Province opened their doors and took various initiatives, as did many other institutions through open days and information services—all to inspire citizens, young and old, with the message that lifelong learning is an essential ingredient in economic, social and cultural development.

Throughout the month, new partnerships were established and old ones strengthened with government departments, the private sector, NGOs and HEIs. There was positive media coverage of Festival events, demonstrating 'from the bottom up' what good educational projects and programs there are and what serious problems learners and educators face. The Festival succeeded in unleashing the goodwill and energy of a wide range of people. This was an important first step in popularising and giving content to the vision of a 'Learning Cape', which works with the tension between economic development on the one hand and social equity and justice on the other.

The Provincial Department of Economic Affairs has agreed that the Festival should become an annual activity. The immediate challenge is how to move from an exciting innovation to deepen and develop the vision and reality of the 'Learning Cape'. The Festival is a means to an end, not an end in itself. It needs to be nested within a much more extensive Learning Cape initiative that is integral to building the human development base of the Province. Developing the initiative further will involve articulating a provincial human resources strategy, seeking indicators to assess learning outcomes and, more diffusely, popularising lifelong learning as lived reality. These activities will no doubt generate contestation, and ambiguous learning outcomes. Progressive educators cannot assume that their interventions will generate wholly positive learning. But they must keep trying.

9

POLICY FORMATION IN ADULT
EDUCATION AND TRAINING

Kjell Rubenson & Francesca Beddie

Internationally, lifelong learning (LLL) is the major contemporary adult education policy focus. In this chapter, Kjell Rubenson argues that history and contemporary context shape LLL policy. He surveys three generations of lifelong learning policy, showing how each has been influenced by economic and political imperatives. He then discusses the crucial role of the state in determining LLL policy. In Nordic countries, with a long tradition of state support for social equality, LLL policy is linked to a longstanding commitment to full employment and is embedded in deep traditions of popular adult education. This contrasts with Anglo-Saxon countries, which have weaker traditions of social provision and are more closely wedded to neoliberal, market-driven economic and social policy. Francesca Beddie illustrates this in her discussion of the difficulties of developing a coherent LLL strategy in Australia.

One lesson that adult educators can take from Rubenson's and Beddie's analyses is that economic and political forces do not mechanically determine adult education policy. Certainly it is important to understand how history, economics and politics shape adult education. But people (politicians, intellectuals and civil servants) set policy directions, and these people can be influenced. In recent years adult educators have become more aware of this and have increasingly engaged in policy activism.

CHANGING MEANINGS OF LIFELONG LEARNING

In the late 1960s, UNESCO introduced lifelong learning as a master concept and guiding principle for restructuring education. For a short period lifelong learning—together with closely related ideas such as recurrent education, championed by the OECD, and *éducation permanent*, presented by the European Council—received considerable attention. When first presented, the appeal of the first generation of LLL was its potential to respond to new challenges caused by rapid and unprecedented economic, political, cultural and social change. Lifelong learning promised to continue the renewal process of knowledge, skills and values throughout life. Humanistic proponents of LLL claimed it would promote a better society and quality of life, and would allow people to adapt to and control change. The focus was on personal development; the catchword became people 'making themselves' rather than 'being made'. Individuals were expected to work towards achieving the central goals of democracy and the development of self, through self-evaluation, self-awareness and self-directed learning. As Wain (1986) concludes, practical questions were never really addressed and the discussion remained at the level of vague ideas before it quickly disappeared from the public discourse.

When the second generation of LLL appeared on the policy scene in the late 1980s the debate was driven almost exclusively by an 'economistic' world view. The broad assumption that industrial countries are undergoing a period of economic transformation in which knowledge and information are becoming the foundations for economic activity has encouraged the state to redefine the connection between the spheres of adult education and the economy. Education is becoming less distinct from the economy (OECD 1989: 17). Lifelong learning, therefore, is the key link between our educational and economic strategies at the beginning of the 21st century (Ontario Premier's Council on Economic Renewal 1994). This understanding also informed the European Union's influential White Paper on the Learning Society (1995).

The restricted view that has dominated the second generation of lifelong learning has been severely criticised. In fact, it has become something of a growth industry among adult education scholars to critically examine the policy documents and to deconstruct the dominant political economic imperative. What this criticism seems to have failed to address so far is a subtle shift in the discourse and the emergence, mainly in Europe, of what might be called the third generation of lifelong learning. We now increasingly find reference in policy documents not only to competitiveness and employability, but also to social inclusion and to some extent also active citizenship and personal development.

The European Union's Memorandum on Lifelong Learning (2000)

argues that any policy on lifelong learning has to start by recognising that contemporary social and economic changes are interrelated. The EU stresses two equally important aims for lifelong learning: promoting active citizenship, and promoting employability. The document states (2000: 4):

> European Union must set an example for the world and show that it is possible both to achieve dynamic economic growth and to strengthen social cohesion. Lifelong learning is an essential policy for the development of citizenship, social cohesion and employment.

The third generation of LLL suggests a different role for, and interrelations between, the three major institutional arrangements—state, market, and civil society. The first generation saw a strong role for civil society, while the second generation privileged the market and downplayed the role of the state, almost totally neglecting civil society. It is important to stress that these institutional arrangements are not static but interrelated. The influence of the market on the state–education relationship cannot fully be understood by reference to shifts away from state control towards privatisation and decentralisation. With economic relevance becoming the key concept driving government policies on adult education and training under the second generation of lifelong learning, the interests of business have been privileged. The business sector is given the lead role in defining what competencies and skills the public educational system should produce. Recognising market failures, and growing concern about large groups not participating fully in social and economic life, the third generation can be read as a shift in balance between the three institutional arrangements. The market is still being given a central role but the responsibilities of the individual and the state are now also visible. The language is one of shared responsibilities.

A closer reading of recent policy texts and the understanding that seems to dominate the present policy debate might lead one to be more sceptical of what looks to be a major shift in the public discourse on lifelong learning. Despite repeated reference to the involvement of all three institutional arrangements, what stands out in recent policy documents is the stress on the responsibility of individuals for their own learning. A fundamental assumption in the second and third generations of LLL is that lifelong learning is an individual project. It becomes the responsibility of persons to make adequate provision for the creation and preservation of their own human capital (Marginson 1997).

This understanding can be seen to reflect the Third Way program and its precept, 'no rights without responsibilities'. According to Giddens (2000: 165), a leading Third Way theorist: 'Governments must maintain a regulatory role in many contexts, but as far as possible it should become a facilitator, providing resources for citizens to assume responsibility for the consequences of what they do.'

THE STATE AND ADULT EDUCATION POLICY

As Carnoy reminds us, there are crucial differences in what adult education attempts to do and can do in different social-political structures. Ultimately, Carnoy argues, 'these differences depend heavily on the possibilities and limits of the state, since it is the state that defines adult education and is the principal beneficiary of its effective implementation' (Carnoy 1995: 3).

Many accounts of globalisation—such as that of Thurow, discussed in chapter 8—posit policy and institutional convergence towards reliance on individual and market incentives rather than on political or institutional mechanisms (Clayton & Pontusson 1998). Yet several empirical studies have found little convergence in the areas of labour market strategy, education and training systems and the welfare state (McBride & Williams 2001; Garrett 1998; Rueda & Pontusson 2000; Thelen & Kume 1999). Distinct models of capitalism (Vogel 2001; Thelen 2000), welfare state (Rieger & Leibfried 1998; Regini 2000) and skills formation systems (Brown et al. 2001; Ashton & Green 1996) persist. Similarly, while concern regarding the knowledge economy, and gradually also social cohesion, is driving adult education policy in almost all countries, this is set within different political economies and welfare state regimes, which affect the direction and outcome of adult education policies. These links are reflected in the findings of the International Adult Literacy Survey (IALS) (OECD 2000b).

The IALS indicates that adult education participation rates are particularly high in the Nordic countries. The average participation rate in the Nordic bloc was 53%, compared with 39% for Australia, Canada, New Zealand, the United Kingdom and the United States. Further, the IALS shows that there is a noticeable relationship between social background, educational attainment and participation in adult education in all 22 countries in the study. However, the relationship is stronger in some countries than in others. This suggests that public policy can help moderate inequality in adult education participation. In the USA, university graduates were 16 times more likely to participate in some form of adult education and training than those with primary school as the highest credential. The comparative ratio in New Zealand was 22 times, while in the Netherlands it was five times and in Sweden six times. The IALS also found a strong relationship between economic inequality and literacy inequality (unequal literacy rates across classes, gender and ethnic groups within countries) (OECD 2000b). Where one type of inequality is high, so is the other.

Countries tend to group themselves in three distinguishable clusters. There are the Nordic countries, with relatively low economic and literacy inequalities. In the middle we can detect a continental European cluster, with Germany, the Netherlands and Belgium having slightly higher inequalities than the first group. Then there is the Anglo-Saxon group, which shows the highest level of inequality. This finding seems to suggest that inequalities in basic capabilities, as defined by literacy rates and participation in adult education, are part of national economic and social structures and can be understood in terms of various forms of welfare state regimes. The Anglo-Saxon liberal welfare state, with its means-tested assistance and modest universal transfers, sees adult education activities mainly as a way of getting people off welfare. Participation is primarily left to market forces, and entitlements are strict and often associated with stigma. The social democratic welfare state, according to Esping-Andersen, rather than tolerating a division between state and market and between working-class and middle-class, promotes an equality of the highest standard, not an equality of minimal needs. Thus, higher and more equal participation rates in the Nordic countries are a function of the Nordic welfare regime, and reflect an active state concerned about inequalities in participation.

A founding pillar of the Nordic strategy is the full employment concept, which has profound effects on adult education policies. As an example, the Social Democratic government of Sweden introduced the Adult Education Initiative (AEI) (Sweden, Government Bill 1995/97: 222) as a cornerstone of its social policy, as a 'special strategy' designed to halve unemployment by 2000. Instead of expanding labour market training programs with their strong vocational focus, the Swedish AEI is attempting to raise the general education level of unemployed adults. A similar emphasis on raising the educational levels of those with a short formal education can be found in recent reforms in Norway (NOU 1997: 25). What is of general interest here is how the state defines what is a reasonable amount of education to be offered to the unemployed.

In accordance with the Nordic welfare state model, the level as defined is quite substantial. In contrast, in Anglo-Saxon countries, labour market training programs tend to be brief and to provide narrow employability skills.

The Nordic adult education strategy should be seen as an instrument in what has been labelled a 'high-road strategy' to economic competitiveness, resulting in a 'virtuous circle' of high skills, high productivity and high wages (Wong & McBride 2003). The opposite is a low-road strategy, which assumes a bifurcated labour market, with a high-skills sector containing 'good jobs' and a large sector of low-paid, low-skilled jobs. The latter characterises labour market strategies in Anglo-Saxon countries and is linked to short, low-end training programs as part of welfare-to-work schemes.

Recent shifts in adult education and labour market policy in the Nordic countries can be seen as a movement towards what Esping-Andersen (1996: 260) labels an 'optimal welfare state [which] . . . shifts the accent of social citizenship from its present preoccupation with income maintenance towards a menu of rights to lifelong learning and qualification'.

The impact of the state on adult education participation is also evident in the structure and financing of the Nordic adult education sector. What sets that sector apart from those of most other countries is the availability of a publicly supported popular adult education. In the late 19th-early 20th centuries, forms of popular adult education such as folk high schools and adult education associations emerged, which had strong links to social movements. Over time these have developed into a relatively unique and highly institutionalised popular adult education system whose distinguishing characteristics, despite considerable state and municipal subsidies, are that it is free and voluntary. Historically, popular adult education has been part of the labour movement's counter-hegemonic ambition to heighten members' consciousness of and commitment to its vision and program for social change and justice.

Historically, popular education must also be understood as part of the Nordic social accord between capital, state and civil society. State subsidies for popular adult education are motivated by the desire of all three parties to support an enterprise that aims to make it possible for people to individually and collectively influence their position in life and participate in the development of society.

The funding regime is one of the key policy instruments available for influencing adult education participation. A crucial issue related to the funding regime is the link between supply of and demand for adult education on the one hand and the processes that govern who gets what kind of adult education on the other. At a time when government policies seek to boost efficiency through the adoption of a more market-oriented approach and outcomes-based funding, there is a growing likelihood that adult education will favour those easiest to recruit and more likely to succeed (see McIntyre et al. 1996). In this context, the comparatively successful recruitment of the less formally educated to adult education in the Nordic countries is a result of the availability of targeted funding for recruiting disadvantaged groups. Earmarked funding for targeted strategies, such as outreach and special study aid, has been the most successful (Rubenson 1996).

The persistence of the Nordic model of adult education should not be interpreted as an absence of hegemonic pressures from neoliberalistic ideas on current adult education policy. A recent Swedish education Act notes that adult education and training has so far concentrated too much on treating the individual as part of a collective with a common background and common needs, with teaching organised in prepackaged forms. The Act states that the challenge for state-supported education and training is to cater to everyone on the basis of individual wishes, needs and requirements. Some of the language in the Bill is reminiscent of the neoliberal discourse that has informed the policy directions of lifelong learning across the globe. However, while the notion of a training market is central to the 2001 Swedish Act, the state is still a central player. Resources allocated for outreach activities, counselling, availability of courses and financial assistance all contribute to the state-supported infrastructure for lifelong learning.

The above discussion raises important questions about the relationship of the state to its citizens and what understanding of democracy should inform state intervention in adult education (see Rothstein 1998). Dworkin (1977: 180ff) argues that the state should treat all its citizens not just with concern and respect but with *equal* concern and respect. In accordance with this principle, both Rawls and Dworkin argue for justice in resource allocation. However, as Amytag Sen (1982) stresses, the resource argument is not a sufficient condition for a just society. He introduces the concept of *basic capability equality*, referring to the need to take into account (among other things) differences in those abilities that are crucial for citizens to function in society. Nussbaum (1990) discusses the fundamental problem occasioned by the fact that people living in difficult social conditions tend to come to accept their fate, as they cannot imagine any reasonable alternative. She argues that instead of accepting this situation, it is the duty of the state, with due respect for its citizens' right to choose different ways of life, to see to it that its citizens are in a position to make well-considered choices. The issue is whether or not one possesses the basic capability to make choices with regard to participating in adult education. Sen's concept helps us understand why a system of adult education that takes it for granted that all adults can make use of available adult education possibilities widens, rather than narrows, existing educational and cultural gaps. The new policy challenge is to devise ways of tackling inequalities in readiness and capability to learn.

The role of the state in equalising opportunities for adult education is further complicated by the fact that opportunities for adult education participation are increasingly linked to the kind of a job a person holds. The IALS study demonstrates that, regardless of country, more than half of the participants in adult education and training attend an employer-supported activity (OECD 1999). The data show how closely linked workplace characteristics are to participation in adult education and training and the vast inequalities that exist in employer-sponsored adult education and training. It is worth noting that while the Nordic welfare state has been very keen to use labour market and educational policy to promote human capital development, it has, despite strong pressure from the unions, been reluctant to regulate employer-sponsored education and training and has largely left this to be settled by the social partners at the bargaining table. Without an active state, large groups are left to rely on the employer and/or their own ability to finance adult education. In a large part of the OECD world this makes today's ambitious goal of *lifelong learning for all* nothing but empty policy rhetoric (Rubenson 1999).

LIFELONG LEARNING IN AUSTRALIA

In Australia there is plenty of rhetoric. Lifelong learning has entered the policy lexicon, but in practice it remains code for workplace learning or preparation for work. Official support for more liberal forms of adult education and informal learning is weak. A significant number of Australians—around 30%—remain outside the system of adult learning (e.g. vocational and educational training, adult education courses, community classes).

The acceptance of the term 'lifelong learning' coincides with the growing diversity of adult education and training in Australia, and with increased recognition of the importance of informal learning, in the workplace and elsewhere. This broadening of the scope of adult learning poses a challenge both for policy makers and advocacy bodies such as Adult Learning Australia (ALA), a national body that promotes and fosters the value of learning (see www.ala.asn.au). All must channel their efforts towards achieving tangible results rather than mouthing platitudes about the value of learning.

For ALA, whose principles are grounded in the liberal adult education tradition and a belief in social justice, the choice of focus is not difficult. It concentrates on those least engaged in learning because, in the knowledge economy, not to learn for life or to have the capacity to learn is a recipe for disadvantage. In the current system, driven by industry demand and individual choice, the disengaged are the people least likely to pursue learning opportunities unless there are state policies in place to provide incentives.

If the priorities are not difficult to formulate, why is it that adult education (as opposed to workplace training) in Australia remains, as in many OECD countries, structurally weak and chronically underfunded? And why do we still lack a comprehensive national policy on lifelong learning for all? The answer is twofold: the absence of a strong learning culture, and the constraints of a federal system.

The policy environment

The most recent Australian policy review of lifelong learning and adult and community education is the Senate report *Beyond Cinderella: Towards a learning society*, published in April 1997. It recommends that the Commonwealth government 'make an unequivocal commitment to the concept of lifelong learning and the promotion of a learning society; and imbue its education policies and associated funding mechanisms with the values and principles of lifelong learning for all Australians'. It also recommends 'an integrated National Adult Community and Vocational Education and Training (NACVET) policy giving effect to the commitment to lifelong learning' (Senate Employment, Education and Training References Committee 1997: vii). No such policy exists at the beginning of 2003. The Senate (whose earlier, 1991 report also refers to Cinderella) certainly got the name of the adult and community education sector right: it remains the Cinderella of education policy, unsupported in any systematic way at a national level, with funds coming almost exclusively from the states, whose definitions of adult education vary considerably and whose main priority remains schools.

Before we examine the reasons for this reticence on the part of the Commonwealth government to frame a national policy, let us look at the efforts that have been made to create a national vocational training system under the auspices of the Australian National Training Authority (ANTA). This is pertinent for two reasons. First, it demonstrates that coordination within the federal system and with industry is possible. Second, it is ANTA, rather than the Commonwealth Department of Education, Science and Training, which has recognised the advantageous connections between learning for life and a more productive workforce, and which is therefore prepared to fund some national adult and community education programs.

Australia's vocational education system is genuinely national, although the states' issues (often unrelated to education) sometimes create obstacles to its efficient functioning. That said, Australia has the fourth-largest coverage of workforce trainees in the world (ANTA 2000: 8). Figures show that this equated to 72.4% of the working-age population participating in lifelong learning in 1997 (primarily in work-related training) (Watson 1999: 6–7).

Another major question for this industry-led system is how to deliver the generic skills people will need to remain employable in the 21st century. For ANTA it seems that part of the answer lies in the embrace of lifelong learning—ensuring that trainees learn to learn and stay ready to learn throughout their working lives—and in finding more flexible arrangements, including by connecting with adult and community educators, to reach neglected or reluctant learners. But ANTA's core business remains workforce training. Its expenditure on lifelong learning is tiny.

Leadership for lifelong learning must come from outside the vocational education sector. The healthy numbers participating in vocational training are not embedded in a culture that values learning for its own sake, for its contribution to the maintenance of our civilisation and the proper functioning of our democracy.

While 1.3 million people do participate in non-vocational adult education courses, these people are usually already passionate learners. University graduates are twice as likely to participate in adult education and training as are people with a high school qualification. That leaves an estimated 46% of Australian adults with insufficient literacy to cope with the everyday demands of life and work in a complex society (OECD 1999). These 'non-learners' tend to be people who are excluded from the lifelong learning system: those who are out of the workforce, where most adult learning takes place, because they are unemployed or suffer a disability, have retired or are raising children. According to recent Australian Bureau of Statistics figures, the unemployment rate for 15–64-year-olds was 2.8% for those with a bachelor's degree or above, compared with 10.8% for those who did not have a non-school qualification and had not completed year 12 (ABS 2002). These people are generally not motivated to raise the question of lifelong learning— nor, if they were, are they likely to have much influence in the political system. The education of adults does not feature on election agendas.

The OECD has made the point that the context of adult learning policies is as important as the policies themselves. It argues that the educational attainment of the population, the effectiveness of the initial education system, the political and social relevance granted to lifelong learning and skills upgrading, are all central to the design of adult learning policies (OECD 2001: 22). With 4.4 million 25–64-year-olds in Australia who have not completed upper secondary education (Watson 1999: 10) and poor literacy skills even among people who have completed school and university, Australia still has much work to do in improving its culture of learning.

The growing knowledge gap is recognised in the 2002 Ministerial Declaration on Adult Community Education (ACE), the latest policy statement to be issued by the federal, state and territory ministers responsible for adult and community education (MCEETYA 2002). The declaration is not a policy document but rather a set of four goals and suggested strategies for achieving them, unaccompanied by enabling funds or any rigorous monitoring system. It is deliberately narrow in focus—despite the current climate in which definitions of lifelong learning are broadening—to ensure that it does not stray into the terri-tory of other parts of the system (e.g. higher education, which was undergoing a thorough review at the time the declaration was being drafted; see http://www.dest.gov.au/crossroads/).

What used to be called adult *and* community education was further reduced in scope by removing the 'and'. We can surmise that this was a bureaucratic sleight of hand employed to remove any financial commit-ments from signatories. Yet its opening statement is couched in terms designed to inject ACE into the mainstream economic debate. It makes some important points about the role of education in community capacity-building through community ownership and acknowledges the importance of ACE as a pathway to further education, in particular for second-chance learners. Its analysis extends beyond the workforce, but the document can in no way be considered a national policy on adult learning—and does not pretend to be.

Nor does the declaration appear to have made much impact at the national level. The federal Department of Education, Science and Training (DEST) has made some references to lifelong learning but these have not been translated into action, for example with the introduction of any comprehensive plan to engage non-learners or those outside the formal system of schools, universities and vocational training institutions. But if, as the Department's 2002 Annual Report suggests, there is potential for lifelong learning to be seen as a cross-cutting issue for all these areas, perhaps there is still hope for Cinderella (DEST 2002a).

Cross-cutting approaches

Australia has a strong record in public education, for example in health promotion and environmental issues. In the early 1990s there were efforts to help people learn about reconciliation with indigenous Australians, and in the past decade governments have shown interest in civics education. Government agencies involved in employment, social welfare and community development also recognise the importance of training, and increasingly of learning, as a key element in the sustainability of their programs.

This suggests the need for a national policy on lifelong learning that takes a whole-of-government approach. The danger here lies in getting no further than motherhood statements about the benefits of learning, with no agency willing to take a lead or, more importantly, to devote funds to the cause. For, whatever the policies, they are of little effect without money, and in this regard adult education is still dressed in rags. The latest ABS figures (December 2002) say that $40 billion per year is spent on education and training in Australia, of which government spends $29.6 billion (74%) and the private sector $10.3 billion (26%). Adult education's share of this funding is paltry, albeit extraordinarily difficult to capture given the ad-hoc nature of funding. One study puts ACE revenue at $240 million, with an estimated 73% obtained from course fees and other charges, 22% from state governments and 5% from the Commonwealth—the reverse of the overall picture in education (Watson 1999: 21). But as Watson and her co-authors note, this is not the full picture: universities, for example, earn $94 million a year from continuing education courses. This suggests that the $350 million figure suggested in another study is closer to the mark (Gelade et al. 2001: v).

While these figures do not take account of other government programs that include a community education component, there is no doubt that the trend has been towards the privatisation of adult education (including courses offered by community-based 'not for profit' providers, which have to offer most courses on a full- or part-cost recovery basis). This reflects the neoliberal philosophy that lifelong learning should be a matter of supply and demand, with the market providing opportunities to learn for those who seek them and are prepared to pay for them. This laissez-faire approach also contends that people should not be forced to learn, and chooses to ignore the possibility that alternative methods of learning (outside the classroom or without a formal teacher–student relationship) could be attractive to non-learners, could rekindle their appetite for education and training and so ultimately generate greater social capital.

While there is no prospect of significant government funding for adult education, other options must be explored, including the pooling of resources currently scattered across public and private programs, and better coordination of educational efforts. These could provide adult learning with a considerable boost. One mechanism for achieving this is the learning community.

Learning communities are springing up around Australia. The idea is simple: learning is an intrinsic part of sustainable development and an essential element in improving the quality of life of an individual and a community. Each learning town, city or region has its own flavour and modus operandi, but they are all characterised by a commitment to build partnerships and encourage greater communication in the community in order to identify learning needs and find the solutions. (For a profile of a number of learning communities in Australia, see the audits of 10 communities carried out with ANTA funds; www.anta.gov.au.)

Learning communities in Australia and elsewhere have shown how crucial it is to have grassroots ownership of initiatives and not to swamp communities with money before they have the capacity to use it properly. The greater need at the moment is for encouragement to build coalitions between the various education sectors, business and government agencies and in the process to change their mentality from one of competition to collaboration. This can result in better use of funding dollars and more effective learning outcomes, as has been the case in learning cities such as Nottingham in the United Kingdom. Such collaborations require government support. This is not to say that there needs to be a totally publicly funded adult education system but that there is an urgent need for policy leadership, enabling funds and dedicated programs to reach non-learners.

Research and evaluation

Unfortunately, however, the lack of a coherent system of adult education at present makes it very difficult to provide tangible evidence of the benefits that learning communities, non-accredited and informal learning can deliver. There is no national mechanism to develop measures of effectiveness, to monitor and improve quality, or to decide on national priorities for public funding (e.g. targeting groups with special needs). Nor is there a funding model in place that would encourage improved governance in providers.

Without such quality assurance, it cannot be expected either that governments will increase funding to the sector or that individuals will pay for services. This is an important area for research and policy action. Given the generally accepted need to ensure that people continue to learn throughout life and to reach out to the non-learner, there is also a need for action research on orientation or guidance systems that would help adults find the most appropriate avenues for learning.

Conclusion

To see real progress in the policy arena, it is necessary to cultivate the idea of a learning society and to gather champions to the cause. Only then will the policy advisers, already burdened with too many competing priorities, take notice of Cinderella. This requires evidence supporting claims for learning. It also demands a major change of attitude about adult education and training:

- that it is not just about either work or recreation, but is an integral part of life;
- that it does not always have to result in a piece of paper; and
- that informal learning and non-formal learning are as much a part of a lifelong learning system as accredited courses and workplace education.

The target audiences for this message are many—policy makers, business, learners and potential learners, and the providers themselves, who do not always find it easy to think differently about learning or their potential customers or to strike up unusual partnerships and change rivals into collaborators. Who will deliver the glass shoe to Cinderella, and how, remains to be seen.

10

RESEARCH IN ADULT EDUCATION AND TRAINING

John McIntyre & Nancy Grudens-Schuck

This chapter assesses the meaning of research in adult education and training. It will explore a number of themes—the divergence of research traditions, the role of research paradigms, and the need to see research in relation to practice. The chapter will examine, too, some of the tensions that occur when academic research is broadened to include other types of inquiry. 'Inquiry' refers to a range of investigative activities that aim to advance the field of adult education by improving theory and practice. We think of inquiry as an act of focused learning that is shared with others. Research is not something confined to universities or research institutes. It occurs also in the everyday work of adult educators. A crucial message here is that research takes place in a context, and needs to make this context visible in order to create knowledge that is accurate and meaningful.

RESEARCH AS SCIENCE

The idea of research as a particular type of science pervades our thinking as educators, and this presents the profession with several challenges. Passages like the following may call up images of white coats and laboratory mice (Kerlinger 1994: 16):

> First, there is doubt, a barrier, an indeterminate situation crying out, so to speak, to be made determinate. The scientist experiences vague

167

doubts, emotional disturbance, inchoate ideas. He struggles to formulate the problem . . . He studies the literature, scans his experience and the experience of others. Often he simply has to wait for an inventive leap of the mind. Maybe it will occur; maybe not. With the problem formulated, with the basic question or questions properly asked, the rest is much easier. Then the hypothesis is constructed, after which its implications are deduced, mainly along experimental lines . . . the relation expressed by the hypothesis is tested by observation and experimentation. On the basis of the research evidence, the hypothesis is accepted or rejected. This information is then fed back to the original problem.

In this view, research is mechanical, male and rather melancholic. The 'problem' is like a key that unlocks a particular rational process, one which is abstract and impersonal. The researcher struggles in isolation to state the problem, and there is little sense of engagement with other people. With precision and control, the researcher acts from outside on the educational field.

This model for research has been called the positivist, empirical-analytic or 'natural science' model, with emphasis on experimental design (Usher & Bryant 1989: 10–14). This approach typically compares a control or comparison group (to which nothing special happens) with a group that is subjected to a treatment or intervention. Through its grip on education and the social sciences, this approach has dominated research in adult education and training. It continues to be recommended to students as the most respectable approach to research—the 'gold standard', at least in the USA (Deshler & Hagan 1990; Merriam & Simpson 1989). However, the approach has been vigorously criticised for its limited assumptions about science, persons and society. These assumptions deny, for example, the power of human beings to make meanings and to create social worlds (e.g. Usher 1996). They may also deny the potential for collaboration with subjects to enhance research, as is practised in the participatory action research tradition (Greenwood & Morton 1998; Heron 1996; Reason 1994; Robinson 1993; Zuber-Skerrit 1996).

For a century there have been challenges to the domination of empirical-analytic science, accompanied by the emergence of alternative paradigms (Carr & Kemmis, 1986; Greenwood & Morton 1998; Lincoln & Guba 1985). Some alternative forms of research are anchored to a philosophical or political stance; others to the idea that particular contexts or purposes favour specific forms of research. It is clear, however, that the contemporary researcher of adult education would benefit from carefully surveying the landscape of ideas about inquiry. Contemporary research, rather than being isolated and singular as in Kerlinger's (1994) portrait, is instead diverse, 'messy' and dynamic. Consequently, research assumptions must be unearthed and tested through dialogue and debate.

Paradigms

The term paradigm is used in multiple senses, both in educational research (e.g. Carr & Kemmis 1986; Merriam 1991; Usher 1996) and in the wider literature of social inquiry (Reason & Rowan 1981). A paradigm, in short, is a framework that is sufficiently influential to organise reality. Paradigms point to broad differences in how people understand adult education and training—to fundamental differences in world view, institutional linkages, political and social values that underlie beliefs about what should be researched, why and how. A paradigm is more than the philosophical preference for one research methodology over another. It is also more than a theoretical perspective that furnishes useful analytical concepts. Three key meanings of 'paradigm' are described below.

The social organisation of science

In this view, 'paradigm' refers to a complex sociological account of the way science is institutionalised and how individuals' behaviours conform. It refers to typical methodologies, the composition of their associated disciplines, and social relationships and world views that underlie, for example, Western behavioural science. This is the rich meaning of paradigm that emerged from the work of Kuhn (see Usher & Bryant 1989: 15–16; McIntyre 1993).

A broad 'philosophy of science'

Here the paradigm is a set of philosophical beliefs supporting an approach to research. We find competing philosophies at work when we consider distinctions between, let's say, empiricist science and naturalistic inquiry (Lincoln & Guba 1985) or collaborative inquiry (Reason 1994). A prevailing North American view, for example, is that there are many traditions with distinct methodologies within the qualitative research paradigm (see LeCompte, Millroy & Preissle 1992). Method, as a concept, is subsumed under paradigm, and typically refers to technique. Thus, it is argued that there are many methods but few truly distinct paradigms.

Types of science

This is a view of paradigms associated with critical theory (Habermas 1987; Bredo & Feinberg 1982; Merriam 1991). There are three main forms human inquiry can take, arrayed according to the knowledge or interest that is dominant. These forms of inquiry are empirical-analytic, interpretive, and critical science (see also chapter 1). This is the well-known view that Carr and Kemmis (1986) popularised when they argued for a *critical educational science* based on action research that goes beyond both empiricist and interpretive science to achieve, for professionals, a better relationship between their theory and practice (see also Zuber-Skerrit 1996).

The advantage of the second and third views of paradigms is that they emphasise that knowledge is always constructed in a social context. Interpretive and critical frameworks assume that there are no absolute answers regarding what research 'is'. Research is deemed legitimate when it conforms to the practices, ideals and values shared by a community of researchers (Usher & Bryant 1989: 16). This view is of great significance for adult educators and trainers. It makes the context of inquiry—and the values and interests that are peculiar to it—central. Because there is a great diversity of adult education contexts, this view of inquiry permits researchers to relish rather than regret diversity in research.

ADULT EDUCATION AS A FIELD OF INQUIRY

The deep differences among adult educators and trainers about the nature and uses of research can be seen in a number of key areas:

- the influence of formal school education on thinking about educational research;
- the impact of conflict between institutional and learner perspectives on adult education and training;
- the domination of research agendas by the state, particularly the impact of government- and industry-led economic reform and educational restructuring; and
- the importance of the context on inquiry with respect to what is researched, who does the research, and to what ends.

School education

Research on adult education and training has been overshadowed by research on school education. It is only quite recently that adult education and training have become 'researchable'. Academic research in the adult education field consequently is not well developed. Perhaps this is why scholars tend to exaggerate the (supposedly) special features that separate adult education from other forms of education, and from the social sciences in general (Deshler & Hagan 1990). This isolationist stance can distance the adult education researcher from rich sources of theory to be found beyond the field of practice, such as in sociology, anthropology, organisational development and evaluation, as well as in education.

Learner versus institution

There is an ongoing tension between an institutional perspective and a learner perspective. Tension exists between an institutional perspective that emphasises teaching practices, curricula, and structural issues like recruitment and retention, and a learner perspective that emphasises the felt experiences and world views of adult learners. The research tradition that focuses on instruction and learning associated with formal institutions is dominated by studies of course recruitment and retention. Such studies typically identify personal characteristics of the people who enrol or attend; their reasons for becoming involved; how frequently or intensively they participate; and what they gain in terms of skills, knowledge, and attitudes (Courtney 1992; McGivney 1990; Sargant et al. 1997; McIntyre, Foley, Morris and Tennant 1995). This research is often empirical-analytic and may use a national sample-survey approach. Its findings emphasise the distribution of adult learning opportunities; barriers to participation; and the instrumental value of gains to learners, to society and to employers.

The state

Since the 1980s, Western governments have intervened to reform education and training. The practice of adult educators and trainers has been affected by continuous restructuring of educational institutions under the political-economic pressures of global capitalism (Yeatman 1990, 1993; chapter 8). The state has used research strategically to engineer policy changes (McIntyre & Wickert 2000). For example, in Australia

171

from the 1990s, nationally agreed policies mandated that vocational education and training respond directly to the needs of industry or learner 'clients', and tried to integrate technical and further education (TAFE) colleges, industry training and community agencies in a national training system. Educational policy has itself become an important field of scholarly research and critique (Peters & Marshall 1996; Marginson 1993; Halpin & Troyna 1995; Taylor, Rivzi, Lingard & Henry 1997; Yeatman 1998). In this case, important questions for researchers might be: In what directions are the policy interventions of national governments driving both practice and research? How should (and do) researchers respond to policy agendas?

Context

The schooling influence, together with interests of the state and industry, have led to an emphasis on adult learning and teaching in formal educational programs. Until recently, researchers have neglected adult learning in non-formal and naturalistic settings. Indeed, some of the most interesting adult education research is on informal learning in workplaces, community organisations, parent or patient support groups, health care and human service systems, multicultural interactions, environmental movements, and other settings (Cassara 1995; Courtenay, Merriam & Reeves 1998; Foley 1991a, 1991b, 1993a, 1993b, 1993c, 1994, 1999; Grudens-Schuck 2000; Horton & Freire 1990; Marsick & Watkins 1991).

We believe that a hallmark of high-quality, contemporary adult education research is *recognition of context*. The practice of research and inquiry is always situated: it takes place in particular organisations or settings. In adult education research the focus needs to be on the ways in which context and learning articulate and intersect. One might consider differences arising from *where* something is learned, *how* it is structured, the relative *power* of participants, the identity and *life world* of learners, and the *type and degree* of incentives or coercion (Welton 1995). Any of these will colour the experiences of both learners and practitioners.

DIVERSITY IN METHODS

The empirical-analytic approach is dominant, but there are well-established, reliable alternatives. Some researchers have reacted directly against empirical-analytic approaches. They argue that experimental, positivist approaches dehumanise and domesticate. They have explored, instead, how adult learning can be understood and theorised as an aspect of life experience in the humanistic tradition using interpretive or qualitative methods (Boud & Griffin 1987; Brookfield 1984; Mezirow et al. 1990). Research findings from interpretive or qualitative studies highlight dimensions of education that empirical-analytic research cannot. Interpretive research may discover ways in which particular education programs lead learners—for example, how incarcerated women define 'self' differently—and suggest ways that adult education may have a role in healing identity (Clark 1997). Interpretive research can also highlight the role that education plays in solidifying self-actualisation, such as the interpretive research that led Jack Mezirow (1991) to develop the theory of transformational learning. Specific traditions of interpretive research have particular terms and procedures associated with them (Creswell 1998), but typically rely on language as data and on patterns of meaning as the outcome or 'findings' (Merriam 1998).

A further tradition within interpretive research engages critically with social and economic institutions, such as Lather and Smithies' (1997) research on the stages of living and learning of women with HIV or AIDS. This type of research drives political questions into the open, exposing the radically different opportunities for learners and the social marginalisation that occurs routinely, often along racial, ethnic, gender and class lines. Research in this tradition is activist and political, intending to change longstanding social policies and practices.

Practitioner and participatory approaches

Our view of inquiry suggests that any adult educator or trainer, not just academics, can develop a framework for critically analysing and conducting research. This is a long way from the textbook approach that equates research to formal inquiry for scientific and scholarly purposes (see Merriam & Simpson 1989). The field of inquiry has opened up, in part due to the divergence of views about research, including populist forms of participatory and action research approaches that demystify the act of research and encourage the involvement of practitioners (see Reason 1994; Sankaran et al. 2001; Wadsworth 1997).

Researchers actively collaborate with learners in the research process when using participatory and action research. This approach to inquiry is relatively new, although a strong foundation was laid by researchers in the 1980s and 90s (Greenwood & Morton 1998; Hall & Kassam 1988; Heron 1996; McTaggart 1991; Reason 1994). Participatory processes look different from conventional interpretive and empirical-analytic research. Two aspects set them apart from other modes of inquiry. First, the research agenda—the 'problem' or focus—is *determined through collaboration* of the professional researcher with insiders, or by insiders (non-professionals) alone. This process favours the questions and concerns of learners, workers, environmentalists, community members, people with disabilities, and others. 'Gaps in the literature' or government policy priorities are secondary, especially when the state is seen as oppressive or marginalising.

Second, people who would typically serve as research 'subjects' are invited to assume a *direct role in the research* by contributing to design, data collection, interpretation and reporting. For example, nurses have collected data on the way they improve patient care (Reason 1994); teachers have collected data about the effects of new practices (Noffke & Stevenson 1995); and farm leaders have collected data on the effectiveness of educational techniques used in programs that teach farmers to farm environmentally (Grudens-Schuck 2001; Grudens-Schuck, Allen, Hargrove & Kilvington 2003).

There is diversity and disagreement among participatory researchers (Greenwood & Morton 1998). Some researchers emphasise direct social action or involvement with social movements, and are dedicated to working with poor or oppressed members of society (Chambers 1997). The social justice approach is often based on a structural political analysis (e.g. Freire 1970). Proponents are often critical of the failure of academics to recognise the ways in which social injustice, power and oppression are present in adult education contexts. Other researchers focus on industrial democracy and community education, involving people from a range of social and economic strata (Reason 1994; Sankaran, Dick, Passfield & Swepson 2001) with an emphasis on democratic approaches to reform rather than radical restructuring (Greenwood & Morton 1998). There is overlap on many occasions of participatory methodology with feminist research methodology (Weedon 1987; Lather 1991a); distance and control are considered unnecessary and unhelpful to the quality of the study as well as to the people involved (Lather & Smithies 1997). Finally, there is a conflict between those participatory researchers that hold that only qualitative data can be generated through participatory research and those that hold that such research can employ much the same methods as any other study, including experimental research and quantitative methodologies (Deshler & Grudens-Schuck 2000; Greenwood & Morton 1998).

This is an unresolved issue, with tricky questions embedded in it, and clearly needs to be addressed by the next generation of adult education researchers.

One must also be open to new approaches that are the result of innovation within the field or through application of established methods from other fields. An example would be application of a novel statistical approach to understanding subjectivity, termed 'Q methodology', that has been used with success in the communication and policy sciences (Brown 1980). Researchers use qualitative methodology to understand diverse viewpoints, and are drawing interesting conclusions for policy and program development (Lipgar, Bair & Fichtner 2000).

We can thus see that adult education research is not a unified field in which the goals and methods of research are settled among experts. Rather, there are deep ideological differences about adult education and training that affect what is seen as the meaning and purpose of research (see McIntyre 1993). There is room for disagreement and room for creativity. There is also a need to attend to the influence of context and a need to hear new voices. In summary, the following points hold for contemporary adult education and training research:

- Research can take different forms. Rigid adherence to particular forms of research method may be less useful than was formerly thought.
- The form of research will depend, to a great extent, on the context, the researcher's theoretical framework, the interests of collaborators and institutions, and the particular problem that comes into focus.
- Research is both a political and a practical process in which the researcher pursues inquiries through a range of activities, including collaborative activities that bring to bear others' points of view.

There is a wide range of other tasks that must be attended to by the researcher, such as development of relationships with others (professional and lay); consideration of ethics in negotiation with participants; decisions related to naming and theorising concepts; choices related to design and method; details related to project management; and communication (and perhaps continued negotiation) of findings and results, including reporting and publishing. These issues are summarised in Table 10.1. The following cases illustrate the range of studies undertaken, and the ways in which they address the foregoing concerns.

Area of inquiry	Key issues
Context of inquiry	What is the setting for the research? is it a formal educational institution or another type of practice? Is the research policy-driven, academic or practitioner based?
Framework	What are the main assumptions the researcher is making about adult education and the kind of research that is appropriate to the context? How are these assumptions reflected in the inquiry process?
Problem-taking	What is the problem that is the focus of the inquiry? Who defines this as a problem? How is the problem formulated by the researcher, and how does it reflect the framework of assumptions?
Theorising	How is the problem understood? What theorises—either formal or informal—are being used to grasp the problem? What key concepts guide inquiry, or emerge from reflection on the process?
Research method	To what extent is research seen in terms of applying a method or technique to the problem? Is the researcher aware of the limitations of the technique? What justifies the use of the method?
Negotiation	How will the interests of other people be affected by the research? How far does research involve collaboration with its participants, rather than coercion? What are the ethical issues?
Meaning of data	In what form is the information collected and from what sources? How are categories of 'data' developed, understood, validated and reported on?
Interpretation	What meanings are made out from the inquiry? What is claimed for the research? What conclusions are communicated to others?
Critique	How is the research used by the researcher or by other interests? For whom is the inquiry significant? What were its strengths and limitations?

Table 10.1: Aspects of inquiry in adult education and training

Case 1: Adaptability of employees

An Australian study illustrates the strengths of empirical-analytic research. Using a quasi-experimental design, John Stevenson (1986a, 1986b) examined adaptability in trainees undergoing formal vocational education and training. National education and training reform has made the concept of 'adaptability' a key concept in Australian policies designed to achieve the flexible and productive workforce demanded by contemporary industrial capitalism. The construct of adaptability suggests that there will not be much 'working smarter' unless workers can become learners who apply their knowledge to new and complex work situations. The 'problem' that was defined by Stevenson's research illustrates how both policy interests and theoretical frameworks can drive research in a fruitful direction. Drawing on his extensive experience in developing curriculum for state vocational education, Stevenson wanted to know whether less structured (less formal) pedagogies might develop higher-order adaptive learning in students. He hypothesised that highly didactic instruction severely limited the scope for learners to achieve such outcomes.

The theoretical framework of this study drew on a well-developed body of literature regarding applications of cognitive theory to human behaviour. Using structural learning theory, the study conceptualised adaptability as a collection of higher-order cognitive capacities that enable learners to apply existing lower-order knowledge (e.g. facts or techniques) to new situations. In other words, adaptability is 'knowing how to apply what you know' to unfamiliar situations. On the basis of this work, Stevenson argued that an 'open environment' was necessary for adaptability to be learned (Stevenson 1986b). He argued that higher-order capacities must be developed through challenging experiences—as when electrical apprentices crawl in underfloor spaces to locate wiring circuits, or hairdressers razor-cut hair to an unfamiliar style without prior instruction. The study critiqued the educational culture of technical and vocational education institutions that had grown out of formal content delivery and examination. Stevenson's work suggested that formal institutions might have difficulty responding to new national training policies that demand deregulated, experiential and flexible training. To achieve adaptability among workers, educators would need to design learning environments that pressed learners into higher-order learning. Such studies also raise questions about what factors can stimulate that kind of 'situated learning' (see Stevenson 1994).

Stevenson's (1986 a & b) research presumed that assisting industrial capitalism (and its attendant objectives of efficiency and profitability) is a proper mission of vocational training and education. Other researchers take a different position. For example, Howell, Carter and Scheid (2002) have produced a body of work that sharply criticises workplace education in the USA. The base of their criticism is a structuralist Marxist analysis, often merging with feminist approaches to inquiry. Their approach contributes to a 'critical theory' intellectual tradition that is well established and opposed to the assumptions that drove Stephenson's research. Such critical studies arrive at quite different conclusions. Howell et al. portray human resource development as part of the reproduction of social systems that oppress workers. They argue that improving vocational education merely makes capitalism more efficient and profitable. Such education results in higher profits for wealthy owners while exhausting workers through higher demands and controls. The researchable 'problem', according to this alternative view, is not a set of deficits among workers (e.g. lack of adaptability as per Stevenson) but unchallenged assumptions about power and control in the workplace.

It is also worth noting that in Stevenson's (1986 a & b) study, the research assumed that similarly designed training programs would cause a uniform response among adults with like characteristics across classrooms and institutions, and even across regional and national boundaries. The notion of context as a unique influence, one culturally constructed by participants and the history of the institution, was altogether absent. To gain a sense of research that is sensitive to context, we need to examine interpretive research.

Case 2: Aboriginal–white relations

Such an interpretive study is Peter Willis's (1988) analysis of the hidden structure of Aboriginal–white relationships in northwestern Australia. In *Patrons and Riders* Willis explores his experiences as a Catholic missionary working in the Kimberley region in the 1970s. He attempts to understand the failure of a community development project on an Aboriginal reserve. Willis relates how members of the Aboriginal congregation included him as a kind of father in their kinship relations. However, community members refused to become obedient clients in response to Willis' assumed patron role when he acted on their behalf. Willis tells how Aboriginal members went along with his attempt to start a market garden and to gain a government grant to purchase a large truck. However, they used the truck mainly to transport others to ceremonies in remote areas. In the final analysis, the community development project did not work the way Willis had expected.

Willis (1988) suggests that the Aborigines in his congregation adopted a 'kinship-rider' role in which they went along with his attempts to achieve community self-determination so long as this served their objectives, too—such as getting transport to remote places associated with traditional family and spiritual life, controlling disturbance from 'young fellas', and increasing the availability of cash and goods on the reserve. Willis concluded that Aboriginal people, made economically dependent on whites by dispossession, had nonetheless developed strategies to manage white control of their lives on remote cattle stations run by all-powerful managers who, while 'protecting' the Aborigines, were instead dependent on their cheap labour. The strategies of 'kinship-riding' continued to be useful in dealing with white welfare and church agencies despite the rapid social and economic changes of the 1970s. The walk-offs from stations, the introduction of award wages, the coming of mission education, the Australian citizenship referendum, legal alcohol, and the shift from assimilation policies to self-determination—all are understood by Willis as aspects of Aboriginal resistance to white colonial domination.

Willis (1988), in his role as community adult educator, looks reflectively into a conflicted past. He attempts to understand its deeper cultural and historical meanings associated with the actions of members of contemporary Aboriginal communities. He struggles to understand how the context, in its cultural complexity, constrained the educational outcomes he wanted. Willis' work links not only to adult education but to important work in other disciplinary sectors, such as sociology and anthropology. Povinelli (2002) has contributed anthropological analysis of the dilemmas facing Australians as they build multiculturalism into policies that define what it is to be indigenous yet contemporary. Adult educators can move back and forth in this way from the work of researchers in other disciplines, such as Povinelli, to find both affirmation and challenges.

Learning about one's identity with others in informal community settings could not be more different from the context of vocational education and training. In the USA, Courtenay et al. (1998) investigated learning by young adults infected with HIV, a precursor to the devastating AIDS disease (see also Baumgartner 2002; Courtenay et al. 2000). These researchers have tried to understand levels of learning: technical learning about the disease, including treatments; and learning how to live with integrity amid the fear and disgust that are often associated with people infected with HIV. The research team overlaid Mezirow's transformational learning theory onto stages of learning to live with

HIV/AIDS. Courtenay et al.'s adult education approach articulated closely with Mezirow's theoretical framework by identifying a 'catalytic experience' and a five-stage process of 'meaning-making' that included exploring and consolidating 'new ways of being' (Courtenay et al. 2000: 103). The researchers have continued this work through follow-up studies (see Baumgartner 2002; Courtenay et al. 2000) that permitted them to test the stability of 'perspective transformation' related to living with a life-threatening illness. The interconnections among studies are what comprise a body of literature about a topic or issue in adult learning, providing opportunities for transfer of knowledge or applications to program development (see also Lather & Smithies 1997).

The common thread among interpretive studies is their reliance on subjectivity and local meanings (Merriam 1998). Crucial themes and patterns are linked to the particular time, place and situation. However, the Willis (1988) study and the studies by Courtenay and associates (1998, 2000) employed different techniques to produce interpretive claims. The Willis study relied on informal observational and conversational techniques sometimes termed 'ethnography' or 'participant observation'. Among the best known is educational ethnography (Hammersley & Atkinson 1995), which takes as a problem how participants make sense of their social world (the classroom, a workshop, a community group, a learning team). Among the best-known Australian research of this kind is Walker's *Louts and Legends* (Walker 1988). Over three years, Walker studied the life of several groups of young men at a Western Sydney high school. These young male pupils were understood as inhabiting 'worlds' constructed by male youth culture and those cultures with which it interacts—the cultures of school, ethnic and language communities, and social class. The identities of young men are shaped by the youth culture and its interactions, but at the same time the boys are shaping the youth culture by imposing or resisting its values and understandings.

Ethnographic study can also involve delving into documents and other media, including local historical records, newspapers, music and art. The Courtenay study, however, relied mainly on semi-structured interviews conducted over time. Creswell (1998) provides a helpful text for sorting out the various traditions of interpretive work.

Case 3: Hidden outcomes of adult community education

The vocational emphasis of education reform has also challenged community adult education (see chapter 9). In Australia, adult community education (ACE) refers mainly to learning that is organised by self-managing community organisations, such as evening colleges, neighbourhood houses or adult learning centres. In the mid-1980s, policy researchers in ACE were forced to justify the value of literacy, leisure, and 'bridging' courses to the state funding bodies. A well-known study, the *Outcomes Report* (Kimberley 1987), used both survey and case history approaches to document the outcomes of selected short courses. Further, the researcher developed a Freirean (1970) framework that looked for evidence of participants becoming more conscious of themselves as learners through courses and other activities organised in neighbourhood houses.

Community providers in this project understood education as the recognition, valuing and promotion of learning. They sought to develop the individual's consciousness of learning so that the learner would be proactive (the 'agent') rather than reactive (the 'recipient'). Kimberley (1996: 31) notes: 'education is about discovering the means by which learning may be directed. It is not only learning how to learn but discovering what uses may be made of one's learning'. It is difficult to demonstrate such processes through empirical-analytic research. Kimberley understood that a central problem of the study was persuading staff of state agencies that community access courses had valuable vocational outcomes, yet these were not always definable as specific job skills. At the core of the institutional education perspective is a bias that considers personal development to be less worthwhile than instrumental 'topical' knowledge or skills. The challenge for the researcher was to systematically collect data that would demonstrate the existence of 'hidden' (i.e. previously unrecognised) educational outcomes. She constructed a research process that emphasised participants' voices and surfaced hidden dimensions of learning through case studies. The learners' stories illustrate the consequences courses often had for their personal life, including reorientation to study and work. But the meaning of such stories is not self-evident. The researcher places them in an interpretive frame that challenges us to see the processes of 'conscientisation' they are meant to represent.

To surface the perspectives of less powerful participants in order to confront oppressive social systems is to adopt a *critical perspective* on research. To achieve this, the researcher had to negotiate the participation of people in the neighbourhood houses who had a vital interest in the continuation of their funding. This kind of negotiation is rarely acknowledged as part of inquiry, particularly in the empirical-analytic science model, where researchers often impose their own reality construction on participants (see McIntyre 1993; Usher 1996). The support of providers ensured that a wealth of case studies was collected. The researcher was able to show how the courses could lead to further education or training by developing affective capacities, such as self-confidence and self-esteem, as well as specific job skills.

In empirical-analytic studies, such voices typically are not heard. Human complexities are simplified and purged of their subjective qualities. For some behavioural scientists, such 'anecdotal' data are also inadequate from the point of view of validity and generalisation. A critical approach, along with interpretive studies, does not isolate and quantify the factors that are believed to prompt learning, such as course features, teacher qualities or learner readiness. The positivist scientist may agree that the stories are moving, but maintains we do not know what the stories represent because there has not been a controlled experiment that would permit analysis of the factors.

We could possibly leave the issue there, but for one crucial point. Today such case-history evidence is less politically compelling, because economic and educational restructuring (see chapters 8 and 9) demand a more sophisticated analysis of outcomes (see McIntyre, Foley, Morris & Tennant 1995; Bagnall 1994). The corporatisation of public education institutions favours highly instrumental research. Empirical-analytic science is attractive to the corporate managerialism of the contemporary state (Yeatman 1990) because it ties down the object of study and restricts the meanings in play. Controlling evidence becomes the priority. The tendency of positivist science to reduce complex information to simplistic generalisations is valued because it serves the corporate agenda. Policy makers and funding bodies are less concerned with real-life complexities associated with the experiences of adult learners than with controlling the policy agenda, assessing policy impacts, and limiting demands on the public purse (McIntyre & Wickert 2000).

Thus the policy interest of government has led to a resurgence of participation studies, but in a very different form from the North American tradition of motivational research, which aimed to develop theory rather than influence social policy (see Darkenwald & Merriam 1982; Long 1983; Courtney 1992). The new wave of policy research demands of researchers social and political relevance, and a robust engagement with social policy debates (see Griffin 1987; Jarvis 1993; McIntyre & Wickert 2000). This new social research, when it is done with social justice goals in mind, does not have to cede control of education to governments and corporations but can also advocate the rights of learners. Exemplary in this regard is the National Institute for Adult Continuing Education in the UK, which through national surveys such as the 'Learning Divide' (Sargant et al. 1997) has revealed social inequalities that challenge the rhetoric of 'lifelong learning for all'.

Case 4: Inquiring practitioners, inquiring learners

The previous case studies represent academic or policy research in the public domain directed by experts or professional researchers. It is also useful to understand the potential of practitioner-based inquiry and learner-controlled inquiry. One of the areas rich in practitioner- and learner-controlled inquiry is the field of environmental education and sustainable development (Cassara 1995). Top-down, standardised forms of agricultural and rural development failed spectacularly in many areas of the world, even as 'Green Revolution' benefits were reaped by some (Chambers 1997). Participation, as part of the sustainable development agenda, was proposed as a way to rectify past problems and to implement development projects that would enlist the knowledge and commitment of local people in solving complex problems (Cassara 1995; Grudens-Schuck, Allen, Hargrove & Kilvington 2003).

In the 1990s, Grudens-Schuck (2001, 2000) directed a research study of a sustainable agriculture education program for farmers in Ontario, Canada. The study combined an interpretive approach (ethnography) with participatory action research. Grudens-Schuck shared control of the research process with agriculture department staff and program administrators by involving them in the development of research questions, in the collection of data, and in interpretation and reporting. She based the methodology on several theorists important to this new mode of inquiry, in particular Greenwood and Morton (1998) (anthropology and sociology) and John Heron (1996) (humanist psychology). The study was based on theories about the politics of curriculum development (Cervero & Wilson 1994; Schwab 1978).

The program, called the Ontario Environmental Farm Plan (hereafter, Farm Plan), began in 1993 and continues even now. Farm Plan was unusual in the degree to which farmers controlled the process, similar to producer-led environmental movements such as Landcare in Australia (Campbell 1998). Farm organisations hired farmers and community members both to conduct workshops and to assess completed farm plans, using participatory instruction. The program worked with ministry extension to develop technical materials and to deliver technical content, but the main leadership was from the farming community, not professional adult educators (i.e. extension educators). Farm Plan was highly successful, involving 20 000 farmers (approximately half the farming community) over six years.

It is interesting to ask what is different about participatory approaches. In truth, there is overlap with other methodologies. Participatory methods are dependent, for example, on a constructivist view of the world, a perspective shared by researchers who employ interpretive and qualitative approaches. The constructivist framework enables both qualitative and participatory researchers to place a high value on an insider's distinct account of reality. The approaches also share methods. Grudens-Schuck (2001, 2000) produced detailed portraits of Farm Plan based on data produced through participant observation and open-ended interviews. Her methods resulted in an ethnographic narrative, full of stories and quotations mixed with analysis.

Unlike Willis, Grudens-Schuck shared control of the research with insiders. She encouraged the involvement of local people, so that insiders' ideas influenced major decisions related to the research. First, she negotiated the purpose and focus of the inquiry with insiders. She collaborated when setting the research agenda, not just to gain access to the site but to improve the accuracy of the research and to exercise the democratic impulse (Greenwood & Morton 1998; Heron 1996). Second, she made it possible for program staff and directors to participate in 'expert' decisions related to the research, such as: (a) who to interview and which workshops to observe (i.e. sampling and selection); (b) determining how different ideas fit together (i.e. coding and the development of themes); and (c) analysis and reporting (i.e. interpretation and representation). In some cases, program insiders also collected data. Participation occurred not just once but many times, and in relation to several dimensions of the research, setting this form of inquiry apart from empirical-analytic, interpretive and qualitative research.

Grudens-Schuck (2001, 2000) and program staff acted on findings of the research—not merely as an 'application phase' but as a way to increase the *accuracy of the findings*. This 'action' phase sets participatory approaches apart from empirical-analytic research, although some forms of interpretive and qualitative research encourage analogous 'natural experiments' (Greenwood & Morton 1998). By acting on findings, Grudens-Schuck uncovered significant tensions between institutional and learner perspectives that had not come to light earlier. The sequence went like this: first, Grudens-Schuck established that a prevalent rumour about the workshops was incorrect. Participative exercises, one of the innovations on which the program was based, were rumoured among some staff to be the cause of lengthy workshops. Community-based, 'grassroots' facilitators taught participative portions of the workshops. In turn, the length of workshops was believed to be associated with a downturn in attendance, threatening the program. The solution? Cut the participative exercises. However, through observation and document searches, Grudens-Schuck established that nearly the opposite was true: (a) the attendance rate was steady; and (b) participative exercises required minimal time. She also learned that a technical/lecture portion of the workshop, taught by government extension staff, took many times longer to complete. The action phase involved sharing the 'facts', and asking staff to: (a) keep participative exercises; (b) reduce the longest technical portion of the workshop; and (c) continue doing a good job enticing farmers to attend workshops.

Several challenges are associated with implementing participatory forms of inquiry. The one who directs the research must be able to stimulate and sustain collaboration. Facilitation skills and knowledge of group dynamics are therefore needed alongside analytic skills (Heron 1996). Participatory approaches also require a willing set of insiders: one cannot force participation. Taking participation seriously can draw criticism from researchers schooled in other traditions. Collaborative processes rely on different ideas of data quality and validity from empirical-analytic, positivist research. Despite decades of success with participatory approaches, adult education researchers may be told that the approach is unacceptable due to the supposed 'bias' resulting from the researcher's intimate involvement with research 'subjects'.

Practitioner-based workplace inquiry

Much workplace inquiry is also participatory (Greenwood & Morton 1998). Workplace education may not be recognised as 'research' because it is informal. Further, practitioner-based research may not be published or accessible in the same way as was the Farm Plan. Rather, workplace inquiry can occur as part of a commitment to democratise the workplace, and may be informal and unofficial (see McTigue in chapter 13).

CONCLUSION

Little has been said in this chapter about the impact on educational research of feminist and post-structuralist approaches (e.g. Weedon 1987;

Lather 1991; Fonow & Cook 1991) and postmodernist thought (Usher & Edwards 1994; Usher, Bryant & Johnston 1997; Garrick & Rhodes 2000). These perspectives on research challenge the notion that there are clearly identifiable research frameworks and suggest, instead, that there is an 'ungovernable' diversity of theoretical approaches, values and research methods.

Knowledge is generated from a particular perspective, and unfolds within a research tradition that features a particular set of assumptions about what is problematic, what is researchable, what counts as 'evidence' and so on. Thus we have maintained in this chapter that the question of understanding and successfully conducting research is not simply a matter of knowing and applying research methods or techniques. Rather, success hinges on careful examination of the way in which methodologies frame or construct knowledge (Usher 1996). At issue then is how we conceptualise the perspectives that in every sense govern the use of methods and techniques.

Our argument has emphasised the variety of research practice in adult education and training, suggesting that this diversity reflects the nature of the field. Researchers differ in the perspectives they take on the field and its problems, according to their assumptions about such factors as the significance of formal courses provided by institutions, the kinds of policy forces driving research, and the nature of the context in which they work. We have also argued that research needs to honour context more than it has in the past. As it is the diversity of context that makes adult education distinct, researchers must develop better ways to understand how learners and settings interact to produce learning in adults.

PART IV

Innovations and Issues

11

ON-LINE ADULT LEARNING

Bruce Spencer

Distance education (DE) has always been an evolving field of educational practice: in terms of individualised study it has moved from mail-in correspondence courses with little tutor support to carefully crafted, instructionally designed, edited and professionally printed courses with telephone and e-mail tutor support. In grouped study it has shifted from audio 'teleconferenced' courses to televisual 'videoconferenced' and now to on-line 'computer-conferenced' courses. Distance education is also being renamed flexible learning, distributive learning or, more specifically, computer-mediated communication, on-line learning or e-learning.

Distance education is essentially a delivery method, and most of the more challenging issues in DE are issues to be found also in education generally and in adult education in particular. For example, questions of access, equity and pedagogy, and the overarching questions as to the purposes of adult learning (for economy, transformation/social change, diversity etc.), are generic to education. The DE perspective adds a twist to these issues: it flavours them without substantially changing their essence. The distinctiveness of DE is also challenged by the increasing use of on-line learning as an add-on to traditional 'face-to-face' (f2f) education, giving traditional classrooms a DE component.

From an adult education (AE) perspective, DE poses a number of problems related to the social processes and purposes of AE that need to be re-examined in light of the shift to on-line learning. This chapter will review some of the major issues sparked by the growth in DE and on-line delivery; it will consider the strengths and weaknesses of on-line learning; it will report on an on-line learning research project; and will consider a number of practical issues for adult educators and trainers based on recent scholarship in the field.

DISTANCE EDUCATION AND THE MOVE TO THE VIRTUAL CLASSROOM

Before progressing to an analysis of on-line learning it may be helpful to review the definitions of DE and its links to issues in AE. Garrison supports a view that 'distance education is a species of education characterised by one structural characteristic, the non-contiguity of teacher and student' (1989: 8). According to Keegan (1980), this 'separation of teacher and student' is the first of six elements present in all well-established definitions of distance education; the others are:

- the influence of an educational organisation, especially in the planning and preparation of learning materials;
- the uses of technical media;
- the provision of two-way communication;
- the possibility of occasional seminars; and
- participation in the most industrialised form of education.

This list illustrates that DE is focused on the techniques of delivery; it distinguishes DE from most of the concerns of traditional f2f education. The list does not address the adult learning issues raised by DE, for example:

- The idea that DE students study at a time and place of their own choosing is linked to ideas of self-directed, lifelong learning.
- The target audience for DE institutions is, typically, adults studying part-time, fitting their studies around work, family and community commitments.
- Although not all DE institutions describe themselves as 'open', many claim 'open access', i.e. no or few entry requirements for their main programs, as illustrated by the names of many DE institutions, including the British Open University (OU) and Athabasca University ('Canada's Open University').

These aspects of DE—self-directed, lifelong, accessible education, open to all adults—can be considered as goals that are shared with adult educators in general. (For a more extensive discussion of openness and accessibility in DE, see Spencer 1998a: ch. 5; and for a critique of DE structures and methods, see Spencer 1998b.)

The move to the electronic classroom (the most significant aspect of on-line learning) within DE does cause us to revisit the definitions and issues raised. For example: Does on-line learning move DE from a focus on individual study towards more classroom study? Does DE, particularly the electronic classroom, enable open, critical, liberal adult education? Does it facilitate authentic dialogue, the blending of experience with other knowledge, and the pursuit of social educational aims (social education can be understood as education for social purposes to achieve social change/transformation, such as the promotion of participatory democracy and active citizenship)?

Adding an on-line—sometimes referred to as computer-mediated communication (CMC)—component to an existing individualised DE course does not have to move that course from individualised self-paced study to group study. The on-line component may be little more than access to Internet resources, or an instructional lesson, or an on-line quiz: it does not have to include a student-to-instructor and/or a student-to-other-students component. But the possibility of on-line discussions via computer conferences does open up traditional individualised DE courses to the possibility of a 'virtual classroom'. Critics of on-line learning often refer to it as moving students away from f2f classrooms and dialogical education. But from a traditional DE perspective, on-line learning creates the possibility of moving students *towards* a classroom and increased dialogue, and *away from* the isolation of individualised study and dialogue limited to the course materials and occasional contact with the course tutor. This may not mean that all courses become instructor-paced courses, as some self-paced courses may have 'rolling' discussions that allow students in when they get to those sections of the courses. But clearly the on-line aspect does favour paced courses, with a cohort of students moving through the courses in the same way as traditional f2f courses.

Some might claim that newer technologies can completely replicate the classroom or that 'computer-mediated communication traverses the oral/written continuum and encompasses qualities associated tradition-ally with both forms of communication' (Harrison & Stephen 1996: 25, drawing on Wilkins 1991). But in most cases computer conferencing remains a written/textual, not 'oral', practice and therefore the many qual-ities of oral communication and the dynamics of the real seminar room are not present. The 'best of both worlds' thesis is thus not sustainable.

191

There are, however, both strengths and weaknesses in using the virtual classroom (reviewed below). Sometimes it will appear to be 'better', at other times 'worse', than a traditional seminar classroom, but it should be noted that the interaction achieved electronically is simply *different* from that achieved in a traditional classroom. (It should also be noted that some academic critics of on-line learning who lambaste it for distancing students from instructional discussion ignore the 'distancing' involved in f2f mass lectures at their own institutions—e.g. see Noble 2001.)

Another trend to note at this juncture is the development of on-line components in traditional courses. In a report in *Guardian Education* (MacLeod 2002), Dr Yoni Ryan of the Queensland University of Technology, Australia, is quoted to illustrate how on-line learning has taken off with traditional campus-based courses, partly because of the more reliable computer access: 'On campus, flexible learning has become the big driver of on-line technologies, and in Australia at least, it's to accommodate the fact that more students work in the paid workforce while studying "full-time". It's changed the old lecture/tutorial model, to give a greater emphasis to accessing resources'. And Kathy Wiles, senior adviser in e-learning at the UK's Learning and Teaching Support Network, is reported as estimating that about 20% of study in traditional British university courses is now e-learning. The optimist might argue that whatever benefits reside in both methods of delivery can now be enjoyed in one course (a pessimist might argue that the opposite is true—the worst aspects of both methods come to the fore). The promotion of on-line learning is being linked to private providers, particularly in the USA. Business rhetoric dominates the debate, and new learning institutions can be described as 'not a university in any conventional sense' but 'a set of faculties, devices, and mechanisms', and students as 'potential consumers' (O'Donaghue, Singh & Dorward 2002: 520).

LIMITATIONS AND STRENGTHS OF ELECTRONIC DELIVERY

As indicated above, there are a number of limitations and strengths of electronic delivery. The asynchronous nature of some conferences, with students entering comments at different times and on different days, works against focused discussion as individuals take up and reply to different points; the structure of an argument and the key issues can get lost in this format. A contradiction that can develop when using computer conferencing is that easier access to the debate may not result in an issue being more fully explored. It can lead to students discussing only the 'easier' aspects of a problem and deflect from the tougher questions that would have been dealt with in a seminar classroom with an alert instructor. It should also be acknowledged that computer conferencing privileges those with typing and computer skills over those without; and it favours written, not oral, communication and therefore discriminates against those with writing disabilities, such as dyslexia (although asynchronous conferencing does give students time to prepare their responses).

There are many positive aspects to the adoption of computer networking techniques; for example:

- Class discussion is not cut off by the end of the traditional class meeting or by a coffee break.
- The student does not have to get the tutor's eye in order to make a contribution.
- It is more difficult for one person to dominate the debate, as all can enter a comment (if one student makes lots of contributions, other students can skip those presentations—they do not have to sit and listen to them).
- Many traditional classrooms are non-dialogical, in contrast with an electronic course with a conferencing component.
- Students gain from not being stereotyped by visual clues, and may find making a presentation easier on-line than in front of a class.
- Students with speech defects are not disadvantaged.

The types of interaction are also simply *different*. A written comment in a conference can be read and reread, while a comment made verbally in a traditional classroom has to be remembered or noted if it is to be recalled.

However, a lot of the claimed 'benefits' of an on-line course have not been carefully or independently researched. For example, do 'shy' students find it easier to contribute? Or are shy students in a classroom also likely to be shy (referred to variously as 'lurkers', 'non-active participants', or 'witness learners') in the conference? Is the quality of contributions greater (reflecting the fact that students have more time to construct an answer before posting it) than those made in a traditional classroom? Or are they in fact shallower (reflecting the ease of adding a quick comment when at the screen—this may be more evident in synchronous courses using a real-time chat-line format)? Can students easily amend a position as they gain more information? Or do they feel bound to defend what was so publicly posted? Are students protected from being easily typecast by their body shape, skin colour, gender (this is likely to be known but is not obvious when a comment is being read) and accent—or disadvantaged by not having the visual and tonal clues associated with traditional classroom communication (although in future computer conferences, verbal and visual presentations may become popular). There may be other repercussions. For example, the fierce debate that can go on in a classroom, the kind that is not personal once the right rapport has been established, may be difficult to reproduce on-line. Also, short comments seem to work better in computer conferences than more expansive and punctuated presentations. This is particularly accentuated in synchronous conferencing, with students typing pithy comments while at the machine. Although some readers might welcome brevity, the point is that it results in a different mix; all of the differences listed above change the educational experience. In sum: on-line learning is different from f2f, and has its own strengths and weaknesses. But how does it relate to the purposes of adult education?

On-line learning as adult education

If we accept Lindeman's argument that 'true adult education is social education' (1947: 55), then a form of learning that is individual, usually print-based, and verbally non-dialogical, would have a hard time qualifying as a viable form of 'adult education'. Even a looser definition of adult education (what Lindeman calls 'education for adults'), which accepted multiple and diverse purposes for adult learning such as education for economy (vocational training), liberal arts education and education for leisure, would not readily recognise the legitimacy of such an individualised and often technologically dependent form of education as 'adult education'. For example, Collins' (1991) plea for all those engaged in adult learning to recognise their 'vocational commitment' makes scarce mention of DE. Collins goes on to question technocratic innovation, and he can therefore be read as a critic of DE, with its formulaic instructional design and delivery and its obsession with technology.

However, given the development within DE of the electronic classroom, we need to revisit this issue. The questions to be resolved include: Does DE, particularly the electronic classroom, enable open, critical, liberal adult education? Does it facilitate authentic dialogue; the blending of experience with other knowledge; and the pursuit of social educational aims (e.g. the promotion of participatory democracy and citizenship)? In order to explore these questions we need first to review DE's claim to critical adult education and social purpose. Second, we need to evaluate the potential offered by the addition to DE of on-line learning.

Critical DE

Three scholars from Deakin University in Geelong, Victoria, have adopted a critical perspective on DE that does support its potential as critical liberal adult education (Evans & Nation 1989; Evans & King 1991). They locate DE within the subject areas of education and social science. They reject a delivery-centred approach, arguing that much DE should be understood as text production and reproduction and that critical theory and critical reflection can rescue DE from the social relations embedded in educational technology and tradition. To achieve this, students need space to dialogue with the text, to create their own text, and to be more self-directed and independent learners. The Deakin-edited DE collections include a number of case studies that address these questions and provide examples of critical practice (some of which are more convincing than others). This kind of work has also proceeded in a number of other locations, with courses being designed with more student choice, more open-ended projects, experientially based assignments and interactive materials. In arguing for critical reflection, for locating study within a broader yet critical understanding of the social, the Deakin (and other) scholars marry critical theory and practice to postmodernist insights.

How then can DE serve the social purposes of adult education? If critical DE is consciously combined with more social educational forms (e.g. group and cooperative learning), and if it is linked to social purposes and movements (environmental movements, peace movements, labour movements), then the social interaction and collective learning potential of an education (including experiential and critical knowledge) leading to diverse social purposes may be realised. For example, instead of emphasising individual learning to fit into the economic designs of a company by becoming a better human resource manager, an individual may be provided with an opportunity to learn how to work with others to establish a genuinely democratic, self-managed enterprise. In these circumstances, the distance learning institution may provide vocational technical knowledge linked to the meetings of a community enterprise group. This work predates the shift to on-line learning: if the dialogical nature of on-line DE is accounted for, it is clear that DE can possess the potential for critical adult education and training.

Adding the virtual classroom

In the examples offered above for overcoming the limitations of DE, its spatial dimension was complemented by existing community links and by 'classroom teaching'. This may indicate that social education requires interactive learning between both students and students and students and tutor, which may best be achieved f2f or via the virtual classroom. The virtual classroom goes beyond the limited possibilities for dialogue with the text, and perhaps a telephone tutor, offered by traditional DE to embrace interaction between students, small-group discussion, and classroom dialogue with the tutor. The computer network can also aid individual contact between students and between students and third parties (e.g. by using 'hot-links' to other sites embedded within the electronic course materials). Thus the educational experience is no longer isolated and individualised: the learning can become a social process and diverse. If we add the Deakin critique and understanding of DE and assert the social purposes of adult education, then the social processes of the on-line experience can enable open, critical, liberal adult education. It can facilitate authentic dialogue; the blending of experience with other knowledge; and the pursuit of social educational aims (Evans & Nation 1989; Evans & King 1991).

Electronic communication allows for easier contact within existing community or interest groups, or it can be a means by which contact is maintained once the group is established. It can also be argued that electronic communication has called forth new social groupings, but whether these are equivalent to new social movements or are narrow interest groups has still to be determined. Our interest here is not so much in the informal learning possibilities of the Internet (the 'information super highway' could in any case be viewed as an essentially corporate transmission conduit) as in the non-formal and formal educational opportunities provided by computer-mediated conferencing and learning. (For interesting discussions of the links between non-formal and informal on-line learning, see Sawchuk 2003a, 2003b.)

THE IMPACT OF COMPUTER-MEDIATED LEARNING

Regardless of how all of these issues around the relative merits of electronic classrooms are resolved, the virtual classroom has changed

DE. It has also made DE a possible method for delivering a fuller range of adult education and training programs, and made it more able to do so across an even wider terrain than previously.

The virtual classroom is a substantial advance on, indeed qualitatively different from, the isolated individualised learning of traditional distance education. Further, when it is combined with existing community, it can support social objectives and do so across a wider terrain than is possible via traditional AE or DE means. But there is a danger of the virtual classroom and the Internet becoming fetishised. It can be used to support narrow aims and behaviourist pedagogy and may not be critically examined by its advocates. It could be argued that these technologies were developed to help achieve economic goals of training and re-education of adults rather than social adult education. Given the shifts in funding and emphasis in educational provision for adults away from non-formal community-based provision, it is important for adult educators and trainers to consider the potential contradictions within the newly developed forms of DE and to try to exploit DE's virtual classrooms, hallways and coffee breaks to achieve the broader purposes traditionally associated with AE. These new technologies do present opportunities for co-operative learning (McConnell 1994; Spronk 1994; Spencer 1998a) and, once the equipment is in place, may be more cost-effective than other alternatives.

Social education on-line

We should not overlook the fact that there is differential access to computer networking: indeed, some commentators have suggested that computer ownership will become a defining characteristic of the 'haves' and 'have-nots' in the new information age. However, this is not an argument for ignoring new technology but rather an argument for making it communally and universally accessible. If we vacate the field it will only ensure that it is completely taken over by the privileged.

When students are linked in a community or environmental group, DE (in common with other education for adults) can become social education. Trying to recreate community in the electronic classroom becomes easier if the students themselves are committed to a real community or shared social purpose. They can then use their 'individualised' studies and their remote classroom as a basis for their community-based social action.

An example of this is provided by a research project undertaken at Athabasca University in conjunction with the Canadian Labour Congress (CLC). This project was part of the pan-Canadian Telelearning Network of Centres of Excellence, and provided an exception to much of the Network's corporate-driven agenda. It should also be noted that this project built on earlier on-line union educational research, directed by Dr Jeffery Taylor since 1992 (see Taylor 1996, 2002; Briton & Taylor 2001). The purpose of the research was to see whether the social purposes and popular peer-tutored traditions of Canadian labour education could be sustained in an on-line learning environment. One of the researchers' workshops was run entirely on-line and brought together labour activists from across the country to plan and strategise the May Day 2000 celebrations. An asynchronous conference (termed 'union hall', using an adapted Virtual U conferencing software) was established and was open for six weeks. It was supported by a separate website with additional resources. Two facilitators were responsible for keeping the discussion moving along (Taylor 2002).

May Day 2000 was the first time the CLC had endorsed the 'workers' holiday' and committed resources and energy to ensure that it was marked in some way in communities across the country. Some 40 activists contributed to the discussions, exchanging views on how best to celebrate May Day 2000 in their communities. Post-workshop analysis of conference transcripts and interviews with participants revealed that 'the experience was most useful for activists in smaller communities and that a combination of online and offline activity created the best learning situations' (Taylor 2002: 156).

Moving adult education and training on-line

Discussions of the educational issues involved in moving adult education and training classes to on-line learning environments are often dominated by the technology and techniques rather than critical pedagogy or the purposes of education. The relative merits of standardising platforms or establishing a 'multi-media Web toolbox' or a bank of 'learning objects' engage the experts in the field. There seems to be a universal and unexamined acceptance of the assumption that training and more of it combined with educational credentials is good for the economy and therefore good for the citizen (an instrumental as opposed to a critical view of education and training): DE techniques are simply layered on top of that assumption. Lockwood and Gooley (2001) provide a useful introduction to technical DE issues. Although the title might suggest that its target audience is those already involved in DE, it mainly addresses those in traditional institutions who are moving towards on-line learning. But there is little in the collection that addresses broader issues.

There are a number of key technical points that can be made to assist institutions, educators and trainers contemplating a shift in delivery. The advantage that dedicated DE or dual (traditional and DE) institutions have over others is that they understand the importance of an infrastructure geared towards distance delivery—tutors, library, counselling services, course materials and computer network support. It is easier for them to shift from more traditional DE to on-line DE. What is needed to ensure a successful switch in traditional delivery institutions is a supportive infra-structure reflecting that of DE institutions. Exactly what is needed will vary from institution to institution and depend on the size of the project, but at a minimum computer and web-based support and a student helpdesk are necessary—unless the instructor is going to provide all of that! Second, traditional instructors need time to learn and experiment with the new technology; training and more specifically 'just-in-time' train-ing is important to success for those instructors who would not claim to be computer experts.

If institutions already have self-contained computerised training packages, these can be made available on the web and in so doing reach larger audiences. The move to the web opens up other possibilities with links out of the courses, but once this is achieved someone will need to monitor the links to see that they remain intact. If an interactive com-ponent is introduced that involves instructors and other students, then that becomes expensive as instructor time soon adds up. Educational administrators tend to look at on-line education as cost-effective once the equipment is in place, but any hope for savings vanishes once an on-line conference is added to a course. A regular class may meet once or twice a week for a maximum of three hours. An e-class never closes. The asynchronous on-line conference is on-line all the time. An instructor will log on every day or every other day if she/he is not to be swamped by postings. Instructors familiar with traditional classes should be aware of this when negotiating an on-line workload.

Just as smaller seminar-sized classes work best f2f, they also are more successful on-line. An active on-line course (electronic classroom) of 40 students may be chaotic. Administrators are fixated on the savings potential of on-line learning, but the experience of those institutions (such as Athabasca University) that provide quality on-line courses is that you cannot expect savings; rather the reverse: on-line courses cost more. The reasons for moving to on-line provision have to be other than cost—such as convenience for the students, adding an important edu-cational dimension to a particular course, reaching students that would otherwise not be able to undertake the courses. Therefore, adequate resources are crucial to success.

The platform used for on-line course conferencing has to be user-friendly, from both instructor and student perspective. Being able to follow the debates is important (threading of messages), as is being able to recognise new messages. To achieve successful asynchronous conferencing it is best not to let a discussion run longer than a week or two—to open a new 'board' every week or every other week. (Some of these practicalities are discussed in Lockwood & Gooley 2001.) Other features will depend on instructor and program preferences.

CONCLUSION

The purpose of this chapter has been to argue that it is possible for DE to support social purpose adult education and broad-based training. The move towards the on-line classroom aids rather than inhibits this move. The technological imperatives of on-line learning offer a challenge to educators and trainers accustomed to f2f education, but the shift from a real to a virtual classroom does not have to have disastrous results for progressive educators. As radical distance educators have argued and demonstrated, on-line education can be dialogical, critical and social (McConnell 1994; Spronk 1994; Taylor 1996, 2002; Spencer 1998a). There are both advantages and disadvantages associated with on-line education compared to traditional delivery, but the essential point is to recognise the *differences* between the two and to explore how those can be exploited educationally. On-line learning can be expected to grow; not all of it will have computer conferencing, but that is the most exciting development from an educational perspective. If there is a recognisable trend, it is the move to add an on-line component to traditional courses, and this represents opportunities as well as challenges to traditional educators and trainers.

Computer-mediated learning is affecting all education. Adults, reach-able via the Internet, are viewed as a new market opportunity by traditional educational institutions, which now see their chance to be distance trainers and adult educators. Adult educators and trainers need to critically influence this form of education; they need to ensure it is properly resourced—that it is broadly based, accessible and adven-turous, providing citizens with the information, skills and learning required for a participatory democracy at work and in society.

12

RETHINKING 'ORGANISATIONAL' LEARNING

Laurie Field

This chapter deals with the contentious claim that organisations learn. While its primary focus is on commercial organisations, the ideas outlined here apply to some extent to most medium- to large-sized organisations.

Judging by the literature, one could easily assume that it is an indisputable fact that organisations can and do learn. Here, I argue that neither 'organisational' learning nor the related term 'the learning organisation' is a helpful or meaningful concept.

This may seem a surprising position for someone whose publications include the book *Managing Organizational Learning* (Field 1995a) and a number of papers and reports (e.g. 1997, 1998a, 1998b) promoting the idea that organisations learn. Nevertheless, after a decade of investigation I have concluded that there are better metaphors for describing the learning taking place in and 'by' organisations. This chapter argues that:

- The literature of 'organisational' learning is distorted by the prominence it gives to learning associated with technical-economic interests.
- Another significant distortion in the 'organisational' learning literature is the tendency to view organisations as unitary, and to downplay differences in the interests of organisational members.
- The key to understanding learning within organisations is the notion of a shared-interest group.

Country	Example
Australia	ICI Botany Operations (now Orica), Carlton & United Breweries, Lend Lease, Westpac
UK	Shell, Mercedes Benz, Rover, Isvor Fiat
USA	Johnsonville Foods, Chaparral Steel, Motorola, Shell, Hanover Insurance

Table12.1: Model 'learning organisations'

- Shared-interest-group learning occurs at three levels of interest within organisations—a technical-economic level, a political level, and an ontological level.
- The implication of this line of thinking is that 'organisational' learning is a special case of shared-interest-group learning that occurs only when the whole organisation approximates a shared-interest group—an unusual, short-term situation that might occur when all organisational members are aligned by a common purpose or threat.

THE CONCEPTS OF 'ORGANISATIONAL' LEARNING AND 'THE LEARNING ORGANISATION'

A growing field of interest

'Organisational learning' emerged in the organisational studies literature in the 1960s, and began to attract considerable attention from the mid-1970s. The most influential early writers were Argyris and Schön, largely through their book *Organizational Learning* (1978).

A second wave of interest in 'organisational' learning followed publication of US author-consultant Peter Senge's (1990) book *The Fifth Discipline*. The ambitious claims made on the book's cover—that it would 'reduce the learning disabilities of any organization', 'help organizations stay on the right path', 'profoundly influence management thinking' and 'lay the foundation for a true alternative to the authoritarian hierarchy'—reflect its idealistic approach.

In the period following the appearance of *The Fifth Discipline*, the body of academic and popular writing about 'organisational' learning grew considerably, particularly in North America (Crossan & Guatto 1996). This writing popularised the ideas that certain enterprises have superior learning capabilities (see Table 12.1 for examples).

Why the interest in 'organisational' learning?

How do we explain this interest in organisational learning and the related idea of organisational knowledge? At least five factors have played a part.

Environmental turbulence

Since the 1960s, the operating environments of many enterprises have become increasingly turbulent, as a result of change associated with the pressure to lower costs and increase profit, and the emergence of new technologies, new competitors and new options. Faced with this environment, it is very attractive to imagine the enterprise as a living organism, which learns and adapts rapidly.

Knowledge as a primary resource

Enterprise success increasingly depends on the capacity to extend knowledge and apply it effectively. In part, this transition results from the growing importance of service and information industries, and the decline of manufacturing in countries like the USA, the UK and Australia. But even within manufacturing itself there is increasing awareness that the vast majority of employees—involved in areas like sales, marketing and purchasing—are primarily involved in service jobs in which knowledge is their key resource.

The increased importance of flexible organisational forms, including alliances, consortia, joint ventures and innovation networks, adds to the pressure to capture and use organisational knowledge in ways that bring competitive advantage. Similarly, the increasing tendency for business to adopt an international focus privileges knowledge about specific markets and cross-cultural learning.

Organisations as complex systems

An enterprise constitutes a complex system, in which events in one area often affect (and are affected by) circumstances in other areas. As discussed elsewhere (Ford 1991; Field 1995b), successful enterprises are those that integrate employee relations, work organisation, skills, technology and information. For this to occur, people in an enterprise need knowledge that overrides narrow specialties. Many managers and employees need a sound understanding of what is happening elsewhere in the organisation and its environment, and learning is the process by which this understanding is acquired.

More permeable, fuzzy boundaries

Within many enterprises, the boundaries between inside and outside are becoming increasingly blurred. In retailing and manufacturing, just-in-time practices are effective only if there is a close relationship with suppliers. Public sector agencies are becoming less insular and more responsive. In many industries, the level of expertise needed to win contracts may be attainable only if long-term alliances are established with subcontractors. Benchmarking within and between enterprises, visits to other sites and intercompany collaboration also span the boundary between enterprise and environment and pave the way for learning that benefits the whole organisation.

Reduced time frames

To access emerging markets, enterprises increasingly have to develop their competence and do things faster. Enterprises have to integrate new software and hardware, and take advantage of new products, services and market conditions. The primary catalyst for reducing time frames in recent years has been networked computing and the Internet. To date, the main advantage of the Internet seems to be not so much fostering new types of businesses, such as on-line retailers, as improving the speed and efficiency of existing businesses. There is a direct correlation between the corporate need to speed up knowledge acquisition and application, and the desire to improve 'organisational' learning.

WEAKNESSES IN THE CONCEPTUAL BASE OF 'ORGANISATIONAL' LEARNING

While many organisations are experiencing the kinds of changes just outlined, in most circumstances they are not actually engaged in 'organisational' learning. However, writers on organisational learning often fail to distinguish between (a) learning by groups of managers or by other organisational groups and (b) learning by the organisation as a whole. This blurring results from conceptual confusion and selective reporting in the literature. In particular:

- The terms 'organisation' and 'learning' are often used in ambiguous and confusing ways.

- The 'organisational' learning literature focuses almost exclusively on learning associated with technical and economic interests.
- Organisations are generally assumed to be unitary, meaning that they constitute a single-interest group.

The 'organisational' learning literature often uses the terms 'organisation' and 'learning' in ambiguous and confusing ways

In discussions of 'organisational' learning, the abstract term 'organisation' is often treated as if it were a tangible entity, possessing the attributes of its members (e.g. goals, a capacity to remember, behaviour, cognitive processes), and thus that something akin to individual learning occurs within organisations. For example, Sandelands and Stablein (1987) claim that 'organizations are mental entities capable of thought' (1987: 136), and propose an 'organizational mind' as a way of understanding 'the commerce of ideas' (1987: 138–9); Cohen and Bacdayan (1994) suggest the existence of an 'organizational unconscious'; Nicholini and Mezner (1995) refer to an organisation's 'cognitive structure', 'identity' and 'memory'. Further, there is no agreement on what actually constitutes 'organisational learning'. Some authors emphasise behavioural change (Swieringa & Wierdsma 1992: 33); others, cognitive change (Argyris 1990; Huber 1991: 89); and yet others, new knowledge and understanding (Thurbin 1994: 7).

The 'organisational' learning literature is almost exclusively concerned with learning associated with the technical-economic interest

The organisational learning literature almost universally assumes that learning relates to 'technical' areas, such as engineering, law and financial management, that are applied to generating profit (as a shorthand device, I'll refer to this as the 'technical-economic assumption'). For example, doctoral studies of organisational learning included in FirstSearch Dissertations Abstracts during 1998 and 1999 dealt exclusively with technical issues like banking management and administration, capital budgeting, new product development, software design and business acquisitions.

Alongside this tendency to assume that 'organisational' learning refers to learning associated with technical and economic interests, the organisational learning literature tends to ignore learning associated with organisational politics and emotions. For example, in Nonaka's influential 1994 paper on organisational learning, discussion of 'making tacit knowledge explicit' assumes commercially valuable, technical knowhow, not learning and knowledge associated with organisational politics or emotions.

Obviously, the technical-economic interests in productivity and profit is the *raison d'être* of commercial organisations. However, learning directly associated with achieving productivity and profit is not the only kind of learning that is significant. People learn for a variety of reasons, including on occasions when their personal interests conflict with the technical-economic interest (as can happen, for example, when there is downsizing, unfair dismissal, an inequitable bonus system, or site relocation). As a result, individuals and groups within organisations are continually learning about areas such as participation and collaboration, management attitudes and behaviours, economic and psychological security, health, creativity and expression, political awareness, the realities of capitalist society, relationships and family, one's history and possible futures.

The 'organisational' learning literature tends to view organisations as unitary, and to downplay different interests within the same organisation

Much of the 'organisational' learning literature is couched in an idealistic language that demonstrates a unitary view of organisational life. Thus, the learning organisation is claimed to be able to 'sustain consistent internal innovation' (Mills & Friesen 1992: 146), to be 'skilled at creating, acquiring, and transferring knowledge' (Garvin 1993: 80), to have an 'intense desire to learn' (Hodgetts, Luthans & Lee 1994: 12), and to 'continuously transform itself . . . empower its people, encourage collaboration and team learning, promote open dialogue, and acknowledge the interdependence of individuals, the organization, and the communities in which they reside' (Marsick & Watkins 1994: 354). Raising the level of extravagant rhetoric even further, Inkpen and Crossan (1995: 597) assert that 'organisational' learning 'is like the fountain of youth . . . [prolonging] the organization's life indefinitely'!

The assumption running through quotes like these is that the activities, values and interests of all organisational members are aligned. Taken to an extreme, the implication of unitary thinking is that, because all members of the organisation think as one, organisational power and politics are unnecessary.

Unitary thinking is nicely illustrated in the following description of a large North American manufacturing plant by its Chief Executive (Melohn 1994: 156):

> [Our employees] are not at all interested in the traditional forms of power. They want power over their job, not over other people . . . We set the goal of sharing power among co-workers. Everyone has to have the same mind-set . . . There can be no sniping between departments because, in reality, all departments simply blend together.

Descriptions like this of work environments free of power and conflict are quite common in the 'organisational' learning literature. While one could dismiss them as naive and unrealistic, it is more useful to see such accounts as part of a spectrum of approaches that managers and author-consultants use to legitimise some concepts (e.g. ' "organisational" learning') while marginalising others (e.g. 'intergroup conflict').

From the unitary perspective, the organisation can be likened to a beehive, where all employees happily surrender their 'honey' (including knowledge and learning) to satisfy the technical-economic interests of the organisation. Much of Senge's popular work on learning organisations, *The Fifth Discipline* (1990), reflects this kind of thinking. Consider, for example, the following passage (Senge 1990: 3):

> Learning organizations are organizations where people continually expand their capacity to create the results they truly desire, where new and expansive patterns of thinking are nurtured, where collective aspiration is set free, and where people are continually learning how to learn together.

In Senge's writing, the individual employee's interest is always assumed to correspond with the organisational interest. Senge reduces 'structural conflict systems' (1990: 156) to tension between an individual's learned feelings of powerlessness and his or her personal vision and aspirations. Senge depicts this tension as an individual learning issue: how can employees 'learn' that they have power to achieve their visions and aspirations? He then introduces the unitary notion of 'alignment' (1990: 234), arguing that individual visions and aspirations need to line up with those of the organisation. As long as this occurs, Senge asserts that the new-found 'personal power' will be put to good (i.e. commercial) use, and conflicts between workers and management will become unnecessary.

The unitary flavour of Senge's influential work recurs throughout the organisational learning literature. For example, according to Stata (1996), 'organisational' learning requires individuals to have common beliefs and goals in order to learn together; Schein (1993: 41) asserts that organisational learning requires 'the evolution of shared mental models that cut across the subcultures of the organization'; and Marsick and Watkins (1994: 354–5) observe that 'employees at all levels share their learning with others . . . so that it becomes part of the organization's memory'.

THE POLITICAL INTEREST AND 'ORGANISATIONAL' LEARNING

The nature of the 'political' interest

At this point I'd like to move away from critiquing the 'organisational' learning literature, and suggest a way of thinking about learning in and 'by' organisations that better accords with reality. The focus here is on learning associated with the political interest and the ontological interest.

I want to emphasise that the line of thinking presented here did not result from any particular theoretical perspective but instead grew out of the experience of working as a researcher-consultant in Australian companies over many years, observing and interviewing. From this experience, it seemed that learning was commonly provoked by such things as changing operating environments; experimentation with new forms of work organisation; the arrival of new senior managers able to draw on experience in other companies or cultures; shock or trauma associated with such events as job losses and site closure; and the disclosure of financial information which creates uncertainty or provocation. Because learning like this was not encompassed by mainstream accounts of organisational learning, I began to look for insights that were consistent with what I observed.

One useful thread was Habermas' (1987) theoretical work on knowledge and interests. For Habermas, human interests relate to goals such as understanding the human condition (e.g. learning relating to people's differences, relationships, response patterns), and achieving personal and group freedom (e.g. learning relating to injustice, autonomy and responsibility, power relations, and the value systems that constrain us). It is goals such as these that I had come to associate with a 'political interest'.

Habermas argues that considerable knowledge and learning result from efforts to avoid becoming hemmed in by such things as bureaucracy, institutions and the financial markets—or what we might colloquially refer to as 'the forces of money and power'. An implication of Habermas' work is that tensions and incompatibilities between technical-economic and political interests may precipitate a great deal of learning within organisations.

Other helpful pointers to the existence of a 'political' interest as a locus of learning can be found in the various 'non-unitary' perspectives on organisational life. I will look briefly at three of these, namely pluralism, critical accounts of the labour process, and postmodernism.

In *pluralist accounts* of organisational life (e.g. Davidson 1994; Darrah, 1996; Badham & Buchanan 1996), shared-interest groups engage in a political struggle for limited resources. In so doing they seek power from wherever they can in order to protect and control their situations and further their interests. As they do so, they learn about such things as people's differing interests, values and agendas; ways in which management exerts pressure to control workers, and ways in which workers can resist excessive control; the nature of alliances; means of achieving sought-after outcomes; and strategies for protecting group interests.

Labour process accounts (e.g. Jermier, Knights & Nord 1994; Thompson & McHugh 1995; Beirne, Ramsay & Panteli 1998) emphasise that workplace relations are contested not only because of the stances taken by management and employees but also because of economic inequities encapsulated in the laws and institutions that regulate finance and international capitalism. The labour process perspective is suggestive of learning relating to such factors as pressure from shareholders, the threat of takeovers, changes in the international marketplace, hidden constraints on empowerment, and the inequitable nature of pay arrangements.

Postmodern accounts of organisational and community life (e.g. Foucault 1979; Gee, Hull & Lankshear 1996; Honneth 1999) view people as enmeshed in webs of practices, discourses and interactions which can be understood only through analysing (or 'deconstructing') particular situations. Postmodern accounts of organisations examine the complexities of work life, including the ways in which organisational members reproduce and challenge organisational practices and discourses. Postmodernism suggests caution about the unitary notion of 'organisational' learning, and points to a more complex, multi-interest and power-imbued view of learning.

While these three 'non-unitary' perspectives conceive of the organisation very differently, each suggests that groups with common political interests are likely to engage in a lot of learning—for example, learning associated with struggles to achieve equity; attempts to maximise group advantage; efforts to protect personal security and job continuity; responses to economic and political dynamics external to the organisation; and attempts to understand the role and nature of prevailing discourses.

Vignette 1 provides an example of learning associated with the political interest, drawn from my own investigations.

Vignette 1: AlphaCo

During the late 1990s, AlphaCo entered what was widely referred to as its 'empowerment' phase. During this period, management encouraged shopfloor employees to be 'empowered' in the service of the company. As described by a middle-level manager:

> *The business had an idealistic vision. We would have maintenance workers on line, who would have ownership of lines, and we would have production workers doing it—everyone would work together, and everyone would know their job, everything would run smoothly.*

However, these efforts, and particularly the emphasis on empowerment, were seen in retrospect to be a mistake. Managers came to believe that they had abdicated their responsibility and expected too much of employees, and had underrecognised the need for substantial training and close guidance. According to one manager:

> *We made a catastrophic mistake. In attempting to empower the workforce, we virtually had anarchy. We had quite a lot of turnover, we had horrendous amounts of damage being done to equipment, and our ability to do what we had to do was seriously impaired.*

Descriptions like this of the 'empowerment' period suggest that there was considerable learning by management as a group about the pluralistic nature of employee relations, and about the limited capacity of managers and employees to work together as one. The promotion of 'empowerment' resulted in what was later perceived by management as a form of anarchy, associated with damage and quality problems.

As a result, management learned that one prerequisite to empowered behaviour was workers having appropriate skills and knowledge. If, as was often the case, employees were underskilled, then 'empowering' them would result in mistakes. As one manager commented:

*I can't empower a four year old to cross the road. That's not empow-
ering, that's abdication. You've got to understand what some people
are capable of, and get them trained until they are capable—then you
are truly empowering them.*

In addition, management learnt about the intimate connection between
empowerment and common vision—that is, that it is unwise to support
empowerment unless managers and employees are focused on the
same sorts of interests, purposes, values and outcomes. The result of this
learning was that management deliberately put a lot more effort into
getting employees focused on organisational goals.

'Organisational' learning or shared-interest-group learning?

In Vignette 1, managers are learning to juggle their wish for empowered, proactive employees against evidence of the need to maintain
control over work and output. This learning is jointly refined through
dialogue and experimentation; it is retained in common accounts and
records of lessons learnt; it is widely shared, at least among managers;
and, in significant ways, it profoundly affects behaviour within the
organisation. On those grounds, one could argue that Vignette 1 is an
example of 'organisational' learning.

However, on closer inspection, it becomes clear that this is actually
an example of learning by a group of managers who share a common
political interest. A lot of so-called 'organisational' learning is actually
like this, learning by groups of people with common political interests—for example members of a board, the membership of a union
at a site, a group of senior managers, a project team, workgroup or
department.

Apart from learning about how to apply pressure to perform (as in
this example), political-level shared-interest-group learning might
include:

- learning about the pluralist nature of work (e.g. people's differences;
inconsistencies in people's beliefs);
- learning to manage information (e.g. about bonuses, profit, workplace change) in ways that meet company needs while avoiding
provocation; and
- learning about alliances (including covert relationships, such as
affairs with senior managers), and how to exploit them.

THE ONTOLOGICAL INTEREST AND 'ORGANISATIONAL' LEARNING

The nature of the 'ontological' interest

The psychoanalytical literature has a great deal to say about efforts to maintain one's sense of security and continuity in the face of internal and external threat. I'll refer to this as the 'ontological interest', borrowing on Laing's (1969) term 'ontological security'. While the psychoanalytical literature is primarily concerned with the individual, it also contains ample evidence that groups with common interests have an unconscious tendency to preserve and protect themselves.

For example, in the context of work, this tendency is evident in the concept of 'social defence against anxiety', popularised by Menzies Lyth (1988) in her descriptions of nurses dealing with the distress of caring for sick patients. Bion's (1961) foundational work on shared-group assumptions also details primitive levels of group functioning that relate to preserving security in the face of threat.

These and more recent investigations (e.g. see Hirschhorn 1990; Fineman 1993; Field 1997; Gabriel 1999) have helped to map out group concerns with such aspects as self-protection and enhancement, maintenance of members' self-esteem, and minimisation of feelings of deep-seated anxiety, shame and powerlessness.

Vignette 2 provides an example of learning associated with the ontological interest.

Vignette 2: BetaCo

The company being described, BetaCo, was taken over by another company during the 1990s, resulting in considerable turbulence, which affected both managers and employees. For employees, the most confronting incident involved maintenance workers. One worker recalled:

> I remember the afternoon very well. We started on the afternoon shift, and the day shift were asked to stay back a little while. Everyone was sent to a different meeting room. While the maintenance workers were being told in the workshop below that they had lost their jobs, and it was not negotiable, and there was an hour to pick up tools and go, other personnel all over the site were being addressed by other company officers, telling them what was happening. It was pretty profound stuff! The way it was done would be considered to be pretty

awful these days. The security guards turn up, and you're called into a meeting, and you're escorted off site, in one day, no time to say good-byes. You had to collect everything, and as you were marching out, the security guards were escorting [maintenance contractors] in. Very emotional stuff, tears everywhere.

A common feeling among employees at the time was that the company had acted unnecessarily harshly towards the maintenance workers. One team leader recalled that the workforce learnt a sobering lesson from the demise of the maintenance workers:

There was an extreme feeling of distrust with the management. It went on for a long period of time throughout the place. Those sorts of things that happen in your lifetime aren't things that you easily forget. If you take production workers here—some of them had been here for 15 to 20 years or longer—those things are just flags in the memory.

The phrase 'flags in the memory' is significant. It suggests that groups can have a shared memory built up around common interests and experiences. This memory is 'flagged' at particular points by incidents that represent threat. 'Flags in the memory' relate to lessons learnt about emotionally laden situations in which the group ontological interest is challenged.

The treatment of the maintenance workers was part of a more general transition that occurred when BetaCo changed ownership, from the previous low-pressure work environment to an environment where 'the almighty dollar' threatened jobs and job security. To some extent this learning was shared, in that both managers and employees faced the same international market forces. A senior manager conceded:

Employees are right when they say, 'Even if we did bust our butts, and we were the site of excellence, someone in the boardroom, for some reason best known to themselves, at a stroke of a pen, could just wipe us off the map'.

A conclusion like this conveys considerable despair about the influence of money and power over both employees and managers. It reflects learning not only by individuals but to an extent by the whole BetaCo site in the face of changes threatening such ontological basics as one's hold on a job and income.

'Organisational' learning or shared-interest-group learning?

Vignette 2 illustrates the emotional charge that can accompany learning associated with the ontological interest. Struggles to protect jobs, feelings of self-worth and economic security can be accompanied by a range of feelings, from terror to rage.

To some extent, Vignette 2 *does* provide an example of 'organis-ational' learning. Here, in the face of threat to jobs and the site, managers and employees are learning common lessons about their powerlessness in the face of the economic interests of a multinational company. For a short time, the whole BetaCo site may approximate a shared-interest group and be capable of learning.

What this suggests is that so-called 'organisational' learning is a special case of shared-interest-group learning, which occurs only for short periods and under particular circumstances when some factor, such as external threat, aligns the disparate interests of organisational members. More commonly, however, learning associated with the ontological interest occurs within smaller groups, such as the group of managers in Vignette 1.

DISCUSSION

The vignettes have illustrated two important things about so-called 'organisational' learning. First, most learning is not 'organisational' at all but resides at the level of shared-interest groups. Second, learning is not restricted to situations where people's interests align with the enter-prise's technical-economic interest. Indeed, a great deal of learning results from tensions and incompatibilities between the technical-economic interest of the enterprise and the interests of organisational members.

These tensions are depicted by the double arrows in Figure 12.1. As I have tried to demonstrate, the 'organisational' learning literature deals almost exclusively with the technical-economic level of learning. The deeper, shaded political and ontological levels tend to be ignored or actively opposed.

This tendency to 'ignore or actively oppose' learning associated with the political and ontological interests is very relevant to consultants involved in areas like HR and organisational change. While there are many ways in which managers can and do support learning associated with the technical-economic interest—by taking care with such factors as feed-back, opportunities for dialogue, group formation, critical reflection and

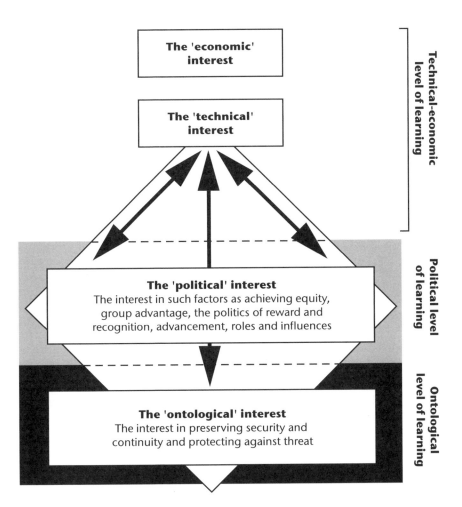

Figure 12.1: Interests and levels of shared-interest-group learning

information retention—they may be reluctant to use these same approaches to support learning associated with the political and ontological interests. In my own consulting work there has often been pressure to restrict the focus to the technical-economic level, and to avoid analysing or intervening at the political and ontological levels.

Thus managers, HR personnel and consultants tread a fine line between (a) creating the conditions necessary to support learning associated with the technical-economic interest and (b) damping down learning at the political and ontological levels which could strengthen interest groups and undermine the dominant technical-economic position.

CONCLUSION

This chapter began by considering the growing prominence of concepts like organisational learning and organisational knowledge, and suggesting reasons for this change. It then focused on problematic aspects of 'organisational' learning, particularly the tendency to adopt a technical-economic assumption and a unitary perspective on inter-group relations.

The chapter then drew on four non-unitary perspectives on organisational life—pluralism, labour process, postmodernism (all of which suggest a 'political' interest'), and the psychoanalytical literature's emphasis on protection and enhancement of the individual and group (or what I have referred to as an 'ontological' interest).

Each of these perspectives suggests that a holistic account of 'organisational' learning needs to go beyond the technical-economic interests of the organisation. As illustrated by the two vignettes, organisational members are continually learning about such issues as applying pressure to perform, managing information, protecting group interests, and the influence of 'money and power' on their lives. Much of this learning relates to tensions between the organisation's technical-economic interests and the political and ontological interests of organisational members.

Not surprisingly, when one looks at the literature of 'organisational' learning, one finds that it echoes the position taken by management (Table 12.2). Learning associated with the technical-economic interest is both recognised and encouraged, whereas learning associated with the political and ontological interest is hidden and discouraged.

In contrast with the assumptions made by the 'organisational' learning literature, I have argued that whole organisations rarely learn. A great deal of what has been referred to in the literature as 'organisational' learning is actually learning by shared-interest groups within organisations. Only in situations in which an enterprise approximates a shared-interest group (e.g. in a small start-up company united by common commitment; or in a company like BetaCo, from Vignette 2, united by common threat) can learning reasonably be considered 'organisational'.

Level of learning	Examples	Typical management stance	Typical coverage in the 'organisational' learning literature
Technical-economic	Learning to improve supply relationships, product design, equipment, processes and software	Encouragement, at least at the level of rhetoric. Informed managers are also likely to encourage in practice	Extensively covered in the literature
Political	Learning about the human condition, about pluralist aspects of work, about getting people to perform, about managing information, and about minimising constraint	Managers encourage learning that protects their position, although their approach may be somewhat uncoordinated. They actively discourage learning that might enhance the position of other shared-interest groups	Rarely covered in the literature, except as an accompaniment to technical-economic-level learning. Organisational learning by groups such as unions, whose interests may be at variance with management, is generally ignored
Ontological	Learning to protect group interests from threat, and about the impacts of money and power on employees' lives	Management ignores or actively opposes shared-interest-group learning at the ontological level	This level of organisational learning is not acknowledged in the literature

Table 12.2: Treatment of learning at the technical-economic, political and ontological levels

Given the evidence presented here, it is time to adopt a more holistic and robust view of 'organisational' learning, one that gives equal weighting to all three levels of learning outlined here: technical-economic, political, and ontological. It is also time to recognise the pluralistic and conflictual nature of organisations and 'organisational' learning, and the crucial role of interests and interest differences. Finally, it is time to examine much more carefully the circumstances, if any, in which learning is actually 'organisational'.

13

WORKPLACE LEARNING

Keith Forrester & Paul McTigue

'Workplace learning' has a long history and many meanings. Apprenticeships, traineeships, work-based degrees, continuing vocational and professional education—all are forms of workplace learning. (For a map of the field, see Evans & Rainbird 2002.) Additionally, the workplace is suffused with informal and incidental learning. People continually learn in their daily experience of work. Just as there are many forms of workplace learning, there are many perspectives on it. Overall, institutional and management views have dominated (Foley 2001: 44–96). This chapter focuses on the worker's interest in workplace learning.

First, Keith Forrester discusses trade union education in the context of the competitive global economy. He argues that when unions enter educational partnerships with employers and government, workers' interests are often sacrificed. To counter this, unions need to develop critical educational programs that help their members negotiate the globalised workplace. Forrester examines one such initiative, a series of work-based certificates developed by Leeds University at the request of unions.

In the second half of the chapter Paul McTigue examines the incidental learning of a group of public sector workers in their changing Australian workplace. He analyses workers' informal learning as management, over several years, introduces first performance management, then enterprise bargaining, then graduate recruits. A manager and union activist, McTigue reveals the complexity and embeddedness of the workers' learning. He shows that those who hope to understand and influence such learning must, like ethnographers or novelists, describe and interpret its often complex and contradictory dynamics.

TRADE UNION EDUCATION IN THE 'NEW' WORKPLACE

The emergence in recent decades of the workplace as a 'site of learning', and as a policy issue, has posed significant problems for trade unions. In countries where trade unions are slowly and hesitatingly emerging from the sustained onslaught of neoliberal economics or are currently being subjected to such pressures, being seen and treated as a significant player within work-based learning policy circles provides a rare opportunity to rebuild or 'modernise' battered images of significance and relevance. The emergence, nearly everywhere it seems, of 'lifelong learning' as a major policy discourse adds to the feelings of 'belonging' being experienced—often for the first time—by trade unions in various parts of the world. The seductive language of 'inclusion', 'non-traditional learners', 'personal development', 'learning workforce' and 'knowledge society' has persuaded unions that workplace education presents an opportunity to address traditional concerns—such as who gets what within workplace training and learning. In the main, unions have enthusiastically grasped the organisational opportunities attached to the emergence of the workplace as a site of learning. In Britain, for example, substantial government funds are currently available for the training and development of union workplace learning representatives. Around 5000 such representatives have been trained over the past three to four years and plans are afoot for a network that totals around 30 000–40 000 over the next decade (Forrester & Payne 1999).

If the rediscovered importance of workplace learning has provided a welcome fillip to the organisational activities for trade unions, the ideological context within which understandings of 'learning' and 'work' are deeply situated has proven more problematic. The emergence of 'workplace learning' and 'lifelong learning' is strongly associated with the drive towards improved economic productivity and performance within a competitive 'modernised' economy. Employee learning is seen as a central characteristic, not only of the knowledge-based economy but of society as a whole. 'Economic healthiness through a knowledge-based workforce entails social inclusion' is a sentiment endorsed by recently converted lifelong learning agencies such as the OECD and World Bank.

The divorce of learning from the socioeconomic realities of the workplace and the wider societal restructuring, however, poses grave risks for trade unions. Masked by calls from employers for 'empowerment', 'autonomy' and 'fulfilment', workplace learning risks becoming a sophisticated corporate strategy for managing 'human resources'. Workplace learning initiatives can be seen as post-Taylorist attempts to capture the commitment, loyalty, trust and sense of belonging of employees (Thompson & Warhurst 1998).

For trade unions, steering a pathway through these ideological labyrinths is fraught with difficulty. The increased political space for workplace learning is naturally welcomed by unions, partly because it promises organisational renewal at the local level. Powerful forces, however, such as expanded technological and informative resources and new managerial ideologies and practices have been reshaping the world of work. Research shows a more complicated reality than that advocated by those who champion 'knowledge workers' and 'the knowledge enterprise'. Most US companies (Milkman 1998) continue to employ traditional managerial strategies that are characterised by low-trust, low-skill, authoritarian routes to competitiveness (see also Thompson & Warhurst 1998).

'Learning for what', then, is a problematic question for all trade unions promoting workplace learning. The answer appears to be 'for employability'—that is, 'the opportunity to increase employees' career chances in a world of rapid changes in markets, technology and work organisation' (Trades Union Congress 1998: 5). Although usually situated within demands for widening participation, guidance, childcare facilities and financial support for study costs, the new union learning framework seems geared towards the 'shared commitment' between employers and unions, in 'partnership'—towards ensuring that the enterprise is able to compete through having a skilled and learning workforce. 'Shared commitment', according to the TUC (1998a: 5), involves commitments from the employer (to invest in job-specific as well as personal development learning), the employees (to own and control their learning throughout their working lives), the state (to provide lifetime entitlement and support for employees) and from the unions (to promote, negotiate and deliver learning to their members).

Workplace learning for trade unions is about employability; for the TUC a learning society is about more than this: it is about 'developing active citizens with the skills to learn and to participate in a democratic society: within their workplace and local community' (TUC 1998: 5). However, it is difficult to identify many learning initiatives that directly engage with the democratisation and wider community perspective. Instead, it is the focus on employability that largely informs the trade union 'modernising' agenda.

What then is the distinctive trade union contribution to 'the new educational framework'? Basic skills, vocational qualifications and career aspirations are legitimate concerns for trade unions, given the historic failure of employers to seriously address these matters. But unions also need to support learning activities that critically engage with the changing organisation and nature of 'work'. In a period when the traditional Taylorist distinction between thinking and doing is supposedly being eroded, there is a corresponding shift in emphasis from an employee's ability to perform to his/her willingness to perform. The so-called 'new politics of production', with its emphasis (in some workplaces, at least) on creativity, initiative and learning, could provide the union entry point for critical considerations of workplace learning. Linking the economic to social and cultural perspectives makes possible a consideration of the often contradictory processes of self and group formation. Similarly a focus, as the TUC puts it, on 'developing active citizens with the skills to learn and to participate in a democratic society' raises questions about 'divisions' within the workplace, over gender and ethnicity, and in the wider community. Interrelated themes such as interculturalism, solidarity, globalisation, ethnic and civil conflict move from the status of agreed motions at national conferences to those that inform local union learning initiatives and practices. It is possible that a preoccupation with 'employability' could encompass such themes.

The promotion of work-based learning by trade unions in Britain is at an early stage of development. In order to explore 'what's possible' and to maximise the organisational regeneration of local union structures and activities, broader learning partnerships will be required. Developing learning alliances between unions and sympathetic colleges, voluntary organisations and campaigning groups will be crucial.

Such partnerships characterised the successful 'employee development' schemes of the early 1990s. In the best-known trade union example of work-based learning, the UK public sector union, Unison, delivers the successful local 'Return to Learn' program throughout the country in partnership with the Workers' Educational Association (WEA). Organised within the union's 'Open College' system and based around project-based group learning ideas, learning in these programs is driven by the encouragement of 'outreach' perspectives and skills development strategies (talking to and involving members in the workplace or local community, interviewing, developing a campaign). Involving 180 hours of directed study, a nine-month program of tutor-supported meetings in participants' homes and two linked residential workshops, 'Return to Learn' has reached an impressive number of workers. To date, more than 10 000 members have completed the program and around 2000 members participate each year at no cost to themselves. Of these participants, 80% are women, 42% work part-time, 90% left school at the first opportunity, 60% have no qualifications, 80% are over the age of 35, and 76% earn less than the Council of Europe's decency threshold. Of the total Return to Learn participants, 59% have progressed to further and higher education (Sutherland 2002; Kennedy 1995).

There are few examples left today of learning partnerships between universities and trade unions. However, at the request of a small number of unions the Continuing Education School at the University of Leeds has developed a series of work-based university-accredited programs. Flexible (face-to-face, on-line and mixed-mode—distance and residential) university-accredited certificates, available as awards equivalent to a third or a sixth of a full degree program, have been developed and promoted as part of the unions' educational program. These programs complement the union's own educational provision but aim to broaden and deepen the learning through encouraging a more reflective and critical appreciation of the wider societal changes within which changes in the workplace and traditional union concerns are situated.

The European Studies Certificate, for example, complements the union's own training courses on European Works Councils by critically examining the 'democratic deficit' within the structures of the European Union and encouraging investigative and campaigning skills around the treatment of refugees and asylum seekers by the British government. The Citizenship and Democracy Certificate seeks to encourage a broader understanding of trade unionism through a critical examination of existing understandings and practices of 'citizenship' and 'democracy'. The Work and Learning Certificate, which in the case of one union all union workplace learning representatives are encouraged to complete, problematises both 'work' and 'learning', and through the development of local action plans encourages a wider conception of 'lifelong learning' in alliance with local community resources and concerns.

Critically engaging with 'given' understandings of workplace learning is a key theme in the Work and Learning Certificate. The social, situated conception of learning underpinning the program moves the focus away from the workplace course to the examination of 'old-fashioned' labour questions like the organisations of work, workplace social relationships and the associated issue of workplace democracy. A workplace learner representative from the manufacturing sector, for example, after critically reviewing government and trade union policies, support and understandings of lifelong learning, concluded that the focus on workplaces hides the need to support unemployed and those in the workplaces where we do not have bargaining rights. Union membership does not end at the factory gates and unions should work together as catalysts for change in the community. Furthermore, if global pressures create the need for workplace learning, then learning is an issue we should address at an international level. As an employee of a recently formed trans-national company, this global perspective could become increasingly important in future domestic negotiations.

Another participant in the Certificate, from the hospital sector, argued that the suggested 'learning agreement' between the local employees and union branch was too narrow:

> There is nothing wrong in seeking a highly skilled workforce, able to adapt to changing technologies and methods, and lifelong learning would seem necessary to keep skills up to date. Should that be the sole aim of lifelong learning? From the employers' point of view this may seem enough. Even persuading employers to provide the training for their own workforce and the time off to undertake it, can seem difficult. But unions have a wider agenda. Lifelong learning is not just about job-specific learning . . . The learning agreement should reflect this and should ensure there is a partnership to promote access to a wide range of learning opportunities.

The Global Labour Certificate has proven the most popular of the Leeds programs. Some 100 trade unionists are currently participating in the Certificate during its 'pilot phase' and four other unions will be joining the partnership in the coming year. The five courses within the Certificate focus on globalisation and work, poverty and inequality, international trade unionism, national and multi-agency policy and practices, and researching globalisation. Participants in these courses examine changing understandings and organisation within the workplace, personal and local retail patterns of consumption, trade and the World Trade Organisation as well as existing anti-poverty policy strategies. The courses all seek to critically enhance the interrelatedness of local community and trade union activity. Program evaluations demonstrate participants' raised awareness of issues like globalisation, fair trade, recycling, human rights, labour migration and refugees.

Assessed activities include writing articles for the union journal arguing for new initiatives or campaigns, preparing reports for a local branch meeting, writing a letter home as an asylum seeker, or writing a speech for the union's general secretary advocating a particular case or union development. A participant in the Global Labour Certificate, for example, develops a case for union involvement in a particular local community campaign, and concludes:

> Unions like ours have always been pioneering and we need to move forward by thinking beyond protectionism and nationalism . . . Unions need to change tactics and work with new social movements.

He outlines a number of campaign strategies, including a joint conference, distribution of campaign literature outside a local retail outlet, establishing 'links with a local union branch in a developing country', and promoting the campaign through the union's participation in European Union confederations. His report concludes:

> The future for a truly international trade union movement and for those concerned with global issues is in building strategic alliances. Our union can forge such alliances with [the campaign group] at the branch, national and international level . . . It is only by working together by pooling resources and sharing knowledge with groups such as [the campaign group] that we can make progress for the common good of improved global workers' rights.

The growing number of trade unionists interested and participating in the Global Labour Certificate is now opening up possibilities for local neighbourhood and/or workplace study circles that can supplement the residential weekends. Finding and exploring new ways of learning as well as themes that engage with current understandings, practices and boundaries of work-based or related learning will be important features of future union learning strategies that 'relate' to and 'connect' with members and new constituencies in ways different from the past.

INFORMAL LEARNING IN A CHANGING WORKPLACE

This case study examines changes that have been unfolding in 'The Department', a large Australian government agency, since the early 1990s. The changes are related in complex and subtle ways, as are their effects and the behaviour they have prompted in the people who work there.

At the outset, readers should know something about their narrator. I've been an employee of The Department for over 20 years. At various times, during the period in question, I've been a manager and a trainer-turned-human resource development (HRD) practitioner. Throughout my employment I've been a union activist.

This era of rapid, ongoing change in The Department raises important questions:

- What are people really learning from workplace change?
- What drives their learning?
- What are its effects?

I'll address these questions by looking at three faces of change in The Department.

1997: Performance management

> If it's worth doing then they should get it right and listen to what their staff are saying. (*Anthony, focus group participant*)

In the early 1990s trainers in The Department, previously responsible for the design and delivery of formal, classroom-based training programs, found themselves redefined as HRD practitioners. This often cast them in the role of corporate change messengers, explaining new initiatives such as performance management.

Introducing a formalised performance management system to The Department had been discussed for a number of years, without any visible signs of change. Performance management was always something that was 'coming soon', to the point that people decided it was never going to eventuate. When it was finally introduced, staff, including middle and line-level managers, felt uninformed, uninvolved and confronted.

Senior management's messages were positive, emphasising 'empowerment', opportunity and reward. However, their efforts were undone by the release of the draft policy. Immediately underneath the policy document's main title appeared the subheading 'managing underperformance'. People saw the inconsistency.

Management seemed primarily concerned with getting the system in place quickly, emphasising form-filling rather than explaining why the system had been introduced. Consequently, staff and managers interpreted performance management as a once-a-year 'performance appraisal' rather than an integrated part of daily work—something that might already be happening informally, to some extent. The result was yet another initiative that most managers and staff decided they didn't like.

Interestingly, this is quite a comfortable position for many people to be in. Why? Argyris (1998: 101–3) points out a basic flaw in many 'empowerment' initiatives: many managers don't really want to empower staff, and many staff, for their part, don't want to be empowered. Argyris contends that for managers it involves letting go of the command-and-control model they are comfortable with, and for staff it involves accepting greater accountability for their actions. Again, this is outside many people's comfort zone. Instead, both groups decide to fulfil their 'contractual obligation' (but nothing more), take heart from previous failed change initiatives, and adopt an attitude of: 'Senior management have tried to do these things to us in the past and failed. I'll ignore this and it will go away as well'.

Along with two other HRD practitioners I was asked to conduct an initial evaluation of The Department's new performance management system. This presented an opportunity to document the concerns, questions and suggestions of people in a number of workplaces and to put this information to constructive use. Feedback was gathered from discussions with small groups of staff and one-to-one interviews with managers.

Earlier messages about lack of information and involvement were repeated. People also raised concerns about:

- giving feedback to their manager;
- giving feedback to and receiving feedback from their peers;
- their behaviour being assessed against 'corporate values';
- being penalised and losing pay rather than being rewarded.

Staff responses, encapsulated by the comment cited at the beginning of this section, produced some changes to the system. Members of senior management acknowledged that they were asking people to take a giant leap and needed to move more slowly. They also made a concerted effort to allay people's fears about losing pay.

I also had the benefit of directly applying what I'd learnt back in my own workplace. This involved continuing to provide people with an avenue for asking questions and getting answers. I was able to organise discussion sessions on a work team basis, allowing people to talk through and agree on some approaches to giving and receiving feedback.

Several years on, managers have abandoned the notion of peer feedback for all staff. They now recognise how confronting it is for most people and the unnecessary damage it might cause to healthy, productive working relationships. Instead, it is used only in assessing the performance of senior managers.

People remain suspicious of the performance management concept. However, at least now their fears have lessened because they are:

- better informed;
- are listened to; and
- beginning to be involved in shaping the change process.

There was still a major aspect of workplace change that people had not recognised but could not afford to ignore. The evaluation indicated that a disturbingly large number of staff and managers didn't understand why performance management had been introduced. They saw it as another senior management initiative and, for its part, senior management portrayed it as such.

This simply wasn't the full story. Globalisation and the creed of competitiveness directly affect decision making at all levels of the economic hierarchy. This includes government decisions that in turn are handed down to departmental heads in the public sector. Performance management and other changes were being driven by forces that would ensure they didn't go away and would be implemented quickly—hence the emphasis that senior management placed on getting the system in place quickly.

Therefore, it was not an initiative exclusive to or driven by The Department's senior management, whose apparent reluctance to provide a full explanation at the time was a worrying aspect of this whole episode. Perhaps this is an illustration of Argyris' claim that those 'in control' are reluctant to be exposed as 'being controlled'.

Certainly it took a while longer for most people fully to appreciate these matters. However, a more complete understanding was not too far away and would be facilitated by an even more profound change in The Department.

2000: Enterprise bargaining

We didn't think the union was doing anything special for us and we figured that we could use the money we saved on our union dues to pay for a [cable TV] subscription. (*Lesley, a colleague, explaining why she and her husband resigned from the union*)

By the end of the 1990s many employees in The Department, some barely 40 years of age, were openly wishing they could retire. The Sydney journalist Adele Horin (2000) reported the same phenomenon among her friends and associates. Relentless workplace change was evoking similar feelings right across the Australian workforce.

How were people coping with feelings of powerlessness in the face of non-stop change? In The Department at least they appeared to be concentrating on issues that had immediate and personal relevance and to be distancing themselves from the rest. Lesley's comment indicates that for one married couple unionism and involvement in workplace issues had given way to cable TV escapism. Was this a sign of the times? Where did this leave unionism?

A decade of effort by the Australian union movement had failed to halt the decline in union membership. For Macken (1997), the most lethal factor was unionism's failure to adapt to the changing face of employment, a key feature of which was the remaking of the traditional employer–employee relationship.

In Australia, this scenario unfolded during the years of the Prices and Incomes Accord, a consensus strategy developed by the federal Labor government and the Australian Council of Trade Unions (ACTU) in February 1983. The ACTU agreed to wage restraint in return for social benefits. The government reasoned that wage restraint would benefit business, thus increasing investment and employment.

Macken argues that during its 13 years the Accord was off-limits to union criticism. Workers saw union leaders obsessed with maintaining Labor's economic credibility (and tenure in office), and the Accord was supported as it was killing unionism (Macken 1997: 59). Workers experienced falling living standards, lower wages, longer hours and growing job insecurity. Why wouldn't union membership decline?

From 1993, the ALP government shifted away from centralised wage-fixing to an enterprise bargaining model. This had major ramifications for public sector workers. Instead of negotiating collectively with government for uniform pay and conditions, they now had to negotiate on an individual enterprise or agency basis. Pay rates began to vary between agencies.

Union negotiators and a management negotiating team stood on new ground, after a union membership vote narrowly opened the door for enterprise bargaining to enter The Department. Time and four subsequent rounds of enterprise bargaining would show this to be a defining moment, as the door opened ever wider to the managerialist agenda.

Management and union signed the inaugural enterprise agreement in 1994. This and the subsequent two bargaining periods featured an energetic, involved union membership, who campaigned strongly and rejected management's initial offers as not good enough. Improvements were gained each time before agreements were signed.

However, by 2000 and the fourth round of bargaining, the energy and involvement had dissipated. The union campaign was hamstrung by the now limited willingness of members to get involved. Management concessions, including assurances about job security, were proving tougher to obtain, and pay rises were linked to more stringent performance standards. Employees again rejected management's initial offer but eventually voted for an almost unchanged second offer.

The union movement's problems now had immediate relevance for The Department's employees. Outsourcing, redundancy and job insecurity were the new coffee-break topics. Why, though, had change produced the effect of a distant, silent workforce? Their silence seemed to be a reluctant acquiescence in the face of change. Was this an accurate interpretation? How to turn this around?

Interviews with members revealed recurring themes. First, people wanted to do a good job and saw their work as important. However, management was making this difficult. Inadequate technology and systems support caused delays and reversed work flows. Employees increasingly had to learn 'on the job', and this wasn't always appropriate. Staff providing this training were still expected to meet their normal work targets. Second, people acknowledged that their level of involvement in workplace issues directly affected their working conditions. However, such developments as the election of a Liberal/National (conservative) government in 1996, subsequent changes to industrial relations legislation and perceptions of growing societal self-interest were restricting that involvement. Members were coming reluctantly to accept that unionism might fade into obscurity.

Union officials and delegates were seen as effective representatives and communicators. This perhaps explains why membership has remained constant in The Department, while diminishing in the workforce generally. However, enterprise bargaining was seen as creating a downward spiral in conditions.

Members valued timely, directly relevant union information, received via e-mail and concise handouts. They were uninterested in the issues facing workers elsewhere. Interestingly, some people indicated that they would attend discussion groups at the union office, outside work hours. (The possibilities that this last point might offer are discussed earlier in this chapter.)

These opinions supported my observations, but left one worrying question unanswered. If members understood that their non-involvement contributed to the erosion of conditions, why did they choose not to get involved?

Collinson (1994) identifies two types of worker resistance to management-induced change: first, 'resistance through distance', as workers symbolically distance themselves from their workplace; second, 'resistance through persistence', as workers seek to exercise their rights and make management more accountable (Collinson 1994: 35–7). The 'resistance through distance' adopted by workers in The Department is defensive and fails to challenge management power. This strategy creates two problems. Workers may accommodate management policy but job security is not guaranteed. Workers are redefined as individuals in competition with each other, rather than as a collective. So 'playing the game' locks people into practices that perpetuate exploitation.

In The Department, union officials and activists have tried to foster 'resistance through persistence', but most workers have opted for 'resistance by distance'. By the end of 2002, union activism and employment conditions were continuing their downward spiral. A fifth round of enterprise bargaining and a lacklustre union campaign culminated in a clear 'yes' vote for management's initial offer. For the first time, employees had accepted the first offer put to them.

The inactivity of union members and the 'union official as representative' model was clearly failing. On a wider scale, a decade of reflection by the labour movement had failed to find a miracle cure. In The Department and other workplaces, collective strength and 'resistance by persistence' were a rapidly fading memory.

Scott (2000: 9) argues that the modernisation of the Labor parties in Britain and Australia has caused division, in both countries, between 'modernisers' and 'traditionalists'. He notes how terms such as 'modernisation' are accorded favourable status whereas terms such as 'traditionalist' are used dismissively. This division and terminology might well describe the maturation of a third face of change in The Department. The 2002 round of enterprise bargaining signalled the full-blown arrival of a new sort of worker—smart, confident and with a different view of the world.

2002: Workforce renewal

> All I want is the opportunity to negotiate my pay and conditions on my own behalf. It may be that I can't do better than the unions but I'd like the chance. (*Amanda, an employee, in a letter to the editor of the weekly in-house journal*)

In 1996, after a long period of workforce stability, The Department began to recruit significant numbers of university graduates. Commencing employment shortly after completing their studies, the new employees undertook a rigorous two-year probationary period of in-house study and work placements. Recruitment was following hot on the heels of a large-scale redundancy program. The new wave of employees were receiving opportunities for rapid career advancement and grabbing them with both hands. The resentment of older employees was palpable.

Management had designed a carefully thought out orientation program for the new recruits. This included messages about the 'negative' attitudes they would encounter with long-term employees and the need to distance themselves from these influences. Most new employees took these messages at face value. An 'us and them' mentality quickly took hold of both groups.

These changes had severe consequences for unionism. Many people, typically within a few years of retirement age and feeling unable to cope with any more change, took redundancy packages. As they walked out of The Department for the last time, a large slice of worker solidarity went with them.

The newer employees did not share this tradition of collectivity, and tended not to join the union. Their numbers grew rapidly over a six-year period, accentuated by the number of people leaving. By 2002 they made up about 20% of The Department's workforce. The combined effect of redundancy and recruitment programs was there for all to see in each successive round of enterprise bargaining, culminating in the easy passage of management's 2002 offer.

Clearly, the priorities and views of the growing number of new employees will have a profound effect on industrial relations and other aspects of The Department over the coming years. They and those longer-serving employees who can ride the current of change are the 'new model' workers in the era of human capital. Increasingly, individuals will have to test their bargaining power on their own. For now at least, collective strength has given way to individualism, a situation that some people feel equipped to deal with while others feel exposed. Is this a case study of a long-term managerialist change agenda coming to fruition? Is worker solidarity dead? Will resistance become ever more individualised and distant?

Over 25 years ago, Terkel interviewed workers across the United States and came to the harsh conclusion that working is, for most of us, an act of daily violence and humiliation (Terkel 1974: xi). To get through the day is a triumph in itself. Loftier goals of leaving a mark and being remembered are for the few. This chilling scenario has certainly proven to be the case for many people in The Department.

More than a decade of change initiatives and their effects have made the 'letters to the editor' section of the weekly staff journal the most widely read piece of information in The Department. The excerpt cited at the start of this section is just one of many that point to further, interesting times ahead.

This case study documents some of the learning, including the drivers and effects, that is taking place all around us in our workplaces. It demonstrates the importance of 'change facilitators' being students of their own workplaces, rather than looking for off-the-shelf 'solutions'. The qualities that make each person and setting unique demand and deserve more than predetermined approaches that don't really begin to work. There are no quick fixes.

14

VOCATIONAL EDUCATION AND TRAINING

Damon Anderson, Mike Brown & Peter Rushbrook

We begin this chapter by defining 'vocational education and training', recognising that the term means different things to different people. We then discuss the economic and political forces currently shaping the VET sector, examine the relationship between vocational and higher education, compare VET systems in different countries, explain VET qualifications and credentials, and discuss VET curriculum, learners and teachers, and pedagogy. We conclude by discussing some tensions in VET and posing some crucial questions about the sector.

DEFINING VET

Vocational education and training is aligned directly to learning for work, and includes training for specific job roles. 'Vocational education and training' is also a contested concept. The 'vocational education' dimension is emphasised by those who contend that VET is (or should be) about the holistic and integrated development of underpinning knowledge and broad-based, transferable work and life skills. The 'training' dimension tends to be emphasised by those who believe that VET should address itself exclusively to the acquisition of a relatively narrow band of employment-related or job-specific skills and competencies. Such distinctions reflect two competing traditions in VET, with the former approach typically advocated by adult educators and high school reformers, and the latter generally promoted by industry trainers and human resource developers (Lakes 1994; Simon et al. 1991; Stevenson 2000; Watkins 1991).

VET harbours a range of tensions, opportunities and threats. Some educational commentators have argued that VET works as a form of control over workers/learners by reproducing existing workplace power relations. The widespread use of competency-based training (CBT) in VET, and the role played by external stakeholders in determining course content and outcomes, also generates criticism. For some commentators, external control of curriculum runs contrary to good practice in adult education and the democratic principles that should inform the development of citizens/workers. VET has also been implicated in the production and maintenance of skill hierarchies that systematically marginalise women, people with disabilities, and racial and ethnic minorities in the labour market (Butler 1999; Kincheloe 1999).

Yet alongside these criticisms stand VET's acknowledged strengths. Historically, VET has provided working people with access to practical skills and 'really useful knowledge' that connect with their everyday struggles and lived experiences. VET provides an education with both the content and form of its programs being appropriate for an array of people with different needs and motivations. Unlike academic schooling, VET provides an education that enables diverse cohorts of learners to experience success by gaining new skills and credentials for work and other purposes. And it addresses some of the access and equity issues raised by earlier forms of vocational preparation (e.g. a male-dominated apprenticeship system).

ECONOMIC CRISIS, NEOLIBERALISM, GLOBALISATION AND VET

Contemporary VET cannot be understood in isolation from changes in the nature of work, technology and work organisation.

Despite VET's significant role in nation-building and industrial development during the 19th and 20th centuries, it has generally attracted little policy or scholarly attention. In recent years, however, VET has risen to almost unprecedented prominence in government policy and public debate. Although the reasons for this are complex and multifaceted, they can be explained to a large extent by the conjunction of deep-seated economic problems, globalisation, and the rise of neoliberal politics and free market economics over the past two decades.

Since the mid-1970s oil crisis, most developed Western nations have experienced major slumps in economic growth and capital accumulation, resulting in mass structural unemployment and related social problems. In an effort to reverse their economic fortunes, many developed nations abandoned the postwar Keynesian settlement that underpinned the development of the social democratic welfare state and its commitment to full employment. Instead, governments have been pursuing a free market agenda through the deregulation of trade, labour markets and financial systems, combined with a restructuring and downsizing of the public sector.

The drift towards smaller government and free markets accelerated after the dismantling of the Berlin Wall in 1989. This event signified not only the historical demise of the centralised command economies of communist countries but also a crisis of faith among Western social democratic nations in the capacity of the state, or central government, to achieve social and economic progress through coordinated planning and resource allocation. Market forces, private enterprise and 'survival of the fittest' were increasingly viewed as superior mechanisms for promoting economic efficiency and social prosperity.

The political vacuum left by the seeming failure of socialism and communism has been rapidly filled by neoliberal ideology. In an effort to kick-start their languishing economies, governments of all persuasions initiated neoliberal reform agendas to 'roll back' the state, eradicate bureaucratic 'red tape', and give free rein to private enterprise and market forces. Such agendas involved, among other things, cutting back expenditure on public services, such as health, welfare and education and training; corporatising and restructuring public services; encouraging private provision; and subjecting public providers to competition (Avis et al. 1996; Green 1997; Pusey 1991).

Correspondingly, government has redefined its own role as one of 'steering at a distance', purchasing (rather than providing) public services, and regulating market transactions 'with a light hand'. Ironically, government has devolved greater responsibility for service delivery on to provider management, while at the same time centralising control of the objectives and outcomes of service delivery via national standards-setting, performance-based contracts and output-based funding. The failure of markets to solve social access and equity problems is partially addressed via targeted funding for 'at-risk' groups, and increasingly punitive measures directed at the victims of neoliberal reform (Avis et al. 1996; Green 1990, 1997).

The rapid advance of economic globalisation, reflected in the ascendancy of transnational corporations and international free trade agreements, has seen greater integration of national market economies and more permeable national boundaries. As a result, national governments have to varying degrees lost control of their economic destinies. Capital has become increasingly mobile, seeking out new markets and cheap labour. Goods and services are designed, produced and distributed via new 'global enterprise webs' that transcend national jurisdictions. The resulting intensification of global economic competition and hyper-volatility in labour markets demand a constant reorganisation and readjustment of national economic structures and work patterns. Such trends have major implications for VET, as they undermine the ability of national governments to predict demand for skills and to plan workforce development over the longer term (Brown et al. 2001; Waters 1995).

National economies, particularly in developed countries with relatively high wages, are left with few options other than to develop their so-called 'human capital'—the knowledge and skills of their workforce. Hence, 'skills formation' becomes central to economic policy. The subordination of VET to 'human capital theory' and the redefinition of VET learners as 'human resources', or units of production to which VET adds value, has in turn displaced the social and educational roles of VET (Brown et al. 2001; Green 1997; Marginson 1993). This fundamental reorientation of the purposes of VET is exemplified in the general attempt to harness VET to national economic objectives and industry demand, and to transfer responsibility for VET policy from education to labour market portfolios. Following economists like Reich (1991), emphasis has also been placed on developing 'symbolic analysts', with the advanced conceptual and analytical skills that attract high premiums in global markets.

Paradoxically, due to the influence of neoliberalism, VET sectors have been subjected to deep funding cuts, business management techniques and a cult of efficiency, or 'doing more with less'. The free market principles of 'competition', 'choice' and 'user pays' have been systematically applied to VET through the creation of demand-driven 'training markets' based on competitive tendering, 'user choice' or voucher schemes, and contracting out. CBT has become the international currency for standardising skills and qualifications with the aim of producing more efficient labour market transactions. Modularisation of courses, work-based delivery and assessment, and contract-based and casual employment for teachers have in turn facilitated private provision of VET (Anderson

1997, 2000; Avis et al. 1996; Hodkinson & Sparkes 1995; Hodkinson et al. 1996; Levin 2001).

Within the new market paradigm, VET administrators have become business managers, VET teachers have been recast as training entrepreneurs, and VET students have been reframed as customers, rather than learners. Starved of government funds and forced to seek new sources of private income, public VET institutions have progressively moved away from serving their traditional constituencies towards commercial training for industry and export markets. The marketisation of VET, however, has been uneven, and is most evident in English-speaking countries.

As national VET systems are increasingly subsumed within the framework of competitive global markets, so too have they been subject to the growing influence of supranational policy 'thinktanks' (Henry et al. 2001; Marginson 1993). Agencies like the Organisation for Economic Cooperation and Development (OECD), the Asian Development Bank (ADB) and the World Bank have been instrumental in standardising VET policy in developed nations and colonising the VET systems of developing nations. Due to their pervasive influence, competitive tendering, performance-based funding and voucher schemes are now features of many national VET systems. The importation of CBT into many African and Asian nations—such as South Africa, which recently introduced 'Outcomes-Based Education and Training' (OBET)—in addition to widespread reliance on private financing and provision of VET, has been promoted through international aid projects funded by such organisations.

In effect, as national economies and labour markets have become increasingly integrated due to the effects of economic globalisation, VET systems have been converging and becoming more homogenised. While historical and cultural differences persist, VET increasingly tends to mirror the demands of global capital and reproduce the 'flexible workers' required by deregulated labour markets. Whether this best serves the interests of working people is questionable, and will be considered below.

THE CHANGING NATURE OF WORK AND VET

In the last quarter of the 20th century, the nature of work changed considerably. Casey (1999) identified three main pressures:

1. *Changes in the development and use of technology.* There has been a sharp rise in the utilisation of digital electronics in nearly all industries.

In particular there has been an increase in the use of information and communication technologies. Skill demands have altered accordingly. Technology has helped to eliminate rigid divisions of labour and the tendency towards specialisation (although other researchers find that new technologies have actually *increased* specialisation, especially at 'higher' levels of the workforce). The manufacturing sector has seen large-scale redundancies, with remaining workers being assisted to 'multi-skill' and 'up-skill'—hence the rise of the 'flexible worker'.

2. *Changes in approaches to workplace organisation and management*. The main tendency has been to restructure organisations by reducing levels of hierarchy and replacing these with flatter and more flexible team-based structures. New management rhetoric also speaks about the participation of the workforce in decision-making processes. Studies of these changes show diverse, and sometimes conflicting, results.

3. *Globalisation*. As noted earlier, this has seen a further rise in the significance of multinational and transnational corporations. Along with this movement comes an increase in the international division of labour and the emergence of the decentred workplace, as 'symbolic analysts' work from laptop computers in home offices and even airline lounges.

Flowing from these 'megatrends' came changes to national economies through structural adjustment and industry restructuring, as large numbers of jobs moved from traditional sectors such as agriculture and manufacturing to services (Brown et al. 2001; Waterhouse et al. 1999; Casey 1999; Levett 2000). Industries such as metal trades and engineering, which were traditionally well represented in VET programs, experienced cutbacks in provision in Western developed countries. Yet the international division of labour meant that these areas were on the increase in other countries, particularly those where labour was much cheaper. Industrially developed countries, such as Australia, saw significant growth in VET programs for new and emerging industries, such as retail, hospitality, tourism, childcare services, and information and communication technologies (Smith 2000). In this way, VET provision was strategically aligned to shifts in labour market demand and thereby facilitated labour market adjustment and economic restructuring.

At the national level, in the 21st century, there have been changes in the distribution of employment, with the formation of so-called 'hourglass' arrangements reflecting job growth at each end of the labour market and a loss of middle-income jobs. These trends have produced winners and losers (ACIRRT 1999). Winners receive higher salaries and improved benefits, while the losers experience job cuts and a reduction in full-time work. Those who have kept their jobs have experienced intensification through longer hours, higher expectations, pressure to retrain, and more demanding work practices.

The flipside of a flexible workforce is job insecurity and 'portfolio' careers. Labour market changes have seen a decrease in full-time and permanent work and an increase in part-time and casual employment. While the number of women in employment has grown, it is mostly in casual and part-time jobs (ACIRRT 1999). Simultaneously, underemployment has risen, despite the preference of many part-time and casual workers for longer hours or full-time employment. There has been a rise in self-employment, partly due to the growth of outsourcing and lengthening employment chains (Waterhouse et al. 1999). Partly as a consequence of recent labour market trends, union membership has also declined.

In many OECD countries, such as the United Kingdom and Australia, traditional career paths for early school leavers and young people on non-academic tracks have largely collapsed, particularly those destined for trades. Many now face an uncertain future of serial employment in casual (and often underpaid and exploitative) jobs, interspersed with periods of unemployment and 'workfare'. Correspondingly, their careers have often become a pastiche of unrelated work experiences, and school-to-work transitions are increasingly fragmented, non-linear and unpredictable (de Goede et al. 1997; Dwyer & Wyn 2001). As employment has become more precarious and employer commitment to workforce development has declined, individuals of all ages have assumed greater responsibility for planning and financing their own learning throughout their working lives.

VET AND HIGHER EDUCATION

In the past, most working people learnt informally on the job, whereas religious and public officials and ruling elites underwent 'higher education' in colleges and universities. With the growth of the factory system from the early 19th century onwards, working-class education 'became an agent of the capitalist system in the reproduction of the necessary labour power' (Coffey 1992: 30). Gradually, working-class education became more structured and institutionalised in the form of apprenticeships and technical schools. Even so, the vocational track was still (and often still is) viewed as inferior to an academic track. Traditionally, therefore, vocational education has been the education offered to those who were regarded, either by birth or circumstance, as citizens of secondary importance (Coffey 1992; Ling 1986; Kliebard 1999; Lipsmeier & Schroeder 1994; Rushbrook & Brown 2001).

Dual-track educational streaming is still prevalent in most developed countries. In fact, the primary function that national governments attribute to the VET sector is the provision of working-class education and training. It should be noted that 'working-class' is interpreted here in two senses. First, in the sense that learners are educated and trained for jobs/occupations described as 'below the professions'. Second, in the sense that people who lack powerful cultural capital in our society due to age, gender, race/ethnicity and socioeconomic background are more highly represented in VET. By contrast, 'higher education' provides the ruling and middle classes with an educational passport to high-status professions, such as law and medicine, and management positions in industry and commerce (Achtenhagen & Grubb 2001).

INTERNATIONAL COMPARISONS

The structure, organisation and delivery of VET vary significantly from country to country. International comparisons need substantial detail and qualification, and are often far from straightforward (Brown et al. 2001; Keating et al. 2002). As comparisons between VET systems in developed and developing nations are even more complex, the following discussion focuses primarily on the former.

Major differences exist between the roles adopted by the state in VET provision. At one end of the spectrum are countries like Japan and Singapore, where VET is largely under the control of highly centralised and interventionist national governments. In between are countries like Germany and Australia, both of which have a federal structure wherein responsibility for VET provision is devolved to state governments within a broader framework of national VET legislation and policy. At the other end of the spectrum is the USA, with its highly decentralised and non-interventionist approach to VET provision. Within and between each of these systems, the degree of autonomy enjoyed by VET institutions varies considerably, although as a general rule they have far less independence than universities. Overall, as noted earlier, there is a global trend towards increasing centralisation and government intervention in

VET provision, albeit coupled with the devolution of managerial responsibility and greater reliance on deregulated training markets (Brown et al. 2001; Green 1997).

Considerable variation also exists between the mix and balance of public and private sector provision in different countries. Private for-profit VET providers have been a longstanding fixture in countries as diverse as the USA and Japan. By contrast, the role of private VET institutions in Germany has been minimal. Until recently, the private VET sector was also relatively small in Australia, New Zealand and the UK, largely because they have long traditions of government ownership, financing and control. However, privatisation trends over the past two decades or so have seen rapid growth in private VET institutions, albeit often heavily reliant on public funding (Anderson 1995; Green 1997; Cantor 1989).

National traditions and patterns of investment by industry in workforce preparation and development are uneven. Historically, large companies in Japan, Germany and the USA have invested substantial amounts of capital in training, and to a lesser extent retraining, for their employees. Employers in Australia, New Zealand and the UK have traditionally invested far less, preferring instead to rely on government provision, 'poaching' staff from competitors, and importing skilled labour (Brown et al. 2001; Green 1997).

From an international perspective, VET covers a broad range of provision. In developing nations, VET programs are delivered anywhere from primary through to middle-level secondary schooling. In developed nations, however, VET provision is most often located in post-compulsory education and training institutions such as upper-secondary schools and technical colleges. In Finland, the Netherlands, Singapore, New Zealand and Australia, there are separate post-school VET institutions. Elsewhere, VET programs run alongside adult, continuing and further education programs. Conversely, VET is delivered mostly on the job in Germany and Japan.

Definitions of 'vocational education and training' also differ significantly. In Germany, for instance, VET covers learning about both technical occupations and the professions. In the past 100 years, the longstanding German apprenticeship system has evolved into a dual system, where workers/learners spend some of their time supervised in workplaces, thereby learning on the job, with the remaining time spent learning off the job in vocational education colleges. This model of apprenticeship training has been adopted by some other countries (Achtenhagen & Grubb 2001; Brand 1998).

Another feature of Germany's VET has been the way that, despite the pressures of the unification program, it has maintained relatively low unemployment, especially among its young people. And, like Denmark, Germany has very high participation rates in post-compulsory education and training. In Germany, two-thirds of all young people undertake and complete an apprenticeship.

The distinctive features of the German system can be attributed in large part to historical and cultural factors. In particular, the 'social partnership' that has long existed between employers, government and unions promotes a high level of cooperation and shared responsibility for financing and managing VET. Other related factors specific to Germany include the tradition of maintaining tight connections between VET and the labour market, relatively high expenditure on VET for young people, and the provision of strongly regulated, institutional pathways from school to work. In Australia, the UK and the USA, relations between employers and unions are more adversarial, VET and the labour market are 'loosely coupled', expenditure on VET is much lower, and post-school pathways are less structured and more diverse and individualised (Burke & Reuling 2002).

In Australia and New Zealand, interest in the dual system has grown over the past two decades and, in part, this has inspired the direction of reform in both countries. Since the early 1990s, the Australian and New Zealand VET sectors have become more integrated and highly systematised. All programs are based on competency standards developed by industry stakeholders, and more recently cross-sectoral pathways have been negotiated. National qualifications frameworks that embrace all the sectors of education and training have facilitated the development of cross-sectoral pathways and credit transfer arrangements. To a greater extent than before, learners can move between the school, VET and university sectors.

Keating at al. (2002) explain that VET in the USA is very difficult to track and is not confined to dedicated VET institutions. Instead, VET provision is widely dispersed. Secondary schools offer general and vocational subjects side by side, with some states having dedicated vocational high schools. Private for-profit vocational schools are also prominent throughout the USA. VET does not have a very high participation rate.

The US economy owes a great deal to the exploitation of its high number of unskilled workers. Ehrenreich (2002), for instance, provides first-hand accounts of the day-to-day struggles of people in low paid jobs.

Following this, Sklar et al. (2001) outline the case for a minimum wage of $US8 per hour for all workers across the USA. Of the 120 million people employed in industry across the USA, one-quarter receive less than this amount.

Despite international differences, in their comparative study of VET across nine countries in three different regions, Keating et al. (2002) find numerous similarities, including:

- Increasingly, national governments have a policy focus on VET.
- There is a growing convergence between VET and general education.
- There has been a tendency towards broader integration across departments within VET institutions in order to offer a wider range of options and increase flexibility.
- VET stakeholders are aware of the need for broader cognitive development of 'soft' skills, core competencies and underpinning knowledge.
- All systems are under pressure to cut costs.
- VET provision is being driven less by governmental and institutional planning than by industry and labour market demand.
- VET has been the testing ground for the development of education and training markets.
- There is a general view that VET has not been sufficiently client-focused.
- VET has traditionally been developed as an alternative to higher-status academic pathways.

For many, the strength of the VET system stems from its connections to the world of work. This connection is formalised through appropriately developed and aligned qualifications and credentials.

VET QUALIFICATIONS AND CREDENTIALS

Depending on the national VET system under consideration, VET qualifications range from certification of basic skills and competencies, through skilled trades, technical and technology areas, to the paraprofessional level. In some instances this can extend into the professions. VET qualifications are generally awarded at certificate and diploma levels, although vocational degrees and graduate-level qualifications are now offered in Finland, the Netherlands and the state of Victoria in Australia.

VET qualifications may be specific to job roles in a particular company, or may be awarded as certification in an occupation or industry.

244

A highly developed VET system offers credentials that have national portability. As a result of globalisation, educational credentials and qualifications are beginning to be exported internationally. For instance, a mutual recognition agreement now exists between Australia and New Zealand.

A developed VET system will offer programs with qualifications that articulate upwards or sidewards into allied programs. Significantly, however, in terms of labour market value and remuneration, a diploma in one industry does not necessarily equate to a diploma in another. Nor do such qualifications necessarily ensure higher wages than those for a lower certificate holder in a different industry. Qualifications are generally not tied to wage levels, though in some circumstances industrial determinations based on qualifications have been negotiated and established.

VET programs gain much of their appeal through their recognition by stakeholders who control access to employment, such as employers, unions, industry associations and, in some instances, government representatives. Although these stakeholders are external to VET, they occupy privileged positions in negotiations over program content and outcomes, and the subordinate role of the primary stakeholders—namely VET learners and teachers—in formal determinations about the content of VET programs remains an issue of concern and debate. For example, common practice in adult education has teachers negotiating content and assessment with learners. This practice empowers the primary stakeholders, but in VET it is seen to detract from industry recognition of qualifications.

VET CURRICULUM

Stevenson (1994) has argued that course design in VET is based on three principles: relevance, responsiveness, and uniqueness. VET courses are considered to be relevant to the extent that they are based on work-related requirements identified by employers. As the buyers of labour in labour market transactions, employers are one of the main stakeholders in VET and have certainly increased their influence in marketised VET systems. For this reason, VET courses typically set out with the primary aim of developing the skills, knowledge and attitudes that employers deem to have value and that they are prepared to purchase.

VET is said to be responsive in the sense that it addresses the current skills and knowledge 'demands' of the market. Stevenson's third principle of uniqueness is not as true today as it was a decade ago. In fact, VET has spilled over into all other sectors of post-compulsory education, with universities offering niche-market VET programs and more vocationally oriented degree programs. It is also true to say that it is unique for another reason: no other sector of education so systematically hands important decisions about curriculum and pedagogy to employers and corporate interests.

Recent VET reforms in most countries have concentrated largely on improving efficiency and responsiveness by finding ways to better fit workers to employer demands. In the main, VET policy makers, practitioners and researchers consider this approach to be unproblematic. From one perspective, it can certainly be argued that one of VET's strengths is that it gives learners access to skills and qualifications that have some value in the labour market. In this regard, VET is empowering for working people. From another perspective, however, this characteristic represents a major weakness of VET, in that it may subordinate the interests of workers/learners to those of capital. The determination of what constitutes 'useful' knowledge for working people is in the hands of employers. Consequently, what working people 'need to know' gets left to managerial prerogative and the market. This may be contrary to the interests of the learners, as it can result in programs that are not only narrow but also disempowering, in that they deny participants access to the knowledge and skills they require to participate actively in workplace and social change.

With the exception of adult literacy and general education programs, the VET curriculum development process typically begins with an analysis of the job role and the identification of competencies. It is the ability to perform these competencies that becomes both the aim and prescribed outcome of the VET program (Mansfield & Mitchell 1996). Globally, most providers of VET use competencies as the basis of their courses in an effort to certificate labour in accordance with the requirements of external stakeholders.

Yet the whole notion of the 'competent worker' remains problematic (Boughton et al. 2002). Curriculum developers visit a range of workplaces in an industry in order to analyse the jobs and define program requirements. At best, however, this produces an artificial and disembodied aggregation of skill requirements, and assumes an idealised notion of a competent worker. Differences relating to technologies and work organisation within an industry or occupation may also be overlooked or ignored, with the requirements of large and medium-sized companies often prevailing in program content.

One of the main pressures on the determination of content is the changing technology associated with a range of work processes. Constant upgrading of technology throughout an industry, even if spasmodic, means that course content must frequently change (Achtenhagen & Grubb 2001).

A common feature of most VET systems now is recognition or accreditation of prior learning systems, which enables learners to obtain credit for skills developed informally and experientially in workplace and community settings. Such credit and recognition systems have fuelled debate on the nature of generic skills and the ability to transfer those understandings from the context in which they were learned to similar or related situations. Some researchers have demonstrated that understandings can be highly situated. They remain unconvinced that these can be transferred to other situations. If they are correct, this has implications for course design, including CBT and the role of off-the-job learning. Such concerns have given rise to programs that utilise authentic work-based projects to facilitate learning (Boud 2001). Other researchers suggest instead that skills and knowledge learned off the job can be transferred (Tennant 1999).

VET Learners and teachers

VET learners come from diverse backgrounds and exhibit a wide range of motivations. Traditionally VET has been strongly male-dominated, although in recent years the number of women in VET programs has increased, especially in OECD countries. However, while gender participation is becoming more equitable, VET programs are still highly segregated, with women overrepresented in lower-paid occupational areas (Butler & Ferrier 2000). Also generally less well represented are socially disadvantaged groups, such as the long-term unemployed, people with disabilities, indigenous peoples, refugees and migrants, and socially and/or geographically isolated people (Powles & Anderson 1996).

Teaching in the sector is complex and demanding. The typical job roles of a VET teacher include development of teaching/learning experiences, resources and assessment tasks for the VET workshop, classroom, laboratory and workplace. Many VET teachers have worked in the industries for which they teach. In fact, a VET teacher's basic qualification is usually in the area in which she/he teaches, rather than in education or teaching. VET teachers are also involved in program planning, industry and employer liaison, marketing, professional development of others, and institute and system-wide research and development projects.

Return-to-industry placements and work-based projects are becoming more frequent in VET professional development (Henry 2001).

VET pedagogy

A wide range of teaching methods are utilised in VET. Lecturing occurs, but teaching and classroom and workshop activities are usually more interactive and seminar-based than didactic and expository. Constructivist learning theories are rising in popularity, and aligned with these are attempts by teachers to increase interaction (Kerka 1997). In this way, VET programs often involve learning through small discussion groups, workplace problems, case studies, assignments and projects. Individualised learning occurs through the use of self-paced instructional materials. Various degrees of reality are used from role-plays and simulation through to the development opportunities afforded by authentic work-based projects (Achtenhagen & Grubb 2001; Print 1993).

Most people are familiar with apprenticeship and its mix of structured and unstructured on- and off-the-job learning. As with all work-based programs, apprentice learners develop their expertise and understandings through participation in both routine and non-routine, goal-directed activities (Ainley & Rainbird 1999; Billett 2001). VET providers often establish practice firms, such as simulated manufacturing and service-oriented workshops, restaurants and hairdressing salons, which are designed to give learners instruction in a realistic context. Many service industry jobs require face-to-face interaction with clients, and this can occur only within highly realistic settings.

According to Billett (1999, 2001), guided support from experts provides learners with access to goals and procedures through joint 'authentic' problem solving. The intention is to get the learner doing the thinking and learning. Rather than prescribing how to do a job, the expert guides the learning process by posing problems and asking questions of the learner—for example: 'What do you think we should do here, in these circumstances, in this situation, and why?' Guided learning is associated with the process of 'cognitive apprenticeship', which involves expert workers assisting learners to understand what might otherwise have remained hidden.

TENSIONS AND QUESTIONS

Competency-based training (CBT) is considered by many to be highly problematic. In the first instance, it is questioned whether complex workplace practices can be broken down into discrete parts and whether the sum of the parts sensibly equates to the whole (Brown 1994; Jackson 1993; Norris 1991). Some have also suggested that CBT reflects gender-based constructions of 'skill' that underpin and reproduce inequitable patterns of access to, and participation in, training and employment for women (Gaskell 1991; Jackson 1991). Yet alternatives to CBT are very hard to find in VET. In fact, except within teacher education, the debate is rarely entered.

It is often argued that basing VET programs on an analysis of job roles is 'efficient'. Indeed, why should learners who hope to be successful in these occupations need to develop skills and knowledge not widely practised in that area? But is there a need for any broader learning? Should these learners be taught for their occupation, for future work, or for the workplace as it at present exists? Does VET cater effectively to the needs of the unemployed and other groups marginalised in the labour market? Should an education for work prepare workers/learners to contribute to debates about the directions that work should take in the future (Lakes 1994; Simon et al. 1991)?

Governments around the world have built their education systems on particular assumptions, such as the correctness of free market economics. But is this the only way forward? Who speaks for the workers/learners? What education do workers/learners need in order to be part of these debates? Is this within the domain of vocational education and training (Avis et al. 1996; Kincheloe 1996, 1999)?

Is VET, by comparison with a 'higher education' in universities, still about 'educating the working class', or does VET deserve equal status with professional education? Why differentiate between these two sectors at all? Why not recognise these barriers as artificial and collapse them by talking about a new field such as 'work-related learning'? Further, does the VET sector harbour patterns of participation and stratification between learners on the basis of socioeconomic class, race and ethnicity, and gender (Kincheloe 1999)? Does the VET sector cater to all stakeholders, or are some stakeholders unfairly privileged (Anderson 1999; Avis et al. 1996)?

Debates, tensions and questions abound in this sector, and most remain unresolved. But at the forefront is concern about the very nature and purposes of VET. If VET is the main sector of education in which the state offers working people an education, then it seems that the struggle remains for analytical and thoughtful educators to be critical and to work towards change, thereby ensuring that VET provides an education that is worthwhile. Some claim that there are 'two measures of labour market success: one is having a job—particularly a secure job—and the other is earning a reasonable income' (ACIRRT 1999: 2). Clearly, vocational education and training keys workers/learners into the current requirements of the labour markets. Unfortunately, though, in a capitalist economy this leaves many people out.

15

RADICAL ADULT EDUCATION AND LEARNING

Joce Jesson & Mike Newman

At the start of a new century, it is useful to look back at the way that education and educators have worked to change society. Much of this change has occurred through very small activities that have drawn in other people and spread. Some of these changes have occurred through people organising for change, and usually there has been some form of education for these social change organisers. However, all of the changes can be traced to the vision that the organisers or the educators involved had of a society that could be more equal, freer, and more humanly empowering.

The history and culture of radical education has largely been an oral one, learned through stories passed on from one generation of activists to another. Formal history usually deals in sifted documents presented as historical outcome or facts. Such history is often devoid of the agency of participants. Popular histories seek to uncover participants' lives and intentions. Histories of social action are found in the stories that reach back into the past to stress the multifarious small victories which advance notions of the 'actions of the ordinary people' that future generations can call up and use. These stories are the learning resources to build and sustain change. The past gives us resources that we can use to change the present to create the future.

This chapter examines forms of adult learning associated with radical social action. Learning in the sense we use here means learning by people acting collectively to bring about radical and emancipatory social change.

DEFINING RADICAL ADULT EDUCATION

To begin, we have to recognise that the field of adult education is continually shaped by the broader political and economic environment (for a fuller discussion, see chapter 8). As we consider adult learning within the context of the 21st century, we are confronted by slogans like 'knowledge economy', 'information society', 'continuous learning', 'intellectual property', 'the learning organisation' and 'knowledge assets'. This clamour occurs against an economic direction that developed from the 1970s and that polarised the world into a series of dualisms: those with technology and money and those with none, those who perceive competitive American society as their goal and those who go in dread of it, those who have plenty of food, shelter and water and those without, those with hope and the hopeless, the socially included and the excluded. The rise of electronic technology and the globalised economy has focused attention on information and skills and learning in organisations; the fragmentation of knowledge has transformed talk about labour needs into chants around skill shortages.

At the same time in this new century, the concept of universal education has itself shifted. The goal of universal secondary education for all has now been superseded by another ideal that has people of all ages participating in some form of education, in the name of lifelong learning. Adult learning has become the new growth commodity. The learning market proclaims free choice yet compounds social inequalities. The social and political gaps widen for those who have the money and interest for participation, those for whom education may give some possibility of control over their lives, those who see education as the mechanism needed to change other people.

What we are interested in discussing here is how the broader political economic environment of a community, a nation and maybe the world can be changed by the active learning and involvement of those who are socially excluded in some way. It is not really relevant where this process of learning takes place, whether it is via the web or in a face-to-face situation, in a regular session or in a more informal way; what is important is the social outcome. Radical social action requires the purposeful engagement of a group: learning, and acting collectively for some agreed greater social goal. This can be called education for organising social action or learning radical action.

Learning radical action takes place in a number of ways. People join together in churches, unions, political parties, action groups, aid organisations, charities and social movements to resist various forces and to bring some social change. Membership of these groups involves action: encounters with other members, attendance at meetings—in short, participation in the regular activities of the group (e.g. singing in the choir). It also involves participation in the extraordinary activities of the group: the activities that aim to bring about social change (e.g. singing on the steps during the local council meeting in protest at the closure of a community hall). Organising social action thus involves purposive learning. People engaged in social action are learning in order to resist unwanted forms of control, understanding their own situation and experiences in order to exercise more control themselves. People in groups are learning for a purpose: to change the way they and others in our society think, feel and act. They are learning to be radical activists. Learning for radical social activism therefore differs from other kinds of adult education.

To develop our definition, we will start from its antithesis. In the liberal tradition, adult learning is for the individual person. Liberal adult education offers learning for individual intellectual stimulation or personal enrichment. Since the 1960s there has been an extraordinary increase in adult education for individual personal growth, group psychotherapy, or life coaching. These courses are focused on the development of individuals that make up the group, rather than the group itself.

In contrast, *learning radical action* is about collective learning. It is about how the whole group learns collectively through action to achieve change.

Another antithesis: the capitalist economy has created various forms of adult learning. Industrial training, human resource development training and often union training all aim to train people for their particular roles in the economy. They are less about personal development than shaping individuals to perform functions in the workplace. Workplace training provides people with skills and the knowledge to perform particular occupations, trades and skills. Human resource development helps people perform particular roles within an organisation, with the purpose of making the whole structure work effectively to achieve the organisation's goals. A trade union education program may help people perform their role as a representative, delegate, advocate or negotiator. This sort of workplace education may help develop people's abilities to deal with and implement change, but the change and its direction will be determined by the existing organisation. The purpose of learning is to enable people to function *within* the existing economic system or within a prevailing set of values and relationships.

In contrast, *learning radical action* is about challenging and changing both the relationships and the structures.

A third antithesis: adult learning can be a social service—learning for excluded members of society. Social service adult education provides courses designed to help socially excluded groups. It will enable them to gain skills to participate more fully in the existing economy and society. The political goal is to 'support lifelong learning' or 'increase capability'. Government funding supports such education for unemployed people, for adults with reading and writing difficulties, people with disabilities, those for whom English is not the home language, adults who have been designated as 'disadvantaged'—all those who have in effect been socially excluded. The economic carrot shapes the development of skills for a quite narrowly defined form of literacy or for immediate employment. The learning is tied into government and charitable bodies that make up the welfare and social services. It is adult education for social service.

In contrast, *learning radical action* involves people challenging social structures, changing the nature and substance of the world they work in, working as collective groups to gain more control over how those structures are formed, and gaining more direct control over their own lives.

DIFFERENT FORMS OF LEARNING RADICAL ACTION

The phrase 'learning radical action' reinforces the idea that all action involves learning. Like other adult education, this can take a number of forms: incidental learning, informal learning, informal education and formal education.

Incidental learning occurs during the action. People in community development projects learn to write submissions, undertake historical research, run an office, canvass community opinion, develop a school and lobby government.

Supporters in an international justice network learn web page development and Internet organising skills to assist in a campaign for human rights. They learn media analysis, about human rights, and the international military and trade linkages. They learn high-level media skills, how to lobby, how to create and sustain campaigns, how to build alliances and how to organise effective continuous letter-writing campaigns.

Activists in a campaign over uranium learn about the mining industry, the workings of different levels of government, legal aspects of the leasehold and ownership of land, Aboriginal land rights, international trade, the nuclear power industry and the arms industry, organisation and direct action.

Such learning is very real and empowering, but the learning is incidental to, although necessary for, the social action taken. Reflection after the event helps participants recognise what learning has taken place. This may not be articulated as learning until someone helps them make it conscious (see Foley 1999).

Informal learning occurs when people become aware of the potential for learning in their activities and then make a decision to learn from those experiences. A management committee of a community organisation may decide to review the operations of their organisation. They will need to learn what is going on in order to effect change strategies. A group campaigning against Asian child-sex tours may regroup after a day of demonstration and action outside a travel agency to consider what they have learnt from the day and what strategies they need next for their campaign. There is no planned and structured educational program, but learning is very consciously done.

Informal education is organised, although not always in a recognisably educational way. This informal education is normally very participant-directed and sometimes one-off or sporadic. Women in trade unions come together to find out about the health effects of a chemical they work with, green activists undertake non-violent direct-action training in the midst of a campaign to stop native timber logging. Community organisers in a New Zealand rural community develop e-mail education resources to help the community better understand what could be the real consequences of a government plan for bridging a harbour.

There are any number of informal educational programs for radical social action. Many have been inspired by the work of Saul Alinsky (Alinsky 1946, 1971). Alinsky pioneered 'community organizing' in Chicago's old stockyards neighbourhood in the late 1930s. By forming an unprecedented coalition between the Catholic Church, the Meatpackers Union, educators and various other community groups, the Back of the Yards Council was able to force several landmark concessions from the meatpacking industry.

Formal education, in contrast, is a structured process that takes place within an institution or is designed or accredited through a state-legitimised body. The accreditation systems are supposed to ensure quality for both the learner and the funding body. There are many examples of formal education about radical action. Some are explicitly educational, others are much more content- or issue-focused. They can range from university courses in third world development studies or radical sociology to short programs in indigenous language or social organising. What distinguishes them from other mainstream adult higher education is their content and their connection to social action.

Formal education for social action may emerge from earlier informal education. What started as an informal consciousness-raising group at a neighbourhood centre may become a credit-bearing women's studies class at a local university, giving entry to a degree program to women without formal qualifications.

In 1994 APHEDA (the international aid wing of the Australian trade union movement) and the Uniting Church gained government funding to undertake educational work among their respective constituents around the issues of international trade, development, and workers' and human rights. The church ran a series of study groups in parishes throughout Australia on these issues, while APHEDA developed a one-hour module on workers' rights and human rights in the Asian region, which was used by union educators in courses for union members.

In 2002 the New Zealand Council of Trade Unions (NZCTU) gained government funds to develop and run a series of one-day programs about the international clothing and footwear industry. The clothing and footwear workers worked out how their particular job fitted into the overall industry, and they gained a better appreciation of the power that international corporate-brand companies such as Nike or The Gap had on their work and other workers internationally. The formal program was funded and approved by the state, although the learners did not gain any transferable credit for the course.

VARIOUS HISTORIES

Learning for radical action has a long history. Education has long been a vehicle for social change, both reformist change through the liberal education of working people and radical change through education for socialism.

In Britain in the 19th century, working people engaged in education in order to improve their lot and gain a greater say in their own affairs and the political and economic affairs of the country. Liberal middle-class philanthropists initiated a number of institutions that were shunned by more radical working-class activists. These radicals (Owenites, trade unionists and Chartists) saw such institutions as offering 'useful knowledge'—that is, knowledge helpful to those who wanted to improve their lot within the class-based, propertied state of the time. The radicals established classes and institutions that offered 'really useful knowledge'. This they understood as knowledge concerned with defining and protecting natural rights, extending democracy, critically examining the propertied nature of the state, promoting concepts of community and cooperation, and explaining the continued existence of poverty amid the production of great wealth (Johnson 1988). This goal continues to inspire radical trade union education (NZCTU 2000):

> ... trade union education is not an end in itself, but one of the steps in the advance towards the emancipation of humankind. The goal will be reached only when the broad masses of the workers and those representing them are in full possession of all the knowledge and experience necessary to change the structures of society and banish want and fear forever. (*Statement of International Confederation of Free Trade Unions Education Conference 1952*)

In North America, radical adult education programs also have a long history. We have already mentioned the work of organisers like Saul Alinsky. In the 1920s and 30s, the Antigonish movement in Nova Scotia, Canada, used adult education to help people of the region establish fishing and farming cooperatives, credit unions, and other community facilities and projects. They used meetings, kitchen circles, radio discussion groups and leadership schools to give people control over the production and distribution of their produce. Moses Coady, a central figure in the Antigonish movement, saw adult education as 'an aggressive agent of change, a mass movement of reform, the peaceful way to social change' (Lovett 1988). (For a fuller account of Antigonish, see chapter 7 and Welton 2001.)

In 1932, Myles Horton founded the Highlander Folk School in the Appalachian Mountains of Tennessee. Highlander has since then offered workshops and educational advice to activists and community organisations. Highlander has been through a number of different phases, reflecting its goal of being at 'the cutting edge of change' (Moyers 1981). In the 1930s Highlander worked with people in the mining and cotton industries to establish unions. In the 1940s and 50s Highlander helped establish adult schools in the South—the citizenship schools— to help people learn to read so they could register to vote. In the late 1950s and 60s Highlander provided workshops for civil rights activists (Horton, Kohl & Kohl 1990; Horton & Friere 1990). Highlander's focus since the late 1960s has been on environmental issues, issues relating to indigenous people, and the struggle of local Appalachian people against the intrusion of transnationals and the ownership of land by absentee landlords (Highlander 2001).

Latin America too has many examples of learning radical action. Against a background of repressive governments, military dictatorships and client states of the superpowers, educators have worked to give people a say in their own lives, to combat poverty and struggle for some kind of human dignity. These educators and activists—sometimes referred to collectively as 'popular educators'—have drawn eclectically on socialism, Marxism, liberal education and liberation theology. The Latin American history includes Paulo Freire working with shanty town dwellers and peasant communities in Brazil and Chile (Taylor, 1993), the national literacy campaign in Sandinista Nicaragua (Lankshear 1987), the Christian base communities (*communidades de base*) (Wickham-Crowley 1992), and the work of theatre activist Augusto Boal (Paterson 1999). Internationally there have been similar examples. The work of Ghandi to liberate the Indian subcontinent from British colonial rule was a massive exercise in learning for radical action. Foley (1993b) writes about kinds of learning that took place in China during a 'democratic moment' in the Chinese liberation struggle during the 1940s and 50s. Education played a significant part in liberation struggles for social change in countries like Tanzania or South Africa (see Samoff 1990).

'Popular education' has become widely practised. Freire's 'conscientization' (1970) process seeks to shift people from a fatalistic or naive consciousness to a critical consciousness, to a state of mind in which they are aware of themselves within their social context and capable of acting to change it. In a sense, 'conscientization' is a process by which learners are propelled into the flow of social history. They cease being objects and become writers of their own and their own communities' stories.

Freire's form of learning has fused with indigenous forms of community development and organising throughout the world. In the years preceding the abandonment of apartheid in South Africa, white and black educators, operating out of universities, community organisations and health centres, used adult education to develop a critical awareness in learners. In an inner-city area of Edinburgh in Scotland, adult educators employed a Freirean framework to provide an educational program addressing local issues of poverty and inequity (chapter 14; Kirkwood & Kirkwood 1989). And in countries like India, for example, cultural and development programs have been inventively linked to adult education (Rogers 1992).

The Maori renaissance movement in New Zealand used this Freirean method in a variety of education initiatives they established outside the state system. Their commitment to the development of Te reo (language), tikanga and kaupapa Maori (ways of thinking, being and acting) underpinned these. Informal early childhood centres, or kohanga, were first established, bringing together Maori values and whole-family education. These were followed by kura kaupapa schools and lately by moves to create autonomous Maori universities and a separate nation-state (Pihama et al. 2000).

Education forms part of the struggle by indigenous people for recognition and equity (Foley & Flowers 1991). Tranby Aboriginal Cooperative College in Sydney was established in 1952 with the help of church and trade union groups and became fully Aboriginal-controlled in 1962. Tranby provides courses to help Aboriginal people enter mainstream education, programs assisting Aboriginal people in their communities, and educational support for Aboriginal communities and organisations. Non-Aboriginal people work at Tranby, but this is an Aboriginal organisation committed to an activist form of adult education on behalf of Aboriginal people (Newman 1993).

SOCIAL CONTROL

Both the kaupapa Maori movement and Tranby provide examples of education contributing to indigenous peoples' struggle for self-determination. As social action is concerned with helping people gain more influence over their lives, radical education involves people learning to understand and then resist social control. Social control can take different forms.

People can be controlled through brute force. Dictatorships use police forces and armies. The Highlander Folk School was the target of the Ku Klux Klan, and in 1959 Highlander was raided and its assets seized by the Tennessee state. In Brazil, Freire was arrested, imprisoned and forced into exile following a military coup in 1964. Popular educators in Nicaragua were the targets of those opposing the Sandinistas. The Egyptian medical educators and novelists Nawal Al Saadawi and her husband Sherif Hetata, who set up the Arab Women's Solidarity Association (AWSA), have faced exile and death threats for promoting Arab women's participation in social, economic, cultural and political life.

People also submit themselves to legitimised institutional control. We give over a range of freedoms to institutions in exchange for member-ship, services or protection. We submit to the order and regulations imposed by government. We abide by the requirements of our employ-ment. We follow the educational processes set by schools, colleges and universities. We accept these intrusions on our privacy of regulation, law and order in exchange for the benefits, while institutional control is everywhere in our lives, and for some groups becomes oppressive or lacks countervailing benefits. The government closes down a successful school and disadvantages the communities that use it. The bureaucracy seeks information about us, or trades the information it has with other bureaucracies without consulting us. A successful and powerful cor-poration 'downsizes' its workforce at a particular plant, throwing people into unemployment and seriously affecting the lives and economy of the surrounding district.

Control by brute force and institutional control is relatively easy to identify and develop action around. There is another, more difficult to identify, form of social control: hegemonic control (Gramsci 1976). This is control by the shaping of the population's consent as 'common sense'. One group of people accepts as normal, natural and as needing no explanation, conditions that are in the interests of another group alto-gether. Peasants working the land to produce food in a developing country accept as inevitable that landowners dispossess them and clear their land to make way for an export crop of coffee, even though food shortages may result. Producers and consumers accept that 'the market', not multinational corporations, determines the price of coffee beans. People accept glaring social inequities and express pride in their ability to manage on less than others by calling themselves 'battlers'. Some women accept lower pay and status as 'inevitable' or 'natural'. People see refugees as 'bludgers', trying to get valued immigration status 'through the back door'.

Hegemonic control is detected in these 'commonsense truths', which are voiced by both oppressors and oppressed. 'Common sense' maintains the way things are. When we live in a part of a city poorly served by schools and say 'Talent will always shine', we remove pressure from the authorities to provide universally available schooling. When people say 'Change is inevitable. It's foolish to stand in the way of progress', they can be moved from their homes to make way for a motorway. And when enough people say 'The private sector is more efficient than the public sector', then the sale of essential public services developed for all people is legitimised. Learning radical education is learning to challenge accepted common sense to create social change.

LEARNING TO CHALLENGE COMMON SENSE

Mezirow (1981, 1991) draws on Jürgen Habermas' analysis of the generation of knowledge, and describes three domains of learning: instrumental, interpretive or communicative, and critical or emancipatory.

Instrumental learning is learning in order to manage and control our environment—to do a job and earn a living, to build things and to manage people when we consider those people as functions and part of the physical environment. In this form we examine and learn about reason and cause and effect. We learn to solve problems by weighing up the options and choosing the most appropriate one. This learning can be complex but is essentially about getting the skills and information necessary to construct systems and devise methods for making those systems work. For radical activists, instrumental learning will provide the skills and information to deal with practical matters, to use existing structures and systems such as governmental and legal processes. But the purpose is always to bring about change, and to challenge social control.

Interpretive learning helps us understand the human condition. The focus is on people, what they are and how they relate, on symbolic interaction, on society and social history. We learn to solve problems by exchanging ideas and opinions, through reflection and insight, and by seeking consensus. For social activists, this learning will help in understanding the social context of the problem they are addressing and the character, background and motives of the people they may be working with as well as those they may be seeking to change.

Critical learning helps us understand the psychological and cultural assumptions that constrain the way we see the world and that influence the way we think, feel and act. We learn not only to see the world more clearly but also *to see ourselves seeing* the world. This learning involves coming to know what 'makes us tick', what makes us adopt particular positions, think in particular ways, react and feel the way we do, and take the actions we take. We learn to solve problems through reflection that may transform our whole way of thinking— that may transform our perspectives. In this kind of learning we can learn to see through ourselves and so may be able better to understand others.

Learning radical action is focused on purposive collective action to challenge social control. Because social control occurs through a complex mix of coercion, different kinds of institutional authority and various attempts to influence people's thinking, effective radical education uses a mix of different kinds of learning to challenge and change social control. Robert Regnier (1991) describes the public relations campaign by the nuclear power industry in the Canadian province of Saskatchewan and the counter-campaign by community groups opposed to the nuclear industry. It is an excellent example of social activists engaging in a variety of forms of education. Similarly, Australians involved in a long-running campaign to save a rainforest learned as they acted (Foley 1991b, 1999).

IT'S ALWAYS ABOUT POWER

Radical action is always a struggle over power. It is a struggle about who should wield power and how it is used. Radical social activists are commonly trying to gain more power for the people they are working with or represent. Often, as in the case of the struggle against the nuclear power industry in Saskatchewan, this struggle is an attempt to redress a gross imbalance of power. Part of the role of radical education, therefore, is to help learners understand the variety of ways in which power can be exercised, whether in localised sites and practices or in large, complex state apparatuses or multinational corporations. And that knowledge itself is socially constructed and situated (Kilgour 2001).

Most social movements exist as untidy patchworks of activist groups. Yet there are times when faiths, ideas, fashions, anxieties and ideologies come together, and people take to the streets in huge numbers. Such protests generally signal deep and sustained social action, as in the movements against war, unregulated and unequal trade, child labour and the logging of tropical rainforests. Sometimes, as in Eastern Europe or East Timor, this mobilisation of people can bring sudden and sweeping social change.

Radical education helps provide learners with the tools and information to permit them to arrive at strong political-economic analyses of the organisations, communities and social structures they are trying to change. It enables activists to broaden their understanding of various kinds of power, and to develop the political skills of lobbying, organisation, advocacy, representation and the like that go with action against that power.

ISSUES FOR ADULT EDUCATORS

Fostering radical learning therefore presents the adult educator with a number of ethical challenges and dilemmas. On what conditions does the adult educator engage with a community, community group or group of activists? Does the radical educator engage only by invitation? How and when should the educator intervene?

Most education is an intervention in the lives of others, and this creates particular ethical dilemmas for radical educators. They often enter communities or groups on their own initiative and use educational processes to gain people's attention and get them thinking and learning. Sometimes their entry into the lives of others will be negotiated, but sometimes it is not. Educators have a mission, a belief that the learning they can offer will benefit a community or group of people. However, radical education is about power and interests. It is never straightforward.

When a team of educators, driven by their own sense of mission, attempt uninvited to enter the lives of a people of a different class or ethnicity or even gender, their action can look like invasion. The initiative can all too easily become an exercise in propaganda and another form of social control. (For an excellent discussion of this issue, see Head 1977.)

In Rajasthan, India, a non-government organisation used puppetry followed by discussion to alert villagers to the dangers of alcohol abuse and to mobilise people to take action (McGivney & Murray 1991: 32–3). The results of this intervention by the puppeteer-educators varied from village to village, but the choice over any action lay with the villagers.

In radical education the relationship of the educator to the learners is always an issue. Is she simply the dispassionate facilitator of learning, is she the neutral provider of information and skills? Is she a stirrer, the person who provokes or challenges? Does he abandon any efforts at detachment and objectivity, espouse the learners' cause, and join with them in the action? Mezirow suggests that adult educators should be 'empathetic provocateurs', and that they should stay outside the dominant culture and help people examine their 'uncritical assimilated assumptions' (Mezirow 1991: 360; Mezirow 1992: 231).

Often a radical educator works with learners who decide to take direct action. As this action may be part of a struggle against authority or some other form of social control, the educator may well find him/herself helping people decide whether or not to take violent action. Horton tells the story of 'facilitating' a group of striking miners in 1933 who were considering whether to kill two professional killers or let them go ahead and kill a mineworkers' leader. Whichever way the decision went, someone would be killed. In recounting this, Horton commented (Horton, Kohl & Kohl 1990: 41):

> Of course any person in their right mind would be for non-violence over violence if it were a simple choice, but that's not the problem the world has to face.

Horton himself was beaten up, imprisoned, and menaced by armed thugs. But he saw education that took educators and learners 'to the line' as liberating. Horton resolved his educator's dilemma by having no qualms about helping people arrive at a decision to take action, so long as that action *would lead to further learning*. He maintains that if he had to make a choice between helping people who were engaged in a struggle achieve their immediate objective or fail to achieve their objective but do some learning, he would choose the learning (Horton, Kohl & Kohl 1990: 180–1).

CONCLUSION

Learning in radical education differs from other forms of adult education traditions. It has a long history, there are no comforting institutional procedures to fall back on, and no guarantees that the learning can be contained within a set time and located in a pre-arranged place. Learning happens in different forms, and is inextricably interwoven with action. Part of the educator's role is to help learners collectively analyse and act on the power relationships and the social and economic structures that shape their lives. The relationship between educator and learners is complex. Both educator and learners are presented with ethical dilemmas. As radical social action is about challenging social control and changing established power relations, there will be times when radical education becomes difficult and even dangerous. But, for learners and educators alike, the action can provide learning that exhilarates and liberates.

16

PROBLEM-BASED LEARNING

Peter Stephenson & Vernon Galloway

The practitioner-centred approach to vocational and professional education (see chapters 1 and 2) has stimulated interest in problem-based pedagogy and curriculum. In this chapter Peter Stephenson defines problem-based learning (PBL) and then examines some of its forms. He pays particular attention to the principles underpinning problem-based learning, and to the recent development of more critical and contextual forms of PBL in university professional education. In the second part of the chapter, Vernon Galloway examines the philosophical basis of community-based 'problem-posing' education. He then examines a long-running example of problem-posing education, the Edinburgh Adult Learning Project.

A TEACHING METHOD

It could be said that every form of teaching makes use of case studies and problems to assist student learning. However, we need to ask why and how problems are used in teaching. Conventional forms of teaching use problems to teach how to apply knowledge after it has been learned, while problem-based curricula use particular forms of problems to drive the learning (Woods 1994). Accordingly, Boud and Feletti describe problem-based learning as 'a way of constructing and teaching courses using problems as the stimulus and focus for student activity' (1997: 2).

Due partly to this broad working definition, multiple interpretations of problem-based learning now exist. All would claim to conform to the generally accepted objectives of PBL (see Ryan & Quinn 1995; Barrows 1986; Ryan 1997; Ross 1997), namely to:

- develop problem-solving ability;
- develop self-directed learning ability;
- integrate learning with the graduate's practice; and
- motivate learners.

Barrows and Tamblyn (1980: 22) set out six principles for a problem-based learning curriculum:

1. Problems need to be encountered at the beginning of the learning sequence.
2. Problem situations must be presented to learners in much the same way as they would present in reality.
3. Students should apply systematic problem-solving approaches in ways that develop their ability to reason.
4. Students need to identify limitations in their knowledge or skills as they work with problems, and to use this information to guide their study.
5. Skills and knowledge acquired through PBL should be applied back to the problem to reinforce and evaluate learning.
6. Skills and knowledge acquired through PBL must be integrated with the learners' existing knowledge and skills.

Boud and Feletti suggest it is also important for students to 'work co-operatively as a group, exploring information in and out of class, with access to a tutor (not necessarily a subject specialist) who knows the problem well and can facilitate the group's learning process' (1997: 2).

Debate over the legitimacy of different interpretations of PBL occurs continually. One outcome has been a proliferation of 'subcategories' expressing deviations from earlier applications and writings. In this way a number of 'second-generation' models of problem-based learning have evolved (Feletti 1993), each with the same educational aims but organised and delivered in different ways (Tegel & Dockett 1995). Examples include the following.

Integrated problem-based learning

This variation of PBL uses an integrative framework for structuring explorations into problems of practice, and for proposing and testing possible solutions. Cowdroy and Maitland's (1995) framework, for example, aims to develop and integrate learners' knowledge, skills and attitudes in relation to 'technical', 'organisational', 'professional' and 'theoretical' elements of the problem under study. They argue that this kind of PBL closely approximates the integrated processes of professional practice, where 'synthesis of highly complex issues into simple conceptual ideas for analysis and resolution' (1995: 186) is needed. They refer to its employment in the education of 'integrative practitioners', such as architects, medical and legal practitioners.

Hybrid models of problem-based learning

Boud and Feletti (1997) comment briefly and Armstrong (1997) reports in detail on the application of this popular adaptation. The hybrid approach employs a range of teaching strategies, including lectures, tutorial discussions, laboratory and research work. While on the surface this may not appear dissimilar to traditional teaching approaches, there is an emphasis on presenting conceptually difficult material as interactively as possible. Lecture material is integrated with laboratory and tutorial activities; and, most importantly, there is dedicated time each week for both self-directed and group problem-solving sessions, where integration of learning across disciplines is facilitated.

Situation-based learning

Curriculum materials in this approach 'include not only problems to be solved but also situations that need to be explained or managed' (Tegel & Dockett 1995: 299) in the context of the learners' professional practice. Rather than focusing on specific problems, situation-based learning aims to develop student competence and confidence in handling new and unknown situations.

Inquiry-based learning

This approach does not start with the assumption that a problem need exist for learning to be effective. Rather it assumes that 'learning may be triggered by *any* experience or simulation' (Feletti 1993). Students involved in inquiry-based learning are encouraged to engage in reflection at all stages of the learning process. Inquiry-based learning acknowledges that important contextual differences exist in workplace practice across the professions, and that these differences require eclectic educational responses. Here problem-based learning gives way to a broader, more diffuse approach to inquiry and learning, and one that has similarities to 'action research' (see McTaggart & Kemmis 1982; Carr & Kemmis 1986; McTaggart 1991; Barnett & Abbatt 1994; and Field 1995a).

None of these second-generation models satisfy the expectations of the problem-based learning purists—the handful of educational theorists and teachers who embraced a radical approach to problem-based learning at the time it was being developed, and who now try to protect the field (Chen et al. 1995). They argue that second-generation programs are inadequately developed and insufficiently radical in their departure from conventional teaching practice.

History and promise of problem-based learning

Writers trace PBL's roots to late 1960s medical education programs of North American universities, such as McMaster (Albanese & Mitchell 1993) and Case Western Reserve (Boud & Feletti 1997), and Maastricht University in the Netherlands (Schmidt 1983). While these accounts tend to rely on institutional and personal experience rather than research data, they remind the reader of the central reason for the shift from traditional education practices to problem-based models. This was the questioning of the value of traditional medical programs that obliged students to retain vast quantities of clinical knowledge *before* providing them with the opportunity to develop practical skills through clinical experience. This 'front-end' approach to learning continues to be condemned as (Boud & Feletti 1997: 2)

> . . . an ineffective and inhumane way to prepare students, given the explosion in medical information and new technology, and the rapidly changing demands of future practice.

Challenges to the effectiveness of traditional 'front-end loading' teaching practices can, however, be identified long before the emergence of problem-based learning. Candy (1991: 377), for example, cites studies by Cantor (1946) and Gross (1948) as early attempts to counter traditional 'empty-vessel' approaches to teaching students through explorations of alternative, self-directed approaches to learning. Later, Rogers' (1969) rejections of the dominant 'telling mode' of teaching and Freire's (1972) demolition of the 'banking' approach to education extended the critique of conventional teaching.

The promise of problem-based learning is that it can develop key generalisable competencies in learners. Engel (1997) lists the competencies he believes can be attained through problem-based learning methods:

- adapting to and participating in change;
- dealing with problems, making reasoned decisions in unfamiliar situations;
- reasoning critically and creatively;
- adopting a more universal or holistic approach to problem solving and learning;
- practising empathy, appreciating the other person's point of view;
- collaborating productively in groups or teams; and
- identifying one's strengths and weaknesses and undertaking appropriate remediation (e.g. through continuing, self-directed learning).

Challenges

As helpful as these attributes may be, they have allowed some educators to make extraordinary claims for problem-based learning. Saldo et al. (1995, in Forrest et al. 1997: 150), for example, maintain that problem-based learning, 'if followed as intended, encompasses all elements for optimum learning'. Critics of PBL seize on such sweeping generalisations. Collins (1995), for example, claims it is naive to think that methods of teaching that rely on self-directed learning (e.g. Knowles' (1980) use of the learning contract) are exempt from social, political and economic influence. Just as traditional 'telling modes' of teaching have been condemned for their tendency to perpetuate dominant forms of knowledge, modern adult educational approaches such as PBL and experiential learning are accused of paying insufficient attention to political, social and historical influences on learning.

This position has significant implications for professional education. It challenges adult educators to reconceptualise andragogy and self-directed learning, and to link them to the critical practice of adult education. Such a reconceptualisation requires 'self-directed', 'inquiry-based', 'situation- or problem-based' and 'experiential' learning programs—under whatever name—to take greater account of political considerations and social context.

Problem-based learning *can* open up new possibilities for effective student learning (see Boud & Feletti 1997; Engel 1997; Margetson 1997), and its processes *can* develop skilled lifelong learners, equipped to work in a rapidly changing world (see Cross 1982; Candy 1991; Woods 1994).

Yet research (see Weil 1988, 1989; Stephenson 2002) has also revealed that for the non-traditional learner, the culturally marginalised and the socially disadvantaged and disenfranchised, contemporary adult education approaches like PBL and experiential learning may provide skills of only limited value. The sorts of daily workplace problems experienced by these groups require a different approach to teaching and learning. This means a different construction of the problem—one that moves away from reliance on individual interpretations of *possible work problems* (or scenarios) to one that takes account of the social and cultural interpretations and implications of *messy, real-life problems*. In this situation, grounded learning is the key. Problems must be grounded in the real-life context of the learners themselves, in their own communities, work organisations or social structural locations.

Strong examples of this kind of program are not easily found in professional education, much of which has traditionally been more concerned with the development of self-actualised, self-directed, individual lifelong learners than it has with the promotion of education as a moral and political endeavour for collective benefit (McWilliam 1997).

The University of Queensland (UQ) program for indigenous Australian primary health care professionals is a possible example of the second sort of PBL. The vast majority of students in the UQ Bachelor of Applied Science (Indigenous Primary Health Care) are indigenous Australians. Only a few hand-picked non-indigenous students have so far been permitted into the program, and then only after they were carefully selected (Hill 2000). Graduates of this course tend to work in community-based health programs, where they deal daily with the results of entrenched Aboriginal and Torres Strait Islander community health issues. Others take up positions in indigenous health agencies or mainstream local, regional and state agencies. PBL is used in their professional education to closely examine factors in the health care environment that influence Aboriginal and Torres Strait Islander communities. Learning situations are as much interested in exploring proposals for change as they are in identifying problems with the system. Learning packages are built around a series of clinical situations which 'trigger' inquiry, discussion and situation analysis of not only the clinical problem at hand but also the related historical, cultural and social factors that surround it (Hill & Samisoni 1993).

Another Australian university where indigenous practitioners use PBL in their professional learning is the University of Western Sydney. In 1997 the UWS became the first Australian university to offer indigenous Australians the opportunity to gain professional qualifications in the field of environmental health. For nearly 20 years before this, UWS delivered a mainstream-accredited environmental health degree through on-campus and distance education modes. PBL was used at each stage of the program alongside conventional teaching. The arrival of indigenous learners provoked a critical analysis of the suitability of both the conventional learning approach and the PBL approach. This review resulted in pedagogical changes in the PBL subjects. These changes aimed to better prepare learners for work in complex, cross-cultural professional settings.

In the final-year PBL subject, for example, the educational purpose shifted from being primarily concerned with the development of the individual towards learning expressed as a collaborative, strategic and action-oriented venture. In its new critical and strategic form, the PBL subject concentrates on developing the ability of learners to *act* on situations and to *reflect* on their actions in a systematic, self-conscious and reflexive way. Students engage with their peers in a variety of challenging yet open and respectful forums. The forums are both face-to-face and Internet-based and involve indigenous and non-indigenous student practitioners. Learners are asked to consider what it might take for indigenous practitioners to effectively meet the environmental health needs of their own communities at the same time as they work with the cultural differences between mainstream bureaucratic agencies and local indigenous community groups. Problems and solutions are explored in their socio-political, historical and cultural contexts. This contextual and critical form of PBL aims to raise students' consciousness through a continuing reflexive dialogue about their learning processes and discoveries, their questions and problems, and their management of individual and group learning. It is a framework as relevant to the learning context of mainstream professionals as it is to the learning circumstances and objectives of socially committed indigenous practitioners. And it is a framework that is driven by and grounded in the messy, real-life experiences of learners in work- and community-based project settings (Stephenson 2002).

PROBLEM-POSING EDUCATION

The messy nature of real-life problems lies in the complex nature of their construction. Their resolute refusal, in many instances, to surrender to the technical rationality of top-down solutions calls for a different construction of the problem. In community and social movement set-tings, problem-based learning has been heavily influenced by Freire's concept of 'problem-posing education' (Freire 1972). What follows is an outline of the philosophical ideas that underpin the approach, and a brief account of one adult education agency's attempt to adopt the problem-posing approach in a community setting.

Often the greatest challenge facing adult educators in a community setting is the overwhelming sense of powerlessness that people feel in relation to the problems they confront on a daily basis. One explanation for this sense of impotence is offered by Fanon (1968) in his work on 'inferiorisation', in which he describes a process by which people's faith in themselves is undermined over generations through the system-atic subversion of their way of life and their potential to effect change. The effect, according to Beveridge and Turnbull (1989), is that people come to believe in the 'myth of their own ignorance' and develop a concomitant dependence on other, 'more worthy' power groups to act on their behalf. Accordingly, if we persist with forms of education, whether problem-based or not, that rely solely on telling modes and top-down approaches, we run the risk of perpetuating the process of inferiorisation.

Problem-posing education proposes a dialogical approach to problem solving, which engages people in the identification of underlying causes of real-life problems and in taking informed action to overcome them. To do this, this pedagogy has to work to dispel the dual myths of ignorance and dependence. Freire's formulation of problem-posing education is based on specific ontological, epistemological and pedagogical princi-ples. Ontologically, Freire proposes the intrinsic equality of all human beings, that we are all imbued with an 'ontological vocation' to 'become fully human' (Freire 1972: 20–1). This is grounded in an epistemological stance, which sees all human beings as knowers of the world who, through continuous critical engagement with it, can come to take control of it. These ontological and epistemological propositions lead to a peda-gogical practice based on dialogue in which all participants, regardless of role, are engaged in a common task of knowing and doing.

For almost 25 years the Adult Learning Project (ALP) has been attempting to adapt problem-posing principles and practice to the inner-city communities of Gorgie and Dalry in Edinburgh, Scotland. Like communities across the globe, Gorgie and Dalry have been subject to the economic, political and social changes that have swept like a riptide through the certainty of people's lives this past 30 years. Problems aren't hard to find in these communities as people try to come to terms with the effects of deindustrialisation, the decline of confidence in representational politics or the social fragmentation of community. The daily-life problems that people identify, however, are not framed in such analytic terms: they are rather experienced as day-to-day hindrances— the lack of money or the size of debt, the short-term contract, the council that won't clean the streets or the neighbour that makes too much noise. These are among the many thousands of everyday worries of local people who live in these communities.

The problematisation of daily life becomes an educational process of making the familiar unfamiliar or, in Shor's terms, helping people find ways of 'extraordinarily re-experiencing the ordinary' (Shor 1985). In the practice of ALP the task of making the familiar unfamiliar begins with the investigation of daily life through the use of what Reason (1994) calls 'participative action research' and Freire (1972) calls co-investigation. Briefly, this cooperative research technique is jointly undertaken by workers from ALP, who recruit local people to become 'co-investigators' (Kirkwood & Kirkwood 1989) of the problems and issues that they face in their daily lives. The research is carried out through interviews and observational methods, called 'listening survey' by Hope and Timmel (1984). In co-investigation meetings, ALP workers along with local people analyse the data as they emerge, seeking out underlying or 'generative themes' (Freire 1972). The generative nature of the themes can be understood in two ways: first, as Kane (2001) explains, they generate most discussion or feelings among people; second, they have the potential to generate links between the specific issues that are raised and wider, more structural roots.

These themes then become the focus of a curriculum-building process, which starts with the design of visual representations of daily life that reflect the issues of concern and have encoded within them the 'links to a wider, integrated reality' (Kane 2001: 40). These 'codes' (see Kirkwood & Kirkwood 1989) are then taken to groups of local people and become the focus of structured discussions in which the issues portrayed are explored. At this early stage of work the process of what Schön (1987) calls 'naming and framing' the problem becomes one that is shared rather than imposed. However, we can also see that the process of naming and framing has itself been problematised through the introduction of a deeper analysis of the familiar, which will be further explored as the structured learning program develops. The exploration of themes now becomes a pedagogical challenge, as the educators attempt to design a learning program where the subject of study and the learning process both have to be problematised for the students.

The educators in ALP developed a learning and teaching design that involved four complementary pedagogical techniques which could be applied across a wide range of subjects—inquiry, critical teaching, dialogue, and action/review. None of these techniques will be unfamiliar to those involved in problem-based learning, but they may bear some exploration in the context of the problem-posing approach in a community setting.

Inquiry refers to the process by which the students are engaged in an ongoing exploration of the relevance of the subject under study in their daily lives. *Critical teaching* involves the teacher in the problematisation of knowledge in relation to the given subject of study in order to excavate its implicit notions of power, material interests and socio-cultural meaning. *Dialogue* as a specific part of the learning encounter indicates a structured space in which ideas and perceptions can be explored and challenged. The *action/review* engages the students in a summative discussion of the main points of learning from the encounter and in an appraisal of the educational experience itself, focusing on issues of participation, balance and flow.

An example of the process in action comes from work undertaken by ALP throughout the 1990s on questions of democracy and representation (Galloway 1999). An investigation into daily life had thrown up a number of issues about representation and the inadequacy of the established democratic process. These were politically historical times in Scotland, with widespread opposition to conservative governments coalescing in a movement for devolved government for Scotland. A range of educational responses were developed by ALP to help people explore their understandings of democracy and to help them engage in the movement for democratic renewal. The main focus for activity became a series of activities under the generic heading of the democracy program.

Throughout the life of the program students were engaged in constant inquiry into the democratic life of the community, looking at questions of decision making and representation in a range of settings, including the family, the workplace and community organisations. Critical teaching considered the historical roots of democracy, political ideologies and radical popular movements. Dialogue was focused on people's experiences of existing democratic processes and the imagining of alternative forms of democracy. Students were involved in action programs that opposed government policies on fuel tax and criminal justice. They also became active in the movements that emerged to demand Scottish political autonomy. The group went on to create a new community organisation based on more open and participative democratic principles, and was instrumental in local campaigns to resist school closures and unwanted land development.

Inquiry, critical teaching, dialogue and action/review are simply techniques. As such, they can stand on their own as educational techniques but become methodology when they are brought into a coherent set by the bond of methodological principle. In terms of its methods, problem posing may look like many other progressive educational approaches, but it is in its politicisation of the educational process that it becomes distinguishable from others.

'Politicisation' is the process by which people are taught to make links between their daily-life problems and wider historical and contemporary cultural changes. Through this process of developing awareness they are encouraged to overcome their sense of powerlessness and act on the world. Each part of the problem-posing methodology adopted by ALP is designed to develop the students' critical capacity and motivate them to act. Paula Allman (1991) talks about the dialogical learning relationship as preparing people for change: 'The preparation hinges upon offering people a glimpse or an abbreviated experience of what it could mean to know, to learn, to be and relate differently'.

CONCLUSION

Learning in a community setting might initially be seen as radically different from the field of professional training. In the older, more conventional formulation, professional training is to do with the accumulation of a restricted set of very specific competences, while it might be argued that community education is concerned with broad principles of human development. However, there is nothing in Stephenson's account of critical PBL above or in this account of ALP to contradict Barrows and Tamblyn's principles of problem-based learning outlined earlier. Problem-posing education is simply more transparent in its politics than most liberal variants of problem-based learning.

17

CULTURE, EQUITY AND LEARNING

Barbara Sparks & Shauna Butterwick

This chapter examines the cultural character of adult education and the links between culture, equity and learning. In what follows, we outline key conceptual resources we believe are useful to a critical analysis of adult education as cultural practice, and offer two case studies using this critical lens. We begin with the assumption that bringing a critical view to how structures and practices of adult education are culturally encoded is a key element of working towards social justice.

A commitment to social justice has a long history in the field of adult education. In 1926, Lindeman called on adult educators to work towards 'a long-time, experimental but resolute policy of changing the social order' (1961: 166). Feminist political scientist Iris Marion Young defines social justice as the 'full participation and inclusion of everyone in a society's major institutions, and the socially substantive opportunity for all to develop and exercise their capacities and realise their choices' (1990: 173). As a social institution, adult education exists within the larger structural framework of society. Thus, an awareness of the structural factors that press on people as they attempt to meet their educational needs and desires for full participation in society and the relationship between social structures and culture becomes central to adult education contexts and activities that work towards social justice.

Adult education is conventionally thought of as a way to enhance one's skills, understandings, knowledge or capabilities. But for some, adult education constrains choices, opportunities and achievements, relegating individuals to programs that do not meet their needs or preparing them with skills and capabilities that are limiting. This duality of function suggests the interconnections, contradictions and consequences of adult education (Giddens 1979). Social interactions, practices, ideologies, rules and mechanisms are all produced and reproduced in action; the dominant society imposes its concept of reality. So while it is possible to transform adult education through a reflexive process of monitoring behaviours, social structures and cultural ideologies or values, there are strong influences that affect motives and processes of knowing.

Nevertheless, practices can be contested, interactions can be critiqued, resources can be used to try to control conditions, and strategic conduct can be developed and maintained. Transformation is possible. To support the development of a critical cultural practice for the transformation of adult education, this chapter presents a conceptual approach to adult education practice that moves beyond notions of cultural pluralism, where the emphasis is on creating the perfectly matched learning situation for each ethnic or class or gender group. We begin by outlining several cultural concepts. Then we examine in detail two cases—first a case of adult literacy practice in the United States, followed by an examination of life skills training programs in western Canada—thus providing concrete examples to facilitate moving from theory to practice. We conclude by refocusing the challenge that lies ahead.

THE CULTURAL STRUCTURES OF ADULT EDUCATION

Conceptualising culture and learning in a critical way raises important questions about differences in learner access, participation and achievement by members of various cultural groups. Such an examination focuses attention on adult education structures and mechanisms that mirror larger societal structures; social interactions where implicit power relations construct both adult educators and learners; and ideologies that guide dominant structures, practices and understandings. This socio-cultural approach also signals an interest in understanding contextualised cultural forms of adult education, where locally produced meanings are created by teachers and learners through interaction within specific contexts (Sparks 2002a). It is important to remember that culture is not fixed but dynamic, it is process not just content, and it is historically and socially contextualised rather than insulated. Several aspects deserve further attention, including culture as systems of meaning, cultural differences as potential dissonance, and the power of discourse to create what is of cultural value.

Systems of meaning

The work of Raymond Williams (1981), a cultural theorist and an adult educator of the British working class, is helpful in understanding the complex and dynamic nature of culture. He defines culture 'as the signifying system through which . . . a social order is communicated, reproduced, experienced and explored' (1981: 13). Involved in all forms of social activity, this signifying system is a distinct 'whole way of life' (1981: 13) which includes not only belief systems, institutions and explicit relationships but social experience, which is still in process. Often the social experience is not even recognised by individuals because it is taken as private or idiosyncratic, perhaps even isolating. Because of their connecting and emergent characteristics, these 'structures of feeling' (Williams 1977: 128) define interactions, both individual and group, and all forms of thought and being that influence meanings particular to and contextualised in everyday life. Culture as a whole way of life is a determining influence in deciding what is to be done or not done in expressing oneself; structures of feeling dictate what is learned.

Cultural meanings are constructed through interaction and what Giddens calls interpretive schemes, which form a core of mutual knowledge and sustain 'what went before' and 'what will come next' (1979: 84). We see this process in adult education classrooms and culturally accepted forms of participation in which reasoned dialogue is favoured. We also see this process of constructed meanings in the context of student evaluation through culturally biased standardised testing. The context of use, such as participation through dialogue or student assessment through testing, is partially shaped and organised as an integral part of that interaction. People draw on historical and/or contemporary contexts while (re)creating certain elements as culturally relevant and valued over other elements. Cultural meanings and values are actively lived and felt.

It is important to avoid essentialising cultural aspects of life among different groups. The dynamic nature of culture points to beliefs, values, institutions and formations that change over time within social relationships, rather than a fixed and unchanging cultural essence that we can know once and for all. Recognising the permeability, fluidity, diversity and complexity within cultures is also crucial to understanding structures of feeling that guide how individuals construct cultural meanings and make sense of life.

Structuration of cultural differences

Differentiated structures of feeling exist among different cultural groups based on varying contextual factors and ideologies. Cultural differences based on race, ethnicity, language, class and gender as well as religion and citizenship status have created inequities in adult education. However, it is not the differences per se that are the issue, but rather how differences are socially constructed and valued or devalued by society (Nieto 2002; Zuss 1994). A critical perspective on the role of cultural structures in adult education leads one to realise that 'equal is not the same' (Nieto 1992: 109). Treating all adult learners in the same way may end up perpetuating the inequality that already exists. A wide range of cultural influences will affect adult learning. Differing learning styles and communication styles, differing perceptions of involvement, as well as the ideology of adult education, all have the potential to produce cultural conflict or tension.

Diouf, Sheckley and Kehrhahn (2000) investigated the reasons for failure of Senegalese agricultural extension programs, and found that Senegalese adults were more interested in continuous learning from elders about religion and social relations than in farming techniques, which they believed they had learned as children. They sought out family members, neighbours or other sources within the village for learning rather than extension agents, who were perceived to lack the social values and cultural norms of the community. The extension program was based on an assumption that all learners are the same, thus program design and strategies did not take into account the materially different realities and cultural ways of learning of the Senegalese. While it is often easier to see how cultural differences are formed beyond one's own nation, community or organisation rather than within the geographical borders of one's more immediate surroundings, it is important to recognise how cultural differences shape local practices and experiences.

There are frequent tensions in social and cultural interactions, between how one is to respond appropriately versus how one responds in practical everyday experience. The reactions of each party in an interaction depend on contingent responses of the other/s with potential sanctions. Cultural sanctions are 'a generic type of resource drawn upon in power relations' (Giddens 1979: 86) and are a feature of all social encounters, however subtle the processes of negotiation may be. Consider the work of Gumperz (1982), which shows the dissonance in cross-cultural interaction. He presents the example of an interview between an East Indian job applicant and English-speaking interviewers.

The exchange of greetings, a basic and seemingly transparent encounter, becomes a problematic beginning to a disastrous interview. Operating from a different cultural perspective, the interviewee gets fewer and fewer clear cues as to what is expected of him. The man has to rely on English-speaking interviewers, participants in the official culture that has determined and regulated the interview process. Such incidents reflect the tension between the practical consciousness of lived reality and the determining influence of the dominant culture or the official consciousness.

Value and the culture of power

The culture that is of more value becomes problematic, of course, especially for members of a non-dominant group. There is a 'culture of power' (Delpit 1988: 2) at work that contains codes and rules relating to communicative strategies, linguistic forms and presentation of self—that is, ways of walking, dressing, writing, interacting. Delpit suggests that the rules of the culture of power reflect the rules of those who have power. These hegemonic criteria and their norms and evaluations are reproduced in the adult classroom as they are in general society through discourse practices (Zuss 1994).

The notion of discourse communities emerges from ethnographic studies of communication from the 1970s. Gee (1992) argues that particular discourses are acquired to deal with everyday life within specific sociocultural contexts that are part of a larger communicative societal system or sociopolitical entity. Certain forms of knowledge and social practices are organised and legitimised at the expense of others. At the institutional level of adult education, unconscious sources of practice and conduct are deeply sedimented and provide everyday life with order and discipline. Structural practices of adult education reflect the dominant society.

For example, the linear style of adult basic education, which moves learners from literacy to secondary to post-secondary tracks established in public schooling for children, does not often serve adults who want to learn reading and writing skills in order to pass a driving test, or to understand safety regulations at the work site, or to learn how to write a formal letter in order to file a complaint against a landlord. Another example is the extensive use of individualised instruction in literacy programs, which is counter to how literacy is often used in everyday life as a social activity. Wikelund (1989) found street youth interacting as a group in dealing with written materials, joking and interpreting the meaning of magazine articles, want ads, assistance forms and crossword puzzles. Working together, some contributed bits of functional knowledge about the item and the consequences of its use, while others offered technical literacy skills in the form of reading or writing. Adult education determines which knowledge and skills are offered to whom in what formats, thus acting, in part, as a mechanism for social control. Pedagogical approaches, program management, plus the limited roles of instructors who are often mandated to use skills-based textbooks and materials according to state or federal guidelines, are all structural aspects of adult education regulated by the dominant discourse.

Dominant discourses have the power to constitute subjects and create social identities of educators by a process of 'learning inside the procedures' (Gee, Hull & Lankshear 1996), or learning by doing, which helps ensure that adult education practitioners take on the perspectives, or world view, of the dominant discourse. Accepting a core set of values the practitioner masters an identity (social position), with little if any critical awareness of how that identity is constructed. Discourse thus creates, or positions, people who either overtly or tacitly define themselves as different, often as better than others, by constructing such binary relationships as insider/outsider (Sparks & Peterson 2000).

Additionally, many adult educators are unaware of their own cultural foundations: as members of the mainstream culture they have been trained within a socially and linguistically homogeneous profession. As a result, many have not learned to value forms of learning that are situated outside the traditional ethnocentric European paradigm. Understanding and challenging the culture of power operating in adult education contexts requires that attention be given to deconstructing privilege, particularly by those who are privileged (Rocco & West 1998: 171). 'Before any discussion can meaningfully address equity, we must reflect upon our privilege. Failure to do so results in . . . objectifying and dehumanising groups of people and thereby further marginalising them'.

There is also potential conflict between the diverse cultural discourses of the learners and the official discourse of the classroom— transmitted, for example, through adult education practices of privileging standard English over black English or the Southern white dialect, the preference for printed text over oral tradition, and the assimilation of non-native English speakers into the dominant language. Alfred (2001) asks some exacting questions: Is it possible to insulate practice from wider institutional and societal hegemonic values? Can instructors truly create an inclusive learning environment without an understanding of the contexts that shape their lives and those of their students? Is it even possible for an inclusive learning environment to exist at all? These are some of the most challenging questions for today's adult educators.

The role of the adult educator: a case of conflict and struggle

The role of the teacher is a structural component of adult education practice. The role that an individual, as teacher, takes on in the classroom is saturated with mainstream cultural values and ideology, as the teacher is the one who regulates what knowledge is accessible to students, the one who carries out the agreed-on or standardised curriculum, and the one who utilises conventional practices of assessment, instruction, discipline and management. The teacher is a social agent of the educational enterprise, and thus occupies a central place in the education of all learners (Sparks 2002b). How an individual interprets and lives that role can vary.

According to a Mexican American woman who had been taking English literacy classes, 'They told us to leave our Spanish outside the classroom. I tell my son it's good to speak two languages—bilingual—try to speak your own language not only just English. They shouldn't make us feel bad about our language' (Sparks 2002b: 113). This was a story that was repeated over and over again by participants in ESL classes in Colorado, an English-only US state. Conventional thinking regarding adult literacy is that the learner should speak only English in the classroom in order to make a more rapid transition from the native language. The ideology of this teaching approach is based on an assimilationist model, where the dominant culture and by extension adult literacy teachers expect Mexican American students to assimilate. The Americanisation perspective of the 1920s (Olneck 1989), which continues to flourish, reflects the belief that minority ethnic groups should adapt to the dominant culture; therefore, it would be inappropriate to teach them how to use their native language to learn English, or to teach them about their own history or culture.

Whether they were fluent or not, using Spanish was highly valued among a group of Mexican Americans in a study of participation/non-participation in adult basic education (ABE) and ESL programs (Sparks 2002b). When they were asked why it is important to speak Spanish, one young man said, 'That's what I was brought up as, that's who I am, that's what I did in the past, that's what I do' (2002b: 78). The importance of language as ethnic and cultural identity was echoed throughout the study, 'because that's our heritage, that is my culture' or 'I'm Mexican; I think all Mexicans should learn Spanish' or 'Anglos say you're dumb if you don't know English. We say we're dumb if we don't know Spanish' (2002b: 79–80). Language as culture, as a whole way of life, is a dynamic and emergent process. This experience of the present, as Williams (1981) terms it, is an act of becoming that is formative and forming.

As literacy and ESL teachers insist that native language be left outside the classroom door, it is one's cultural identity that is seen as being pushed to one side. According to one woman, 'you are a Chicano [Mexican American], and that's all there is to it. My ethnic background was pushed aside like I was supposed to forget about it' (Sparks 1998a: 254). Learners are not inclined to enrol in adult education programs where there is a lack of intercultural understanding and a breakdown in cultural respect between teachers and learners.

The role the teacher takes on has significant consequences for any student learning. Mexican Americans told of being left on their own to 'figure things out', creating a sense of invisibility, exclusion and inferior status. Feelings of exclusion were expressed in relation to other students and teachers. Invisibility related to a lack of care and attention on the part of the teacher, whereas inferior status was created by the comments and attitudes of the teacher (Sparks 1998a). Typical student comments were: 'Nobody seemed to notice if I was there or not. The teachers didn't seem to care', 'They acted as if we weren't there', 'Let's see how can I get through to your kind of people. She didn't come out and tell us "It's you brown people", but she could sure say it another way and it meant the same thing' (1998a: 252). Mainstream bias and blatant racism were part of the educational experience of these adult learners.

Distinguishing between individual teachers who are not interested or not prepared to work with Mexican Americans and other Hispanic adults, and the hegemonic role of the teacher as agent of the state in the class-room who models, trains and monitors the socialisation of individuals into mainstream culture, helps us understand how social systems work. Instructors are expected to use the dominant teaching materials, methods and techniques, such as self-paced individualised instruction, which although counter to the social process of learning (Jarvis 1992) are widely used; and they are expected to have an interest in assisting people in learning basic academic skills to help them move around in the world more easily and effectively. But it is a standardised world that is seen—one that conforms to a normative local community, society and nation. This is

283

not to say that individual teachers should not be held accountable for their actions and attitudes, or that retraining teachers would be futile. Rather, it suggests the hegemonic nature of all aspects of adult education and the intensity of the restructuring job ahead.

While teacher professionalism has been a salient feature of the recent school reform movement in the United States, adult literacy teachers are typically part-time workers who hold full-time teaching positions in elementary or high schools, are retired from a variety of professions and work as volunteer literacy tutors, or are piecing together employment in order to make ends meet. This does not mean that literacy instructors are not dedicated and enthusiastic, nor that they are uneducated; it is simply to say that they are usually not professionally prepared to become adult literacy teachers. The insufficient number of professionally prepared practitioners available for adult literacy programs sends a clear message that literacy students do not deserve them.

There is a hierarchy of power from the national level to the state level where teacher education and development are controlled by laws and procedures. What type of training is offered, for whom and under what circumstances, serves to funnel low-status educators into what is perceived by many as low-status literacy education. To deal with a transient and temporary workforce, subsequent to relying on volunteers and part-time instructors, standardised curriculum such as Equipped for the Future and standardised assessment such as the Comprehensive Adult Student Assessment System (CASAS) are instituted, making instruction regulated and teaching accountable. What this does is to deskill and disempower teachers. They become subjects of educational policy, which serves to differentiate and exploit them. While they are expected to act like professionals, they are offered few of the benefits of other professionals, including livable wages. Agnello (2001) suggests that because teachers comply with standards and regulated curriculum they come to expect standard performance from students. Unless teachers question how they are positioned within the classroom they will not be able to assist their students in similar questioning and critique of social and cultural worlds.

Moving more purposefully from theory to practice requires specific strategies, and one of the most important is reconceptualising the hegemonic role of the adult literacy teacher (Sparks 1998b). As agents of the state, teachers are expected to morally and economically socialise adult learners into the dominant culture. More time must be spent on critiquing the teacher's role as social agent, thus moving away from personal attacks on individual teachers, and on investigating how the role of teacher might support the genuine needs of the learners. By interrogating the hegemonic role of the teacher, we make visible how discriminatory practice continues to occur. From there we must look to individual practices of discrimination, and ask those teachers who engage in discriminatory practices to leave or change their attitudes. Changing attitudes is the first step; from there teachers must teach critically about difference and give way to learner-centred programs rather than teacher-centred programs, which dampen student engagement.

THE CULTURE OF CURRICULUM: LIFE SKILLS TRAINING

Life skills training is common to many programs for the unemployed, and for groups and individuals who face multiple barriers to accessing the paid workforce, such as single mothers on welfare. A variety of definitions of life skills can be found, but for the purpose of this discussion they 'are problem-solving behaviours appropriately and responsibly used in the management of personal affairs' (Saskatchewan NewStart 1982). What is included in the realm of problem-solving behaviours and how 'appropriate' and 'responsible' are interpreted reflects particular cultural norms and values. 'Whose life?', 'Which skills?', 'To what end?', 'In whose interest?' are questions rarely posed within a dominant policy and program discourse that positions life skills as part of the key to success for new immigrants, poor women and those with long unemployment histories.

Life skills discourse takes on various meanings, depending on the context in which the notion is invoked. Within the context of welfare-to-work policies and programs, the discourse of life skills often reflects a deficit model, where adult learners are regarded as lacking or needing to be fixed. Within the discourse of jobs in the high-tech sector, life skills or 'soft skills' are regarded as 'value-added'; workers should have knowledge and expertise of their specific industry and they also need to develop and acquire communication, team-building and problem-solving skills.

Analysis of life skills programs has pointed to the corporate agenda at work in how life skills are defined (Gaskell 1986; Griffith 1988): 'The complexity of the individual judgements . . . are reduced here to a set of agreed upon procedures for acting, procedures which assume the employers' interest is the same as the students' (Gaskell 1986: 435). The white masculine and middle-class norms operating in life skills programs have also been illustrated. Ainley and Corbett (1994), in their study of a British program for students with learning disabilities, found that the skills and attitudes promoted by these programs were 'divorce[d] from their real cultural context' and presented as 'equally accessible to all students whatever their class, culture, background, gender or race' (1994: 371–2).

In a study of government-funded re-entry programs for women (Butterwick 1993), life skills classes were key components of the curriculum in all programs, although each program approached these classes somewhat differently. The goal of one program, where most of the participants were receiving social assistance, was to help women find clerical jobs. There were tensions and contradictions in this program, as women's roles as mothers were both valued and devalued. Naming and honouring the caring and organising work in the home and community the participants did was part of one lesson. These stories had then to be translated into a skills inventory—into a language that employers would value. Not only was the language of the home place actively removed from the official vocabulary, but the different cultural values of being a home-maker and mother were not drawn out. This program also included a 'dress for success' class where, despite the cultural diversity of the classroom, students were urged to discard their 'housewife' garments and don the corporate image of business suit: jacket, skirt, pantyhose, simple blouse and sensible shoes. The irony that entry-level wages made it difficult to purchase this 'uniform' was not lost on the participants; there was also no discussion of cultural differences in relation to dress.

Another program that purposefully recruited immigrant women (most of whom were women of colour) to train as bookkeepers emphasised assertiveness training, improving English language skills (including diminishing their accents) and learning the Canadian system. Despite the fact that many women had been professionals in their home country, these women were encouraged to 'start at the bottom'. The lack of recognition of their skills by employers and the racism and sexism of immigration policy that exacerbated this situation were not raised in the classroom. The dominant theme running through this program was a deficit orientation, where these women's lack of Canadian experience and their different cultural backgrounds were regarded as a problem. It is ironic that, at the conclusion of the program, one Latin American participant found a well-paying job in an international firm because of her Latin American experience and her ability to speak Spanish.

In another program run by a native women's organisation for native women, the life skills classes were reworked on the basis of the 'Medicine wheel', such that the spiritual, physical, emotional and intellectual capacities and needs of the women were integrated into the activities. Each morning began with a talking circle, physical exercise was part of each day's activities, art-based approaches were used, as were more traditional exercises that focused on language and math skills. This program had its struggles as well, as there were many different indigenous tribes represented in the group and different experiences of living on- and off-reserve. The difference between the native cultures of on-reserve and off-reserve became a source of tension when instructors, most of whom had not lived on-reserve, made assumptions about the women's experiences.

More recent research, which involved interviews with life skills instructors and coaches as well as learners, illustrates the enabling and disabling aspects of life skills curricula and programs (Butterwick 2003; Butterwick & Ripley 2001). One life skills coach came to his work through his own experience as a participant in a life skills program. A few years prior to the interview, he had been unemployed and was sent to a life skills program by his case worker. Although initially very resistant, he changed his mind and saw the program's value: 'I would see my own self-esteem and confidence going up, my communication skills were better, I was listening more actively'. Another life skills instructor had grown sceptical of this emphasis on raising self-esteem: 'It's like telling the participants that what you have isn't good enough. I will teach you self-esteem because you don't have it, which is just an impossible situation for a student to be in'.

Including a life skills component is now required by many government funding sources for those agencies submitting proposals to run employment-related programs for individuals on employment insurance and social assistance. One student, who had been in an exploratory trades program for women, was furious that students in that program were required to take life skills classes: 'I actually had a life that was happening—I didn't need to sit and discuss how to do my life. I'm not having problems with my life. I'm having trouble finding a job!' An indigenous instructor was also critical of the requirement of government funding to include life skills in programs for native communities. He no longer runs such programs because, in his view, there was too much dissonance between the Western assumptions of life skills and indigenous world views. The individualistic orientation, in particular, was viewed as problematic: 'it [worked] against pursuing harmony and balance within the family'.

Other instructors felt there was a way to reframe and reorient the life skills classes so that they reflected a critical sociocultural analysis. A First Nations instructor who ran a life skills program in schools brought a community-based approach to her curriculum: 'We invite students, potential students, their parents, administration and anyone else from the community. We hold a round of introductions, coaches talk about their experiences and we do a mini lesson'. Another instructor, a woman of colour, felt that most of the educators in her agency had no analysis of oppression; they were unaware of how structural elements (fuelled by sexism, racism and classism) were at work in creating barriers for individual participants. Instead they used an individualistic and deficit-oriented model, which focused on 'fixing' the individual learners, ignoring the larger context of their lives. Failing to address these cultural and systemic issues, in her view, meant that oppression would then be reproduced. In contrast, she made a point in her life skills classes to look at 'employment standards, rights, racism, discrimination in the workplace, at home and in society and what you do with these situations'.

Examining the curricula of life skills training, a common (and often required) element (at least in Canada) of many programs that train the excluded—those at the margins of the economy and dominant society—can help shed light on how dominant discourses have the power to constitute subjects and create social identities. What is also illustrated is how such structures can be resisted and recreated. Like English language training programs, life skills training is a fascinating area for examining adult education as a site of cultural practice and noting the ways dominant cultural views are reinscribed and resisted. As Luke (1995) argues, the curriculum that gets used by educators is central to the operations and reproduction of social/cultural power relations within institutions.

CONCLUSION

bell hooks argues that 'cultural criticism can be an agent of change, educating for critical consciousness in liberatory ways, only if we start with a mind-set and a progressive politics that is fundamentally anti-colonist, that negates cultural imperialism in all its manifestations' (1994: 6). Critically reflective work is hard work because it requires an openness in how we do things, and in how we think of not just our world but the worlds and realities of all of our students. Through this hard work, adult education can be reconstructed for equitable learning.

As adult educators we must become critically reflective of how culturally encoded our own world views are and how all policies, programs and institutions of adult education reflect and reproduce certain world views. This approach suggests that a reflective mode 'starts from a sceptical approach to what appears at a superficial glance as unproblematic replicas of the way reality functions' (Alvesson & Skoldberg 2000: 5). One potential response to an increasing awareness of the relationship between culture and structure in adult education is to become immobilised. To expand our horizons we need to move beyond feeling immobilised and take action, all the while recognising how our social relations and practices are shaped by power and difference. As Young (1997: 59) argues:

By means of openness and questioning, as well as efforts to express experience and values from different perspectives, people sometimes understand one another across difference, even when they do not identify with each other. Through such dialogue that recognizes the asymmetry of others, moreover, people can enlarge their thinking in at least two ways. Their own assumptions and point of view become relativised for them as they are set in relation to those of others. By learning from others how the world and the collective relations they have forged through interaction look to them, moreover, everyone can develop an enlarged understanding of that world and those relations that is unavailable to any of them from their own perspective alone.

NOTES

CHAPTER 2   THE NEW PROFESSIONAL AND VOCATIONAL EDUCATION

1   The key competencies should be seen as being relational. They bring together attributes possessed by individuals and the contexts in which, through performance, these attributes are demonstrated. They are at a higher level of complexity than other more simple competencies, i.e. they bring together more attributes, but they do not exist without a context. So 'problem solving' or 'collecting, analysing and organising information', for example, should not be thought of as discrete competencies *additional to* other competencies or as somehow underpinning other competencies. There is no such thing as the generic competency of problem solving—only individuals bringing together the appropriate attributes in a particular context to solve the specific problem that confronts them. Thus the key competencies are really no more than 'complex' competencies as defined in the integrated model of competence. They will almost always be employed in combination with other simple competencies where single attributes (e.g. recalling some aspect of knowledge) are necessary but not sufficient to complete a task. In effect, the key competencies will never stand alone.

There are likely to be some similarities between the combinations of attributes required to solve a problem in similar contexts. So in solving problems in social work with troubled juveniles, for example, different social workers will use many of the same combinations of attributes. Even in this restricted arena, however, every problem will be unique, and different combinations of attributes will often be needed to solve what seem, ostensibly, to be similar problems. Although in social work with the aged substantially different combinations of attributes will be needed to solve problems, it is possible that some will still be common to social work with juveniles. The attributes needed, however, will have to be rethought and recontextualised rather then simply transferred.

It is also dangerous to think of the key competencies as discrete, stand-alone competencies. In real-world situations many tasks are complex. The more complex the work (i.e. the tasks that have to be performed), the more combinations of the key competencies will be required to perform successfully. The assumption that these key competencies are discrete and that they can be divided into levels is another instance of the tendency towards atomistic or reductionist thinking discussed earlier in this essay.

CHAPTER 4   UNDERSTANDING ADULT LEARNERS

1 A 'discourse' is a system of cultural practices, norms, values and words that reinforce particular beliefs and behaviours, framing life in a particular way. A particular discourse endorses some ways of acting as 'normal' or desirable, depicts others as bad or irrational, and completely ignores still others by not naming them.

CHAPTER 8   ECONOMICS, POLITICS AND ADULT EDUCATION

1 See, for example, literature in connection with the Ontario-directed project NALL (New Approaches to Lifelong Learning), directed by David W. Livingstone of the Ontario Institute for Studies in Education/University of Toronto (www.nall.ca), and PEN (Popular Education Network), coordinated by a group of scholars/activists from the University of Edinburgh (www.neskes.net/pen).

BIBLIOGRAPHY

Abbreviations

NIACE: National Institute of Adult Continuing Education (Leicester, England)
NCVER: National Centre for Vocational Education Research (Adelaide, Australia)

Mass media sources

ABC *Australian Broadcasting Commission* various programs
SMH *Sydney Morning Herald* various issues

Print sources

Achtenhagen, F. & Grubb, W.N. 2001 'Vocational and occupational education: pedagogical complexity, institutional diversity' in V. Richardson (ed.) *Handbook of Research on Teaching* (4th edn) Washington: American Educational Research Association pp. 604–39

Adams, F. 1975 *Unearthing Seeds of Fire: The idea of Highlander* Winston-Salem, NC: John Blair

Agnello, M. 2001 *A Postmodern Literacy Policy Analysis* New York: Peter Lang

Ainley, P. & Corbett. J. 1994 'From vocationalism to enterprise: Social and life skills become personable and transferable' *British Journal of Sociology of Education* 15(3), 365–74

Ainley, P. & Rainbird, H. 1999 'Introduction' in P. Ainley & H. Rainbird (eds) *Apprenticeship: Towards a new paradigm of learning* London: Kogan Page

Albanese, M.A. & Mitchell, S. 1993 'Problem-based learning: A review of literature on its outcomes and implementation issues' *Academic Medicine* 68(1), 52–81

Alfred, M. 2001 'Expanding theories of career development: Adding the voices of African American women in the White academy' *Adult Education Quarterly* 51(2), 108–27

Alinsky, S. 1946 *Reveille for Radicals* New York: Vintage Books

——1971 *Rules for Radicals: A pragmatic primer for realistic radicals* New York: Vintage Books

Allman, P. 1991 'Adult education fallacy: Positive discrimination leads to liberation' in B. O'Hagan (ed.) *The Charnwood Papers: Fallacies in community education* Ticknall, Derbyshire: Education Now

——2001 *Critical Education Against Capitalism: Karl Marx and revolutionary critical education* London: Bergin Garvey

Alvesson, M. & Skoldberg, K. 2000 *Reflexive Methodology: New vistas for qualitative research* London: Sage

Anderson, D. 1995 'Private training provision in Australia: An overview of recent research' in F. Ferrier & C. Selby Smith (eds) *The Economics of Education and Training 1995* Canberra: Australian Government Publishing Service

——1997 *Competition and Market Reform in the Australian VET Sector* Adelaide: NCVER

——1999 'Vocational education reform and students: Redressing silences and omissions' *Australian Educational Researcher* 26(2), 99–125

——2000 'Quasi-markets in vocational education and training in Australia' in F. Beven, C. Kanes & D. Roebuck (eds) *Learning Together, Working Together: Building communities for the 21st century* Proceedings of the 8th Annual International Conference on Post-compulsory Education and Training Griffith University, Brisbane: Australian Academic Press (vol. 2) pp. 108–15

Anderson, P. 1980 *Arguments within English Marxism* Verso: London

ANTA (Australian National Training Authority) 2000 *National Marketing Strategy for Skills and Lifelong Learning* Brisbane: ANTA

——2002a *Annual Report on Operations 2001–2002* Brisbane: ANTA

——2002b *Learning Communities Audit Reports* Brisbane: ANTA

Apple, M.W. 1990 *Ideology and Curriculum* (2nd edn) New York: Routledge

Argyris, C. 1990 *Overcoming Organizational Defenses: Facilitating organizational learning* Boston: Allyn & Bacon

——1998 'Empowerment: The Emperor's new clothes' *Harvard Business Review* May/June, 98–105

Argyris, C. & Schön, D. 1974 *Theory in Practice: Increasing professional effectiveness* San Francisco: Jossey-Bass

——1978 *Organizational Learning: A theory of action perspective* Reading, MA: Addison-Wesley

Armstrong, E. 1997 'A hybrid model of problem-based learning' in D. Boud & G. Feletti (eds) *The Challenge of Problem-Based Learning* London: Kogan Page pp. 137–50

Arnold, R. & Burke, B. 1984 *A Popular Education Handbook: An educational experience taken from Central America and adapted to the Canadian context* Toronto: CUSO

Ashton, D. & Green, F. 1996 *Education, Training and the Global Economy* Cheltenham: Edward Elgar

Atkinson, M. (ed.) 1915 *Trade Unionism in Australia: Report of the conference held in 1915* Sydney: WEA

Atkinson, M. 1919 *The New Social Order: A study of post-war reconstruction* Sydney: WEA

Attwood, B. & Foster, S.G. 2003 *Frontier Conflict: The Australian experience* Canberra: National Museum of Australia

Australian Bureau of Statistics (ABS) 2002 News Release 17/1/2002 on the Education and Training Indicators, Canberra: ABS (cat. no. 4230.0)

Australian Centre for Industrial Relations Research and Training (ACIRRT) 1999 *Australia at Work: Just managing?* Sydney: Prentice Hall

Australian Human Rights and Equal Opportunity Commission (HREOC) 1997 *Bringing Them Home: Report of the National Inquiry into the Separation of Aboriginal and Torres Strait Islander Children from Their Families* Sydney: HREOC

Ausubel, D.P. 1963 *The Psychology of Meaningful Verbal Learning: An introduction to school learning* New York: Grune & Stratten

Ausubel, D.P. et al. 1968 *Educational Psychology: A cognitive view* New York: Holt, Rinehart & Winston

Avis, J., Bloomer, M., Esland, G., Gleeson, D. & Hodkinson, P. 1996 *Knowledge and Nationhood: Education, politics and work* London: Cassell

Badham, R. & Buchanan, D. 1996 'Power-assisted steering and the micropolitics of organizational change: A research agenda', Paper presented to the Australian and New Zealand Academy of Management Conference, Wollongong, December

Bagnall, R. 1994 'Performance indicators and outcomes as measures of educational quality: A cautionary critique' *International Journal of Lifelong Education* 13(1), 19–32

Barcan, A. 1988 *Two Centuries of Education in New South Wales* Sydney: NSW University Press

Barnett, L. & Abbatt, F. 1994 *District Action Research and Education: A resource book for problem-solving in health systems* London: Macmillan

Barnett, R. 1997 *Higher Education: A critical business* Buckingham, England: Open University Press

Barr, R. & Dreeben, R. 1978 'Instruction in classrooms' in L.S. Shulman (ed.) *Review of Research in Education* (vol. 5) Itasca, IL: F.E. Peacock

Barrows, H.S. 1986 'A taxonomy of problem-based learning methods' *Medical Education* 20, 481–6

Barrows, H.S. & Tamblyn, R.M. 1980 'Selection of the appropriate problems for learning' in S. Jonas (ed.) *Problem-Based Learning: An approach to medical education* New York: Springer pp. 156–62

Baumgartner, L.M. 2002 'Living and learning with HIV/AIDS: Transformational tales continued' *Adult Education Quarterly* 53(1), 44–59

Beckett, D. & Hager, P. 2000 'Making judgments as the basis for workplace learning: Towards an epistemology of practice *International Journal of Lifelong Education* 19(4), 300–11

Beirne, M., Ramsay, H. & Panteli, A. 1998 'Developments in computing work: Control and contradiction in the software labour process' in P. Thompson & C. Warhurst (eds) *Workplaces of the Future* London: Macmillan Business pp. 142–62

Belenky, M., Clinchy, B., Goldberger, N. & Tarule, J. 1986 *Women's Ways of Knowing: The development of self, voice and mind* New York: Basic Books

Bell, B., Gaventa, J. & Peters, J. 1990 *We Make the Road by Walking* Philadelphia, PA: Temple University Press.

Bereiter, C. 2000 'Keeping the brain in mind' *Australian Journal of Education* 44(3), 226–38

Bereiter, C. & Scardamalia, M. 1996 'Rethinking learning' in David R. Olson and Nancy Torrance (eds) *The Handbook of Education and Human Development: New Models of Learning, Teaching, and Schooling* Cambridge, Mass., USA: Blackwell Publishers

Beveridge, C. & Turnbull, R. 1989 *The Eclipse of Scottish Culture* Edinburgh: Polygon

Bhavani, K. 1997 'Women's studies and its interconnection with "race", ethinicity and sexuality' in V. Robinson & D. Richardson (eds) *Introducing Women's Studies: Feminist theory and practice* (2nd edn) London: Macmillan

Biddle, B.J. & Dunkin, M.J. 1987 'Effects of teaching' in M.J. Dunkin (ed.) *The International Handbook of Teaching and Teacher Education* Oxford: Pergamon Press

Billett, S. 1999 'Guided learning at work' in D. Boud & J. Garrick (eds) *Understanding Learning at Work* New York: Routledge pp. 151–64

——2001 *Learning in the Workplace: Strategies for effective practice* Sydney: Allen & Unwin

Bion, W.R. 1961 *Experiences in Groups and Other Papers* London: Routledge

Boone, E.J., Safrit, R.D. & Jones, J. 2002 *Developing Programs in Adult Education: A conceptual programming model* (2nd edn) Prospect Heights, IL: Waveland Press

Borg, C. & Mayo, P. 2002 'The EU Memorandum of Lifelong Learning. Diluted Old Wine in New Bottles?' Paper presented at the BAICE conference, *Lifelong Learning and the Building of Human and Social Capital* University of Nottingham, 6–8 September

Boud, D. 2001 'Creating a work-based curriculum' in D. Boud & N. Solomon (eds) *Work-Based Learning: A new higher education?* Buckingham: Society for Research in Higher Education & Open University

Boud, D. & Feletti, G. (eds) 1997 *The Challenge of Problem-Based Learning* London: Kogan Page

Boud, D. & Griffin, V. (eds) 1987 *Appreciating Adults Learning: From the learner's perspective* London: Kogan Page

Boud, D. & Walker, D. 1991 *Experience and Learning: Reflection at work* Geelong: Deakin University Press

Boud, D., Keogh, R. & Walker, D. (eds) 1985 *Reflection: Turning experience into learning* London: Kogan Page

Boughton, B. 1996 'Does popular education have a past?' in B. Boughton, T. Brown & G. Foley (eds) *New Directions in Australian Adult Education* Sydney: Centre for Popular Education, University of Technology, Sydney (Also available electronically on the Adult Education History Forum, Adult Learning Australia website, at www.ala.asn.au)

——1999 '"Just as impelled as ever to try the liberal racket": The influence of communism and anti-communism on Australian adult education history, as seen through the life of Esmonde Higgins' in E. Reid-Smith (ed.), *Some Topics on Adult Education in Australia: Papers presented at a seminar on the history of adult education* Canberra: Adult Learning Australia Research Network and Centre for Learning and Work Research, Griffith University (Also available electronically on the Adult Education History Forum, Adult Learning Australia website, at www.ala.asn.au)

——2001 'The Communist Party of Australia's involvement in the struggle for Aboriginal and Torres Strait Islander people's rights 1920–1970' in R. Markey (ed.) *Labour and Community: Historical essays* Wollongong: University of Wollongong Press

Boughton, R., Brown, M., Merlyn, T. & Rushbrook, P. 2002 'Constructing the good worker: A dialogue-in-progress' in Conference proceedings for *Envisioning Practice: Implementing change* Brisbane: Centre for Learning and Work, Griffith University pp. 156–64

Bowles, S. & Gintis, H. 1976 *Schooling in Capitalist America: Educational reform and the contradictions of economic life* London: Routledge & Kegan Paul

Brand, W. 1998 'Change and consensus in vocational education and training: The case of the German "dual system"' in I. Finlay, S. Niven & S. Young (eds) *Changing Vocational Education and Training: an international comparative perspective* London: Routledge pp. 103–22

Bredo, E. & Feinberg, W. (eds) 1982 *Knowledge and Values in Social and Educational Research* Philadelphia: Temple

Brenner, R. 1998 'The economics of global turbulence' *New Left Review* 229, 1–265

Brine, J. 1999 *Undereducating Women: Globalizing inequality* Milton Keynes: Open University Press

Briton, D. & Taylor, J. 2001 'Online workers' education: How do we tame the technology?' *International Journal of Instructional Media* 28(2), 117–35

Brockett, R.G. & Hiemstra, R. 1998 'Philosophical and ethical considerations' in P.S. Cookson (ed.) *Program Planning for the Education and Continuing Education of Adults: North American perspectives* Malabar, FL: Kreiger Publishing

Brodney, M. 1940 'Miss May Brodney suggests a Labor college for New South Wales' *AEU Monthly Journal and Report* May, 16–17

Brookfield, S. 1984 'Self-directed adult learning: A critical paradigm' *Adult Education Quarterly* 35(2), 59–71

——1985 *Self-Directed Learning: From theory to practice* San Francisco: Jossey-Bass

——1986 *Understanding and Facilitating Adult Learning* San Francisco: Jossey-Bass

——1987 'Eduard Lindeman' in P. Jarvis (ed.) *Twentieth Century Thinkers in Adult Education* Beckenham, Kent: Croom Helm

——1989 *Developing Critical Thinkers* San Francisco: Jossey-Bass

——1990 *The Skilful Teacher* San Francisco: Jossey-Bass

——1995 *Becoming a Critical Reflective Teacher* San Francisco: Jossey-Bass

——2000 'The concept of critically reflective practice' in A.L. Wilson & E.R. Hayes (eds) *Handbook of Adult and Continuing Education* San Francisco: Jossey-Bass

——2001 'Repositioning ideology critique in a critical theory of adult education' *Adult Education Quarterly* 52(9), 7–22

Brookfield, S.D. & Preskill, S. 1999 *Discussion as a Way of Teaching* San Francisco: Jossey-Bass

Brown, G.A. 1987 'Lectures and lecturing' in M.J. Dunkin (ed.) *The International Handbook of Teaching and Teacher Education* Oxford: Pergamon Press

Brown, M. 1994 'Competency-based training: Skill formation for the workplace or classroom Taylorism?' in J Kenway (ed.) *Economising Education: The post-Fordist directions* Geelong: Deakin University Press pp. 153–84

Brown, P., Green, A. & Lauder, H. 2001 *High Skills: Globalisation, competitiveness and skill formation* New York: Oxford University Press

Brown, S. 1980 *Political Subjectivity: Applications of Q methodology in political science* New Haven, CT: Yale University Press

Brundage, D. & Mackeracher, D. 1980 *Adult Learning Principles and their Application to Program Planning* Toronto: Ontario Ministry of Education

Brysk, A. 2000 *From Tribal Village to Global Village: Indian rights and international relations in Latin America* Stanford, CA: Stanford University Press

Burgmann, V. 1995 *Revolutionary Industrial Unionism: The industrial workers of the world in Australia* Melbourne: Cambridge University Press

Burke, G. & Reuling, J. (eds) 2002 *Vocational Training and Lifelong Learning in Australia and Germany* Australia Centre Series (vol. 5) Adelaide: NCVER

Butler, E. 1999 'Technologising equity: The politics and practices of work-related learning' in D. Boud & J. Garrick (eds) *Understanding Learning at Work* London: Routledge pp. 132–50

Butler, E. & Ferrier, F. 2000 *Don't be too polite, girls! Women, work and vocational education and training: A critical review of the literature* Adelaide: NCVER

Butterwick, S. 1993 *The politics of needs interpretation: A study of three CJS-funded job-entry programs for women* Unpublished doctoral dissertation, Department of Administrative, Adult and Higher Education, University of British Columbia

——2003 'Life skills training: Open for discussion' in M.G. Cohen (ed.) *Training the Excluded for Work: Access and equity for women, immigrants, first nations, youth, and people with low income* Vancouver: University of British Columbia Press

Butterwick, S. & Ripley, L. 2001 'Life skills coach training: The forest and the trees *Proceedings of the Fifth Annual Conference of the Western Research Network on Education and Training (WRNET)* Vancouver: University of British Columbia, 30–31 March

Buzan, T. 1978 *Use Your Head* London: BBC Productions

Cabral, A. 1974 *Revolution in Guinea: An African people's struggle* London: Stage 1

Caffarella, R.S. 2002 *Planning Programs for Adult Learners: A practical guide for educators, trainers, and staff developers* San Francisco: Jossey-Bass

Campbell, A. 1998 'Fomenting synergy: Experiences with facilitating Landcare in Australia' in N.G. Roling & M.A.E. Wagemakers (eds) *Facilitating Sustainable Agriculture* Cambridge, UK: Cambridge University Press pp. 232–49

Campbell, J. 1973 *Myths to Live By* New York: Bantam

Candy, P.C. 1991 *Self-Direction for Lifelong Learning: A comprehensive guide to theory and practice* San Francisco: Jossey-Bass

Cantor, L. 1989 *Vocational Education and Training in the Developed World: A comparative study* London: Routledge

Cantor, N. 1946 *The Dynamics of Learning* Buffalo, NY: Foster & Stewart

Carnoy, M. 1995 'Foreword: How should we study adult education?' in C.A. Torres (ed.) *The Politics of Nonformal Education in Latin America* New York: Praeger

Carr, W. & Kemmis, S. 1986 *Becoming Critical: Education, knowledge and action research* Geelong: Deakin University Press

Casey, C. 1999 'The changing context of work' in D. Boud & J. Garrick (eds) *Understanding Learning at Work* New York: Routledge pp. 15–28

Cassara, B. (ed.) 1995 *Adult Education through World Collaboration* Malabar, FL: Krieger

Cattell, R.B. 1963 'Theory of fluid and crystallized intelligence: A critical approach' *Journal of Educational Psychology* 54(1), 1–22

CEC 1994 *Employment, Growth, Competitiveness* Luxembourg: Office for Official Publications, Commission of the European Communities

——2000 *A Memorandum on Lifelong Learning* Commission Staff Working Paper, Brussels: European Commission

——2001 *Making a European Area of Lifelong Learning a Reality* Communication from the Commission, Brussels: European Commission

——2002 *Official Journal of European Communities 20/7/2002* Call for Proposals EAC/ 41/02, Brussels: European Commission

Cedefop/Eurydice 2001 *National Actions to Implement Lifelong Learning in Europe*, Thessaloniki & Brussels: Cedefop/Eurydice

Cervero, R.M. & Wilson, A.L. 1994 *Planning Responsibly for Adult Education: A Guide to negotiating power and interests* San Francisco: Jossey-Bass

Cervero, R.M. & Wilson, A.L. (eds) 1996 *What Really Matters in Adult Education Program Planning: Lessons in negotiating power and interests* New Directions for Adult and Continuing Education no. 69, San Francisco: Jossey-Bass

Cervero, R.M., Wilson, A.L. & Associates 2001 *Power in Practice* San Francisco: Jossey-Bass

Chaiklin, S. & Lave, J. (eds) 1993 *Understanding Practice: Perspectives in activity and context* New York: Cambridge University Press

Chambers, R. 1997 *Whose Reality Counts? Putting the first last* London: Intermediate Technology Publications

Chase, W. & Simon, H. 1973 'Perception in chess' *Cognitive Psychology* 4, 55–81

Chen, S.E., Cowdroy, R., Kingsland, A. & Ostwald, M. (eds) 1995 *Reflections on Problem Based Learning* Sydney: Australian Problem-Based Learning Network

Chi, M.T.H., Glaser, R. & Farr, M.J. (eds) 1998 *The Nature of Expertise* Hillsdale, NJ: Lawrence Erlbaum

Clark, A. 1997 *Being There: Putting brain, body, and world together again* Cambridge, MA: MIT Press

Clayton, R. & Pontusson, J. 1998 'Welfare-state retrenchment revisited: Entitlement cuts, public sector restructuring and inegalitarian trends in advanced capitalist societies' *World Politics* 51, 67–98

Coffey, D. 1992 *Schools and Work: Developments in vocational education* London: Cassell

Cohen, M.D. & Bacdayan, P. 1994 'Organizational routines are stored as procedural memory—Evidence from a laboratory study' *Organization Science* 5(4), 554–68

Coleman, J.S. et al. 1966 *Equality of Educational Opportunity* Washington, DC: US Government Printing Office

Collins, M. 1991 *Adult Education as Vocation* London: Routledge

——1995 'Critical commentaries on the role of the adult educator: From self-directed learning to postmodernist sensibilities' in M. Welton (ed.) *In Defense of the Lifeworld: Critical perspectives on adult education* New York: State University of New York Press pp. 71–97

Collinson, D. 1994 'Strategies of Resistance: Power, knowledge and subjectivity in the workplace' in J.M. Jermier, D. Knights & W.R. Nord (eds) *Resistance and Power in Organizations* Routledge: London

Commission for a Nation of Lifelong Learners 1997 *A Nation Learning: Vision for the 21st century* Albany, NY: Regents College

Connell, R.W. & Irving, T.H. 1980 *Class Structure in Australian History: Documents, narrative and argument* Melbourne: Longman Cheshire

Cook, S.D.N. & Yanow, D. 1993 'Culture and organizational learning' *Journal of Management Inquiry* 2(4), 373–90

Cornford, I. 2002 'Generic Competencies: A review of some recent literature and analysis from a historical perspective' Working paper, Research Centre for Vocational Education and Training, University of Technology, Sydney (http://www.rcvet.uts.edu.au)

Cornford, I. & Athanasou, J. 1995 'Developing expertise through training' *Industrial and Commercial Training* 27(2), 10–18

Council for Adult and Experiential Learning 1999 *Serving Adult Learners in Higher Education* Chicago: Author

Courtenay, B.C., Merriam, S.B. & Reeves, P.M. 1998 'The centrality of meaning making in transformational learning: How HIV-positive adults make sense of their lives' *Adult Education Quarterly* 48(2), 65–84

Courtenay, B.C., Merriam, S.B., Reeves, P.M. & Baumgartner, L. 2000 'Perspective transformation over time: A 2-year follow-up study of NIV positive adults' *Adult Education Quarterly* 50(2), pp. 102–19

Courtney, S. 1992 *Why Adults Learn: Towards a theory of participation in adult education* London & New York: Routledge

Cowdroy, R. & Maitland, B. 1995 'Integration, assessment and problem-based learning' in S.E. Chen, R. Cowdroy, A. Kingsland & M. Ostwald (eds) *Reflections on Problem Based Learning* Sydney: Australian Problem-Based Learning Network pp. 175–87

Creswell, J.W. 1998 *Qualitative Inquiry and Research Design: Choosing among five traditions* Thousand Oaks, CA: Sage

Cropley, A.J. & Dave, R.H. 1978 *Lifelong Education and the Training of Teachers: Developing a curriculum for teacher education on the basis of the principles of lifelong education* Hamburg: UNESCO Institute for Education & Pergamon Press

Cross, K.P. 1982 *Adults as Learners* San Francisco: Jossey-Bass

Crossan, M.M. & Guatto, T. 1996 'Organizational learning research profile' *Journal of Organizational Change Management* 9(1), 107–12

Cross-Durrant, A. 1987 'John Dewey and lifelong education' in P. Jarvis, *Twentieth Century Thinkers in Adult Education* London: Croom Helm

Dale, R. & Robertson, S. 2002 'The varying effects of regional organizations as subjects of globalization of education' *Comparative Education Review* 46(1), 10–36

Damasio, A. 1996 *Descartes' Error: Emotion, reason, and the human brain* London: Macmillan

——2000 *The Feeling of What Happens: Body and emotion in the making of consciousness* London: Vintage

Damousi, J. 1994 *Women Come Rally: Socialism, communism and gender in Australia 1890–1950* Melbourne: Oxford University Press

Darkenwald, G.G. & Merriam, S.B. 1982 'Participation' in *Adult Education: Foundations of practice* New York: Harper & Row

Darrah, C.N. 1996 *Learning and Work: An exploration in industrial ethnography* New York: Garland Publishing

Davidson, A. 1969 *The Communist Party of Australia: A short history* Stanford, CA: Hoover Institution Press

Davidson, J. 1994 'The sources and limits of resistance in a privatized utility' in J. Jermier, D. Knights & W. Nord (eds) *Resistance and Power in Organizations* London: Routledge

Davis, B., Sumara, D.J. & Luce-Kapler, R. 2000 *Engaging Minds: Learning and teaching in a complex world* Mahwah, NJ: Erlbaum

de Goede, M.P.M. et al. 1997 *Youth: Unemployment, identity and policy* Brookfield, VT: Avebury

Delpit, L. 1988 'The silenced dialogue: Power and pedagogy in educating other people's children' *Harvard Educational Review* 58(3), 280–98

Department of Education, Science and Training (DEST) 2002a *Annual Report 2001–2002* Canberra: DEST (http://www.dest.gov.au/annualreport/2002/1.htm)

——2002b *Higher Education at the Crossroads: Ministerial discussion papers* Canberra: DEST

Deshler, D. & Grudens-Schuck, N. 2000 'The politics of knowledge construction' in A.L. Wilson & E.R. Hayes (eds) *Handbook of Adult and Continuing Education* San Francisco: Jossey-Bass pp. 592–611

Deshler, D. & Hagan, D. 1990 'Adult education research: Issues and directions' in S. Merriam & P. Cunningham (eds) *Handbook of Adult and Continuing Education* San Francisco: Jossey-Bass

Diouf, W., Sheckley, B. & Kehrhahn, M. 2000 'Adult learning in a non-western context: The influence of culture in a Senegalese farming village' *Adult Education Quarterly* 51(1), 32–45

Division for Lifelong Learning (DLL) 2001 *Developing the Learning Cape* Paper commissioned by the Western Cape Department of Economic Development, University of Western Cape, South Africa

Dominicé, P. 2000 *Learning From Our Lives: Using educational biographies with adults* San Francisco: Jossey-Bass/Wiley

Dorsey, E. 1997 'The Global Women's Movement: Articulating a new vision of global governance' in P. Diehl (ed.) *The Politics of Global Governance: International organizations in an interdependent world* Boulder, CO: Lynne Rienner

Dworkin, R. 1977 *Taking Rights Seriously* London: Duckworth

Dwyer, P. & Wyn, J. 2001 *Youth, Education and Risk: Facing the future* London & New York: Routledge/Falmer

Earsman, W.P. 1920 *The Proletariat and Education: The necessity for Labor Colleges* Melbourne: Andrades

Edelmann, G. 2001 *Universe of Consciousness* New York: Basic Books

Ehrenreich, B. 2002 *Nickel and Dimed: On (not) getting by in America* New York: Henry Holt

Eldridge, J.C. 1924 'Education and science in working-class ideology', *Social Science Series of Labor Publications, no. 1* Sydney: NSW Amalgamated Printing Trades Union

Engel, C. 1997 'Not just a method but a way of learning' in D. Boud & G. Feletti (eds) *The Challenge of Problem-Based Learning* London: Kogan Page pp. 17–27

Engeström, Y. 1995 *Training for Change* Geneva: ILO

Engeström, Y., Miettinen, R. & Punamaki, R.-L. (eds) 1999 *Perspectives on Activity Theory* Cambridge: Cambridge University Press

Entwistle, N. 1984 *Styles of Learning and Teaching* Chichester: Wiley

Esping-Andersen (ed.) 1996 *Welfare States in Transition: National adaptations in global economies* London: Sage

European Union (EU) 1995 *Teaching and Learning: Towards the learning society* Brussels: EU

European Union (EU) 2000 *A Memorandum on Lifelong Learning* Brussels: EU

Evans, K. & Rainbird, H. 2002 'The significance of workplace learning for a "learning society"' in K. Evans, P. Hodkinson & L. Unwin (eds) *Working to Learn: Transforming learning in the workplace* London: Kogan Page

Evans, T. & King, B. 1991 *Beyond the Text: Contemporary writing on distance education* Geelong: Deakin University Press

Evans, T. & Nation, D. (eds) 1989 *Critical Reflections on Distance Education* London: Falmer Press

Fanon, F. 1968 *The Wretched of the Earth* Harmondsworth: Penguin

Feletti, G. 1993 'Inquiry-based and problem-based learning: How similar are these approaches to nursing and medical education?' in G. Ryan (ed.) *Research and Development in Problem-Based Learning* Sydney: Australian Problem-Based Learning Network pp. 289–98

Field, J. 1998 'Globalization, social capital and lifelong learning: Connections for our times?' in A. Bron, J. Field & E. Kurantowicz (eds) *Adult Education and Democratic Citizenship II* Krakow: Impulse Publishers

——2001 'Lifelong education' *International Journal of Lifelong Education* 20(1&2), 3–15

——2002 'Building a European dimension: A realistic response to globalisation?' in J. Field (ed.) *Promoting European Dimensions in Lifelong Learning* Leicester: NIACE

Field, L. 1990 *Skilling Australia* Sydney: Longman Cheshire

——1995a *Managing Organizational Learning: From rhetoric to reality* Melbourne: Longman Australia

——1995b 'Organisational learning: Basic concepts' in G. Foley (ed.) *Understanding Adult Education and Training* (1st edn) Sydney: Allen & Unwin pp. 151–64

——1997 'Impediments to empowerment and learning in organisations' *The Learning Organisation* 4(4), 149–58

——1998a 'The challenge of empowered learning' *Asia Pacific Journal of Human Resources* 36(1), 72–85

——1998b 'Shifting the focus from "training" to "learning": The case of Australian small business' *Australian and New Zealand Journal of Vocational Education Research* 6(1)

Fineman, S. 1993 'Organizations as emotional arenas' in S. Fineman (ed.) *Emotion in Organizations* London: Sage pp. 9–35

Foley, G. 1991a 'Terania Creek: Learning in a Green Campaign' *Australian Journal of Adult and Community Education* 31(3), 160–76

——1991b 'Radical adult education' in M. Tennant (ed.) *Adult and Continuing Education in Australia: Issues and Practices* London: Routledge

——1992 'Self-directed learning in vocational adult education' in A. Gonczi (ed.) *Teaching and Learning for the Productive Society* Adelaide: TAFE National Centre for Research and Development

——1993a 'The neighbourhood house: Site of struggle, site of learning' *British Journal of Sociology of Education* 14(1), 21–37

——1993b 'Political education in the Chinese liberation struggle' *International Journal of Lifelong Education* 13(1), 323–42

——1993c 'Progressive but not socialist: Political education in the Zimbabwe liberation struggle' *Convergence* 23(4), 79–88

——1994 'Adult education and capitalist reorganisation' *Studies in the Education of Adults* 26(2), 121–43

——1995 (ed.) *Understanding Adult Education and Training* (1st edn) Sydney: Allen & Unwin

——1997 *Best Practice in HIV-AIDS Adult Education Project: Discussion Paper* Sydney: Australian Federation of AIDS Organisations

——1999 *Learning in Social Action: A contribution to understanding informal learning* London: Zed

——2000 (ed.) *Understanding Adult Education and Training* (2nd edn) Sydney: Allen & Unwin

——2001 *Strategic Learning: Understanding and facilitating organisational change* Sydney: Centre for Popular Education, University of Technology, Sydney

Foley, G. & Flowers, R. 1991 *Strategies for Self-Determination: Aboriginal Adult education, training and community development in NSW* Sydney: Faculty of Education, University of Technology, Sydney

Foley, G. & Morris, R. 1995 'The history and political economy of Australian adult education' in G. Foley (ed.) *Understanding Adult Education and Training* Sydney: Allen & Unwin

Fonow, M. & Cook, J. 1991 *Beyond Methodology: Feminist scholarship and lived research* Bloomington, IN: Indiana University Press

Ford, G.W. 1991 'Integrating technology, work organization and skill formation: Lessons from the manufacturing ports' in M. Costa & M. Easson (eds) *Australian Industry: What policy?* Sydney: Pluto Press

Forester, J. 1989 *Planning in the Face of Power* Berkeley: University of California Press

——1993 *Critical Theory, Public Policy, and Planning Practice* Albany: State University of New York Press

Forrest, A.S., Walsh, L.J., Isaacs, G. & Williams, L. 1997 'PBL as a tool for integration of basic sciences into the dental curriculum' in J. Conway, R. Fisher, L. Sheridan-Burns & G. Ryan (eds), *Research in Development in Problem-Based Learning: Integrity, innovation, integration* Newcastle: Australian Problem-Based Learning Network pp. 149–56

Forrester, K. & Payne, J. (1999) 'A Sort of Metamorphosis: The role of trade unions in widening participation in lifelong learning' *Widening Participation & Lifelong Learning* 1(2), 24–32

Foucault, M. 1979 *Discipline and Punish: The birth of the prison* New York: Vintage Books

Freire, P. 1972 *Pedagogy of the Oppressed* New York: Herder & Herder

Freudenberg, N. 1990 'AIDS prevention in the United States: Lessons from the first decade' *International Journal of Health Services* 20(4), 589–99

Friesen, G. & Taksa, L. 1996 'Workers' education in Australia and Canada: A comparative approach to labour's cultural history' in G.S. Kealey & G. Patmore (eds) *Australia and Canada: Labour compared* Special Joint Issue of *Labour/Le Travail* 38 and *Labour History* 71

Gabriel, Y. 1999 *Organizations in Depth* London: Sage Publications

Galloway, V. 1999 'Building a pedagogy of hope: The experience of the adult learning project' in J. Crowther, I. Martin & M. Shaw (eds) *Popular Education and Social Movements in Scotland Today* Leicester: NIACE

Gardner, H. 1993 *Multiple Intelligences: The theory in practice* New York: Basic Books

Garrett, G. 1998 'Global markets and national policies: Collision course or virtuous circle?' *International Organisation* 52(4), 791–823

Garrick, J. 1999 'The dominant discourses of learning at work' in D. Boud & J. Garrick (eds) *Understanding Learning in Work* London: Routledge pp. 216–31

Garrick, J. & Rhodes, C. (eds) 2000 *Research and Knowledge at Work* London & New York: Routledge

Garrison, D.R. 1989 *Understanding Distance Education* London: Routledge

Garvin, D.A. 1993 'Building a learning organization' *Harvard Business Review* July–August, 78–91

——1991 'Gender and skill' in D.W. Livingstone (ed.) *Critical Pedagogy and Cultural Power* Boston: Bergen & Harvey

Gee, J.P. 1992 *The Social Mind: Language, ideology and social practice* New York: Bergin & Garvey

Gee, J.P., Hull, G. & Lankshear, C. 1996 *The New Work Order: Behind the language of the new capitalism* Sydney: Allen & Unwin

Gelade, S., Harris, R. & Mason, D. 2001 *Accounting for Change: Adult and community education organisations and the GST* Canberra: Adult Learning Australia

Gelpi, E. 1985 'Lifelong education and international relations' in K. Wain (ed.) *Lifelong Education and Participation* Papers Presented at the Conference on Lifelong Education Initiatives in Mediterranean Countries 5-7 Nov. 1984, Malta: University of Malta Press

Gergen, K. 2001 *Social Construction in Context* London: Sage

Gibbons, M., Limoges, C. & Nowotny, H. 1994 *The New Production of Knowledge: The dynamics of science and research in contemporary society* London: Sage

Gibbs, G. 1996 *Improving Student Learning* Oxford: Oxford Centre for Staff Development

Giddens, A. 1979 *Central Problems in Social Theory: Action, structure and contradiction in social analysis* Berkeley: University of California Press

——2000 *The Third Way and its Critics* Cambridge: Polity Press

Gold, J., Watson, S. & Rix, M. 2000 'Learning for change by telling stories' in J. McGoldrick, J. Stewart & S. Watson (eds) *Understanding Human Resource Development: A resource based approach* London: Routledge

Goldberg, E. 2001 *The Executive Brain* Oxford: Oxford University Press

Goleman, D. 1998 *Working with Emotional Intelligence* New York: Bantam

Gonczi, A., Hager, P. & Oliver, E. 1990 *Establishing Competency Based Standards in the Professions* Canberra: Australian Government Publishing Service

Gore, J. 1992 'What we can do for you! What can "we" do for "you"? Struggling over empowerment in critical and feminist pedagogy' in C. Luke & J. Gore (eds) *Feminisms and Critical Pedagogy* New York: Routledge

Grace, A.P. 1996 'Striking a critical pose: Andragogy—missing links, missing values' *International Journal of Lifelong Education* 15(3), 382-92

Gramsci, A. 1976 *Selections from the Prison Notebooks* London: Lawrence & Wishart

Green, A. 1990 *Education and State Formation: The rise of educational systems in England, France and the USA* London: Macmillan

——1997 *Education, Globalisation and the Nation State* London: Macmillan

Greenfield, S. (ed.) 1996 *The Human Mind Explained: The control centre of the living machine* London: Cassell

Greeno, J. 1997 'On claims that answer the wrong question' *Educational Researcher* 27(1), 5–17

Greenwood, D.J. & Levin, J. 1998 *Introduction to Action Research: Research for social change* Thousand Oaks, CA: Sage

Griffin, C. 1987 *Adult Education as Social Policy* London: Croom Helm

Griffith, A. 1988 'Skilling for life/living for skill: The social construction of life skills in Ontario schools' *Journal of Educational Thought* 22, 198–208

Gross, L. 1948 'An experiential study of the validity of the non-directive method of teaching' *Journal of Psychology* 26, 243–8

Grudens-Schuck, N. 2000 'Conflict and engagement: An empirical study of a farmer-extension partnership in a sustainable agriculture program' *Journal of Agricultural and Environmental Ethics* 13(1), 79–100

——2001 'Stakeholder effect: A qualitative study of the influence of farm leaders' ideas on a sustainable agriculture education program' *Journal of Agricultural Education* 42(4), 1–11

——2003 *The Mainstream Environmentalist: Learning through participatory education* Westport, CT: Greenwood Publishing Group

Grudens-Schuck, N., Allen, W., Hargrove, T.A. & Kilvington, M. 2003 'Renovation of dependency and self-reliance for participatory sustainable development' *Journal of Agriculture and Human Values* 20(1), 53–64

Grundy, S. 1987 *Curriculum: Product or praxis?* London: Falmer

Gumperz, J.J. 1982 *Language and Social Identity* Cambridge: Cambridge University Press

Gwyn, J. 1998 *Excessive Expectations: Maritime commerce and the economic development of Nova Scotia, 1740–1870* Montreal & Kingston: McGill/Queen's University Press

Habermas, J. 1987 *Knowledge and Human Interests* Cambridge: Polity Press (originally published 1968)

Hager, P. 2001 'Towards a productive conception of learning' *Research in Adult and Vocational Learning Seminar Series* Sydney: Faculty of Education, University of Technology, Sydney (http://www.ravl.uts.edu.au)

Hager, P., Moy, J. & Gonczi, A. 1997 *Key Competencies Pilots in VET* Canberra: UTS/DEETYA

Haig-Brown, C. 1995 *Taking control: Power and contradiction in first nations adult education* Vancouver, Canada: UBC Press

Hall, B. & Kassam, Y. 1998 'Participatory research' in T. Husen & T.N. Postlethwaite (eds) *International Encyclopedia of Education* Oxford: Pergamon

Halpin, D. & Troyna, B. (eds) 1995 *Researching Educational Policy* London: Falmer

Hammersley, M. & Atkinson, P. 1995 *Ethnography: Principles into practice* (2nd edn) London: Routledge

Hardy, F. 1968 *The Unlucky Australians* Melbourne: Thomas Nelson

Harrison, T. & Stephen, T. (eds) 1996 *Computer Networking and Scholarly Communication in the Twenty-First-Century University* New York: SUNY

Head, D. 1977 'Education at the Bottom' *Studies in Adult Education* 9(2), 127–52

——1978 *There's No Politics Here* London: The City Lit

Henry, J. 2001 *Work-Based Learning and the VET Sector of Australia: A literature review* (URL: http://www.reframingthefuture.net/resources/Literature%20Review.pdf)

Henry, M. et al. 2001 *The OECD, Globalisation and Education Policy* Amsterdam & New York: IAU Press/Pergamon

Heron, J. 1989 *The Facilitator's Handbook* London: Kogan Page

——1993 *Group Facilitation* London: Kogan Page

——1996 *Co-Operative Inquiry: Research into the Human Condition* Thousand Oaks, CA: Sage Publications

Highlander 2001 *Welcome to Highlander Home Page* (web page) Highlander Research and Education Center (Available: http://www.highlander-center.org/ 05-01-2003)

Hill, P. 2000 'Distance education: strategies for maintaining relationships' *Pacific Health Dialog* 7(2), 71–3

Hill, P. & Samisoni, J. 1993 'Two models of primary health care training' *Medical Education* 27, 69–73

Hirschhorn, L. 1990 *The workplace within: Psychodynamics of organisational life* Cambridge, Mass: MIT Press

Hodgetts, R.M., Luthans, F. & Lee, S.M. 1994 'New paradigm organizations: From total quality to learning to world class' *Organizational Dynamics* 22(3), 5–19

Hodkinson, P. & Sparkes, A.C. 1995 'Markets and vouchers: The inadequacy of individualist policies for vocational education and training in England and Wales' *Journal of Educational Policy* 10(2), 189–207

Hodkinson, P., Sparkes, A.C. & Hodkinson, H. 1996 *Triumphs and Tears: Young people, markets and the transition from school to work* London: David Fulton

Hofmaier, B. 1999 'Regional development and learning: Case studies in South Sweden' in B. Nyhan, G. Attwell & L. Deitmer (eds) *Towards a Learning Region: Education and regional innovation in the EU and USA* Brussels: CEDEFOP-European Centre for Development of Vocational Training

Honneth, A. 1999 'The social dynamics of disrespect: Situating critical theory today' in P. Drews (ed.) *Habermas: A critical reader* Oxford: Blackwell pp. 320–37

hooks, b. 1994 *Teaching to Transgress* New York: Routledge

Hope, A. & Timmel, S. 1984 *Training for Transformation* London: Intermediate Technology Publishers

Horin, A. 2000 'A survival guide for mid-life malcontents' *Sydney Morning Herald* 19 Feb., 49

Horsman J. 1999 *Too Scared to Learn: Women, violence and education* Toronto: McGilligan Books

Horton, M. & Freire, P. 1990 *We Make the Road by Walking* Philadelphia, PA: Temple University Press

Horton, M., Kohl, J. & Kohl, H. 1990 *The Long Haul* New York: Doubleday

Houle, C.O. 1996 *The Design of Education* (2nd edn) San Francisco: Jossey-Bass

Howell, S.L., Carter, V. K. & Scheid, F.M. 2002 'Gender and women's experiences at work: A critical and feminist perspective on human resource development' *Adult Education Quarterly* 52(2), 112-27

Huber, G. 1991 'Organizational learning: The contributing processes and the literatures' *Organizational Science* 2(1), 88-15

Hughes, R. 1987 *The Fatal Shore: A history of the transportation of convicts to Australia, 1787-1868* London: Collins Harvill

Inkpen, A. & Crossan, M.M. 1995 'Believing is seeing: Joint ventures and organizational learning' *Journal of Management Studies* 32, 291-308

Jackson, N. (ed.) 1991 *Skills Formation and Gender Relations: The politics of who knows what* Geelong: Deakin University Press

——1993 'Reforming vocational learning? Contradictions of competence' in B. Hall (ed.) *What Future for Technical and Vocational Education and Training?* Adelaide: NCVER pp. 105-22

Jarvis, P. 1992 *Paradoxes of Learning: On becoming an individual in society* San Francisco: Jossey-Bass

——1993 *Adult Education and the State: Towards a politics of adult education* London: Routledge

Jarvis, P. (ed.) 2002 *The Theory and Practice of Teaching* London: Kogan Page

Jermier, J.M., Knights, D. & Nord, W.R. (eds) 1994 *Resistance and Power in Organizations* London: Routledge

Johnson, A. 1988 *Bread and Roses: A personal history of three militant women and their friends 1902-1988* Sydney: Left Book Club

Johnson, R. 1979 ' "Really useful knowledge": Radical education and working class culture' in J. Clarke, C. Critcher & R. Johnson (eds) *Working Class Culture: Studies in history and theory* London: Hutchinson

——1988 '"Really Useful Knowledge" 1790-1850: Memories for education in the 1980s' in T. Lovett (ed.) *Radical Approaches to Adult Education: A reader* London: Routledge

Kane, L. 2001 *Popular Education and Social Change in Latin America* London: Latin American Bureau

Keating, J., Medrich, E., Volkoff, V. & Perry, J. 2002 *Comparative Study of Vocational Education and Training Systems: National vocational education and training systems across three regions under pressure of change* Adelaide: NCVER

Keck, M. & Sikkin, K. 1998 *Activists Beyond Borders: Advocacy networks in international politics* Ithaca, NY: Cornell University Press

Keddie, N. 1971 'Classroom knowledge' in M. Young (ed.) *Knowledge and Control* London: Collier Macmillan

Keegan, D.J. 1980 'On defining distance education' *Distance Education* 1(1), 13–36

Kennedy, H. 1995 *Return to Learn: Unison's fresh approach to trade union education* London: Unison

Kerka, S. 1997 *Constructivism, Workplace Learning and Vocational Education* Columbus, OH: ERIC (ED407573)

Kerlinger, F. 1994 *Foundations of Behavioural Research* (4th edn) New York: Rinehart & Winston

Kilgour, D. 2001 'Critical and postmodern perspectives on adult learning' *New Directions for Adult and Continuing Education* 89 Spring, 53–61

Kimberley, H. 1987 *The Outcomes Report* Melbourne: TAFE Board of Victoria

Kincheloe, J. 1996 *Toil and Trouble: Good work, smart workers and the integration of academic and vocational education* New York: Peter Lang

——1999 *How Do We Tell the Workers? The socioeconomic foundations of work and vocational education* Boulder: Westview Press

Kirkwood, G. & Kirkwood, C. 1989 *Living Adult Education: Freire in Scotland* Buckingham: Open University Press

Kliebard, H.M. 1999 *Schooled to Work: Vocationalism and the American curriculum, 1876–1946* New York: Teachers College Press, Columbia University

Knowles, M.S. 1970 *The Modern Practice of Adult Education: Andragogy versus pedagogy* New York: Association Press

——1980 *The Modern Practice of Adult Education: From pedagogy to andragogy* (rev. edn) Chicago: Association Press/Follet Publishing

Knowles, M.S. & Associates 1984 *Andragogy in Action* San Francisco: Jossey-Bass

Kolb, D. 1984 *Experiential Learning: Experience as the source of learning and development* Englewood Cliffs, NJ: Prentice-Hall

Kovel, J. 1987 *A Complete Guide to Therapy* Harmondsworth: Penguin

Kuhn, T.S. 1970 *The Structure of Scientific Revolutions* (2nd edn) Chicago: University of Chicago Press

Kumar, A. (ed.) 1997 *Class Issues: Pedagogy, cultural studies, and the public sphere* New York: New York University Press

Laing, R.D. 1969 *The Divided Self: An existential study in sanity and madness* Harmondsworth, UK: Penguin

Lakes, R. (ed.) 1994 *Critical Education for Work: Multidisciplinary approaches* Norwood, NJ: Ablex Publishing

Lankshear, C. 1987 *Literacy, Schooling and Revolution* New York: The Falmer Press

Lather, P. 1991 *Getting Smart: Feminist Research and Pedagogy With/in the Postmodern* New York: Routledge

Lather, P.A. & Smithies, C. 1997 *Troubling the Angels: Women living with HIV-AIDS* Boulder, CO: Westview Press

Latour, B. 1993 *We Have Never Been Modern* trans. Porter C. Hemel Hempstead: Harvester Wheatsheaf

Lave, J. & Wenger, E. 1991 *Situated Learning: Legitimate peripheral participation* New York: Cambridge Press

Law, J. & Hassard, J. 1999 *Actor Network Theory and After* Oxford: Blackwell

Leach, L. 2000 *Self-Directed Learning: Theory and practice* Unpublished thesis, University of Technology, Sydney

LeCompte, M.D., Millroy, W.L. & Preissle, J. (eds) 1992 *The Handbook of Qualitative Research in Education* San Diego, CA: Academic Press

Levett, A. 2000 'Changes in work and social life at the dawn of the twenty-first century' in R. Gerber & C. Lankshear (eds) *Training for a Smart Workforce* London & New York: Routledge pp. 13–43

Levin, J.S. 2001 *Globalizing the Community College: Strategies for change in the twenty-first century* New York: Palgrave

Lincoln, Y. & Guba, E.G. 1985 *Naturalistic Inquiry* Beverly Hills, Ca.: Sage

Lindeman, E.C. 1947 'Methods of democratic adult education' in S. Brookfield (ed.) *Learning Democracy: Eduard Lindeman on adult education and social change* London: Croom Helm

——1961 *The Meaning of Adult Education* Oklahoma Research Center for Continuing Professional and Higher Education, New York: New Republic

Ling, P. 1986 'The educability of the ordinary man: Eastern Australia 1880-1914' in *Melbourne Studies in Education* Melbourne: Melbourne University Press pp. 62–92

Lipgar, R.M., Bair, J.P. & Fichtner, C.G. 2000 'Integrating research with conference learning: Ten years of Q methodology studies exploring experiential learning in the Tavistock tradition' *Operant Subjectivity* 24(1), 1–24

Lipsmeier, A. & Schroeder, H. 1994 'History of vocational training' in T. Husen & T.N. Postlethwaite (eds) *The International Encyclopaedia of Education* (2nd edn) Oxford: Pergamon

Lockwood, F. & Gooley A. (eds) 2001 *Innovation in Open and Distance Learning: Successful development of online and web-based learning* London: Kogan Page

Long, H.B. 1983 'Reasons, motives and barriers in participation' and 'Models of adult participation' in *Adult Learning: Research and practice* New York: Cambridge University Press

Longworth, N. 1999 *Making Lifelong Learning Work: Learning cities for a learning century* London: Kogan Page

Lovett, T. 1975 *Adult Education: Community development and the working class* London: Ward Lock Educational

Lovett, T. (ed.) 1988 *Radical Approaches to Adult Education* London: Routledge

Luke, M. 1995 'Text as discourse in education: An introduction to critical discourse analysis' in M. Apple (ed.) *Review of Research in Education* 21, 3–48

Lundgren, U.P. 1981 *Model Analysis on Pedagogical Processes* (2nd edn) Lund: CWK/Gleerup

Macintyre, S. 1980 *A Proletarian Science: Marxism in Britain 1917-1933* New York: Cambridge University Press

Macken, J. 1997 *Australia's Unions: A death or a difficult birth?* Sydney: Federation Press

MacLeod, D. 2002 'Back to home base' *Guardian Education* 17 Dec. p. 9

Magno, C. 2002 'Minding the political gap: The educational imperative of NGOs' *Current Issues in Comparative Education* 4(1) (http://www.tcrecord.org)

Maher, F. & Tetreault, M. 1994 *The Feminist Classroom* New York: Basic Books

Mainsbridge, A. 1920 *An Adventure in Working Class Education* London:

Mansfield, B. & Mitchell, L. 1996 *Towards a Competent Workforce* Hampshire, England: Aldershot

Margetson, D. 1997 'Why is problem-based learning a challenge?' in D. Boud & G. Feletti *The Challenge of Problem-Based Learning* London: Kogan Page pp. 36–44

Marginson, S. 1993 *Education and Public Policy in Australia* Cambridge: Cambridge University Press

——1997 *Markets in education* Sydney: Allen & Unwin

Margolis, E. (ed.) 2001 *The Hidden Curriculum in Higher Education* New York: Routledge

Marr, D. & Wilkinson, M. 2003 *Dark Victory* Sydney: Allen & Unwin

Marshall, J. 1997 'Globalisation from below: The trade union connections' in S. Walters (ed.) *Globalization, Adult Education and Training. Impact and Issues* London: Zed Books

Marshment, M. 1997 'The picture is political: Representation of women in contemporary popular culture' in V. Robinson & D. Richardson (eds) *Intro-*

ducing Women's Studies: Feminist theory and practice (2nd edn) London: Macmillan

Marsick, V. & Watkins, K. 1991 *Informal and Incidental Learning in the Workplace* London: Routledge

——1994 'The learning organization: An integrative vision for human resource development' *Human Resource Development Quarterly* 5(4), 353–60

Martin, I. 2001 'Reconstituting the agora: Towards an alternative politics of lifelong learning' *Concept* 2(1), 4–8

Marton, F., Hounsell, D. & Entwistle, N. (eds) 1984 *The Experience of Learning* Edinburgh: Scottish University Press

Maturana, H. & Varela, F. 1987 *The Tree Of Knowledge: The biological roots of human understanding* Boston: Shambhala

Mayer, R.E. 1981 *The Promise of Cognitive Psychology* San Francisco: Freeman

Mayo, E. 1919 *WEA Series 1—Democracy and Freedom: An essay in social logic* Melbourne: Macmillan

Mayo, P. 1998 *Gramsci, Freire and Adult Education: Possibilities for transformative action* London: Zed Books

Mazey, S. & Richardson, J. 2001 'Interest groups and EU policy-making: Organisational logic and venue shopping' in J. Richardson (ed.) *European Union Power and Policy Making* (2nd edn) London: Routledge

McBride, S. & Williams, R. 2001 'Globalization, the restructuring of labour markets and policy convergence: The OECD "Jobs Strategy"' *Global Social Policy* 1(3)

McConnell, D. 1994 *Implementing Computer Supported Cooperative Learning* London: Kogan Page

MCEETYA (Ministerial Council on Education, Employment, Training and Youth Affairs) 2002 *Declaration on Adult Community Education* Melbourne: Department of Education and Training

McGivney, V. 1990 *Education's for Other People: Access to education for non-participant adults* Leicester: NIACE & Hillcroft College

McGivney, V. & Murray, F. 1991 *Adult Education Development: Methods and approaches from changing societies* Leicester: NIACE

McIntyre, J. 1993 'Research paradigms and adult education' *Studies in Continuing Education* 15(2), 80–97

McIntyre, J. & Wickert, R. 2000 'The negotiated management of meanings: Research for policy' in J. Garrick & C. Rhodes, J. (eds) *Research and Knowledge at Work* pp. 158–77

McIntyre, J., Brown, A. & Ferrier, F. 1996 *The Economics of ACE Delivery* Sydney: NSW Board of Adult & Community Education

McIntyre, J., Foley, G., Morris, R. & Tennant, M. 1995 *ACE Works: The vocational outcomes of ACE courses in NSW* Sydney: Board of Adult and Community Education

313

McLaren, P. 1988 'Foreword: Critical theory and the meaning of hope' in H. Giroux (ed.) *Teachers as Intellectuals: Toward a critical pedagogy of learning* New York: Bergin & Garvey

McQueen, H. 1997 *Suspect History: Manning Clark and the future of Australia's past* Adelaide: Wakefield Press

McTaggart, R. 1991 'Action research for Aboriginal pedagogy: Beyond "both-ways" education?' in O. Zuber-Skerritt (ed.) *Action Research for Change and Development* London: Gower pp. 157–78

McTaggart, R. & Kemmis, S. 1982 *The Action Research Planner* Geelong: Deakin University Press

McWilliam, E. 1997 'Beyond the missionary position: Teacher desire and radical pedagogy' in S. Todd (ed.) *Learning Desire: Perspectives on pedagogy, culture and the unsaid* New York: Routledge pp. 217–36

Melohn, T. 1994 *The New Partnership* Essex Junction, VT: Omneo

Melucci, A. 1988 'Getting involved: Identity and mobilization in social movements' *International Social Movement Research* 1, 329–48

——1989 *Nomads of the Present: Social movements and individual needs in contemporary society* London: Century Hutchinson

Menzies Lyth, I.E. 1988 *Containing Anxiety in Institutions* London: Free Association Books

Merlyn, T. 2001 'The longest war: The two traditions of adult education' *Australian Journal of Adult Learning* 41(3), 297–313

Merriam, S. 1991 'How research produces knowledge' in J. Peters & P. Jarvis (eds) *Adult Education: Evolution, achievements in a developing field of study* San Francisco: Jossey-Bass

——1998 *Qualitative Research and Case Study Applications in Education* San Francisco: Jossey-Bass

Merriam, S. & Simpson, E. 1989 *A Guide to Research for Educators of Adults and Trainers* Malabar, FL: Krieger

Mezirow, J. 1981 'A critical theory of adult learning and education' *Adult Education* 32(1), 3–27

——1991 *Transformative Dimensions of Adult Learning* San Francisco: Jossey-Bass

——1992 'Understanding transformation theory' *Adult Education Quarterly* 44(4), 222–32

Mezirow, J. & Associates 1990 *Fostering Critical Reflection in Adulthood. A guide to transformative and emancipatory learning* San Francisco: Jossey-Bass

——2000 *Learning as Transformation: Critical perspectives on a theory in practice* San Francisco: Jossey-Bass

Milkman, R. 1998 'The new American workplace: High road or low road?' in P. Thompson & C. Warhurst (eds) *Workplaces of the Future* London: Macmillan

Mills, D. & Friesen, B. 1992 'The learning organization' *European Management Journal* 10(2), 146–56

Moyers, B. 1981 *Adventures of a Radical Hillbilly* (video) New York: WNET

Murphy, M. 1997 'Capital, class and adult education: The international political economy of lifelong learning in the European Union' in P. Armstrong, N. Miller & M. Zukas (eds) *Crossing Borders, Breaking Boundaries: Research in the education of adults* Proceedings of the 27th Annual SCUTREA Conference, London: Birkbeck College, University of London

Nadler, L. & Nadler, Z. 1994 *Designing Training Programs: The critical events model* (2nd edn) Houston, TX: Gulf Publishing

Nesbit, T. 1998 'Teaching in adult education: Opening the black box' *Adult Education Quarterly* 48(3), 157–70

Newman, M. 1979 *The Poor Cousin* London: Allen & Unwin

——1993 *The Third Contract: Theory and practice in trade union training* Sydney: Stewart Victor

——1994 *Defining the Enemy: Adult education in social action* Sydney: Stewart Victor

——1999 *Maeler's Regard: Images of adult learning* Sydney: Stewart Victor

——2000 'Program development' in G. Foley (ed.) *Understanding Adult Education and Training* Sydney: Allen & Unwin

Nicolini, D. & Mezner, M.B. 1995 'The social construction of organizational learning: Conceptual and practical issues in the field' *Human Relations* 48(7), 727–46

Nieto, S. 1992 *Affirming Diversity: The sociopolitical context of multicultural education* New York: Longman

——2002 *Language, Culture and Teaching: Critical perspectives for a new century* Mahwah, NJ: Lawrence Erlbaum

Noble, D. 2001 *Digital Diploma Mills: The automation of higher education* New York: Monthly Review Press

Noffke, S.E. & Stevenson, R.B. (eds) 1995 *Educational Action Research: Becoming practically critical* New York: Teachers College Press

Nonaka, I. 1994 'A dynamic theory of knowledge creation' *Organisational Science* 5 (1) 14–37

Nonaka, I. & Takeuchi, H. 1995 *The Knowledge-Creating Company* Oxford: Oxford University Press

NOU (Norges Offentliga Utredningar) *Ny kompetens* (New Competence) Oslo: Government of Norway, 1997:25

Norris, N. 1991 'The trouble with competence' *Cambridge Journal of Education* 21(3), 331–41

Novak, J.D. & Gowin, D.B. 1984 *Learning How to Learn* New York: Cambridge University Press

Nussbaum, M. 1990 'Aristotelian social democracy' in R.B. Douglass, G.M. Mara & H.S. Richardsson (eds) *Liberalism and the Good* New York: Routledge

NZCTU (New Zealand Council of Trade Unions) 2000 *Advancing Union Education* (Poster) Wellington: NZCTU

O'Donaghue, J., Singh, G. & Dorward, L. 2002 'Virtual education in universities: A technological imperative' *British Journal of Educational Technology* 32(5), 511–23

OECD (Organisation for Economic Cooperation and Development) 1989 *Education and the Economy in a Changing Society* Paris: OECD

——1999 *International Adult Literacy Survey (IALS)* Paris: OECD

——2000a *Management of Knowledge in the New Learning Society* Paris: OECD

——2000b *Literacy in the Information Age* Paris: OECD

——2001 *Thematic Survey of Adult Learning* Paris: OECD

Olneck, M. 1989 'Americanization and the education of immigrants, 1900–1925: An analysis of symbolic action' *American Journal of Education* August, 398–423

Ontario Premier's Council on Economic Renewal 1994 *Lifelong Learning and the New Economy* Toronto: OPCER

Ottoson, J.M. 1997 'After the applause: Exploring multiple influences on application following an adult education program' *Adult Education Quarterly* 47(2), 92–107

Palmer, P. 1998 *The Courage to Teach: Exploring the inner landscape of a teacher's life* San Francisco: Jossey-Bass

Parnell, B. 1996a *What Do They Want Us to Do Now? The use of health communication campaigns and social marketing in the response to HIV epidemic amongst homosexually active men in Australia* Sydney: Australian Federation of AIDS Organisations

——1996b *'No, we don't use condoms'. What educational processes may now help us avoid further HIV transmission amongst men in gay communities in Australia?* Draft paper. Sydney: Australian Federation of AIDS Organisations

Paterson, D. 1999 & December 2001 *Brief Biography of Augusto Boal* (Web page) *Pedagogy and Theatre of the Oppressed* (Available: http://www.unomaha.edu/~pto/January 2003)

Patmore, G. 1985 *A History of Industrial Relations in the NSW Railways, 1855-1929* Unpublished PhD thesis, University of Sydney

Perry, W. 1970 *Forms of Intellectual and Ethical Development in the College Years* New York: Holt, Rinehart & Winston

Peters, M. & Marshall, J. 1996 *Individualism and Community: Education and social policy in the postmodern condition* London: Falmer Press

Piaget, J. 1966 *The Psychology of Intelligence* Totowa, NJ: Littlefield, Adams

Pihama, L., Cram, F. & Walker, S. 2000 *Kaupapa Maori Priniciples and Practices: A literature review—Research Report to Te Puni Kokiri, Wellington* Auckland: IRI Maori Research Development, University of Auckland

Pinker, S. 2002 *The Blank Slate: The modern denial of human nature* New York: Viking

Police Reports on political meetings held in Sydney Domain 1918–1921, State Records of NSW, 7/5589, 7/5594

Piore, M. & Sabel, C. 1984 *The Second Industrial Divide*, New York: Basic Books

Povinelli, Elizabeth A. 2002 *The Cunning of Recognition: Indigenous Alterities and the Making of Australian Multiculturalism* Durham, NC: Duke University Press

Powles, M. & Anderson, D. 1996 'Participation and access in TAFE: Economic utility or social service?' *Australian and New Zealand Journal of Vocational Education Research* 4(1), 97–129

Pratt, D. 1981 'Teacher effectiveness—Future directions for adult education' *Studies in Adult Education* 13(2), 112–19

Pratt, D. & Associates 1998 *Five Perspectives on Teaching in Adult and Higher Education* Malabar, FL: Krieger

Pratt, D.D. & Nesbit, T. (2000) 'Discourses and cultures of teaching' in A.L. Wilson & E.R. Hayes (eds) *Handbook of Adult and Continuing Education* pp. 117–31

Prawat, R.S. 1996 'Constructivisms modern and postmodern' *Educational Psychologist* 31(3/4), 215–25

Print, M. 1993 *Curriculum Development and Design* Sydney: Allen & Unwin

Provincial Administration of the Western Cape (PAWC) March 2001 *Preparing the Western Cape for the Knowledge Economy of the 21st Century* White Paper, Cape Town: Department of Economic Affairs, Agriculture and Tourism, Provincial Administration of the Western Cape

Pusey, M. 1991 *Economic Rationalism in Canberra: A nation building state changes its mind* New York: Cambridge University Press

Reason, P. (ed.) 1994 *Participation in Human Inquiry: Research with people* Thousand Oaks, CA: Sage

Reason, P. & Rowan, J. (eds) 1981 *Human Inquiry: A sourcebook of new paradigm research* Chichester: Wiley

Regini, M. 2000 'Between deregulation and social pacts: The responses of European economies to globalization' *Politics and Society* 28(1)

Regnier, R. 1991 'Nuclear advocacy and adult education: A case for counter-hegemonic struggle' *Canadian Journal for the Study of Adult Education* 5(2)

Reich, R. 1991 *The Work of Nations: A blueprint for the future* New York: Vintage

Reimer, A. 2003 'Raise the red flag, comrade', *Sydney Morning Herald Spectrum* 11–12/1, 10

Resnick, L. 1987 'Learning in school and out' *Educational Researcher* 16(9), 13–20

Richardson, J. 2001 'Policy-making in the EU: Interests, ideas and garbage cans of primeval soup' in J. Richardson (ed.) *European Union: Power and policy making* (2nd edn) London: Routledge

Rieger, E. & Liebfried, S. 1998 'Welfare state limits to globalization' *Politics and Society* 26(3)

Rist, R. 1970 'Student social class and teacher expectations' *Harvard Educational Review* 40(3), 411–51

Robinson, V. 1997 'Introducing women's studies' in V. Robinson & D. Richardson (eds) *Introducing Women's Studies: Feminist theory and practice* (2nd edn) London: Macmillan

Robinson, V.M. 1993 *Problem-Based Methodology* Oxford: Pergamon Press

Rogers, A. 1992 *Adults Learning for Development* London: Cassell

Rogers, C. 1969 *Freedom to Learn: A view of what education might become* Westerville, OH: Merrill

Rogoff, B. 1990 *Apprenticeship in Thinking: Cognitive development in social context* New York: Oxford University Press

Ross, B. 1997 'Towards a framework for problem-based curricula' in D. Boud & G. Feletti (eds) *The Challenge of Problem-Based Learning* London: Kogan Page pp. 28–35

Rothstein, B. 1998 *Just Institutions Matter: The moral and political logic of the welfare state* Cambridge: Cambridge University Press

Rowan, J. 1976 *Ordinary Ecstasy: Humanistic psychology in action* London: Routledge & Kegan Paul

Rowse, T. 1978 *Australian Liberalism and the National Character* Melbourne: Kibble

Rubenson, K. 1996 'The role of popular adult education: Reflections in connection to an analysis of surveys on living conditions, 1975 to 1993' in *Parliamentary Commission on Popular Adult Education: Three Studies on Popular Adult Education* Stockholm: Fritzes

——1999 'Adult education and training: The poor cousin. An analysis of OECD reviews of national polices for education' *Scottish Journal of Adult Education* 5(2), 5–32

——2002 *Measuring Motivation and Barriers in the AETS: A critical review* Ottawa: HRDC

Rueda, D. & Pontusson, J. 2000 'Wage inequality and varieties of capitalism' *World Politics* 52, 350–83

Rumelhart, D.E. et al 1986 *Parallel Distributed Processes* Cambridge MA: MIT Press

Rumelhart, D.W. & Norman, D.A. 1978 'Accretion, tuning and restructuring: Three models of learning' in J.W. Cotton & R.L. Klatsky (eds) *Semantic Factors in Cognition* Hillsdale, NJ: Erlbaum

Rushbrook, P. & Brown, M. 2001 'The VET Heritage Curriculum Project' in F. Beven, C. Kanes & D. Roebuck (eds) *Knowledge Demands and the New Economy: Proceedings of the 9th International Conference on Post-compulsory Education & Training* Brisbane: Centre for Learning and Work Research, Griffith University

Ryan, G. 1997 'Ensuring that students develop an adequate and well-structured knowledge-base' in D. Boud & G. Feletti (eds) *The Challenge of Problem-Based Learning* London: Kogan Page pp. 125–36

Ryan, G. & Quinn, C. 1995 'Cognitive apprenticeship and problem-based learning' in S.E. Chen, R. Cowdroy, A. Kingsland & M. Ostwald (eds) *Reflections on Problem Based Learning* Sydney: Australian Problem-Based Learning Network pp. 15–33

St Julien, J. 2000 'Changing conceptions of intelligence and reasoning: Implications for the classroom' *Australian Journal of Education* 44

Samoff, J. 1990 ' "Modernizing" a socialist vision: Education in Tanzania' in M. Carnoy & J. Samoff (eds) *Education and Social Transition in the Third World* Princeton, NJ: Princeton University Press

Sandelands, L.E. & Stablein, R.E. 1987 'The concept of organization mind' in S. Bachrach & N. DiTomaso (eds) *Research in the Sociology of Organizations* Greenwich: JAI Press pp. 135–62

Sankaran, S. et al. (eds) 2001 *Effective Change Management Using Action Learning and Action Research* Lismore, NSW: Southern Cross University Press

Sargant, N. with J. Field, H. Francis, T. Schuller & A. Tuckett 1997 *The Learning Divide: A study of participation in adult learning in the United Kingdom* Leicester: NIACE

Sarup, M. 1978 *Marxism and Education* London: Routledge & Kegan Paul

Saskatchewan NewStart 1982 *The Dynamics of Life Skills Coaching* Prince Albert, Sask: Training Research and Development Station Department of Manpower and Immigration

SAUVCA (South African Universities Vice-Chancellors Association) 2001 *Response to the National Plan on Higher Education* Pretoria, South Africa: SAUVCA

Sawchuk, P. 2003a *Adult Learning and Technology in Working-Class Life* Cambridge/New York: Cambridge University Press

——2003b 'On-line learning for union activists? Findings from a Canadian study' *Studies in Continuing Education* 25(1)

Schein, E. 1993 'On dialogue, culture and organizational learning' *Organizational Dynamics* 22(2), 40–51

Schmidt, H. 1983 'Problem Based Learning: Rationale and description' *Medical Education* 17, 11–16

Schön, D. 1983 *The Reflective Practitioner: How professionals think in action* New York: Basic Books

——1987 *Educating the Reflective Practitioner* San Francisco: Jossey-Bass

Schugurensky, D. 2000 'Adult education and social transformation: On Gramsci, Freire, and the challenge of comparing comparisons *Comparative Education Review* 44(4), 515–22

Schwab, J.J. 1978 'Science and civil discourse: The uses of diversity' in I. Westbury & N.J. Wilkof (eds) *Science, Curriculum and Liberal Education: Selected essays* Chicago, IL: University of Chicago Press pp. 133–48

Scott, A. 2000 *Running on Empty: 'Modernising' the British and Australian Labour Parties* Sydney: Pluto Press

Scribner, S. 1984 'Studying working intelligence' in B. Rogoff & J. Lave (eds) *Everyday Cognition: Its development in social context* Cambridge, MA: Harvard University Press

Sen, A. 1982 *Choice, Welfare and Measurement* Cambridge, MA: MIT Press

Senate Employment, Education and Training Reference Committee, Commonwealth of Australia 1997 *Beyond Cinderella: Towards a learning society* Canberra: Australian Government Printing Service

Senate Standing Committee on Employment, Education and Training, Commonwealth of Australia 1991 *Come in Cinderella: The emergence of adult and community education* Canberra: Australian Government Printing Service

Senge, P.M. 1990 *The Fifth Discipline: The art and practice of the learning organization* New York: Doubleday

Sharp, R. & Green, A. 1975 *Education and Social Control: A study in progressive primary education* London: Routledge & Kegan Paul

Shor, I. 1980 *Critical Teaching and Everyday Life* Boston: South End Press

——1985 *Critical Teaching for Everyday Life* Chicago: Black Rose Books

——1992 *Empowering Education* Chicago: University of Chicago Press

——1996 *When Students Have Power* Chicago: University of Chicago Press

Shulman, L. 1986 'Paradigms and research programs in the study of teaching: A contemporary perspective' in M. Wittrock (ed.) *Handbook of Research on Teaching* (3rd edn) New York: Macmillan

Simon, R.I., Dippo, D. & Schenke, A. 1991 *Learning Work: A critical pedagogy of work education* New York: Bergin & Garvey

Sklar, H., Mykyta, L. & Wefald, S. 2001 *Raise the Floor: Wages and policies that work for all of us* New York: Ms Foundation for Women

Smith, P. 2000 *Tales from the New Shop Floor: Inside the real jobs of the information economy* Sydney: Pluto Press

Soloman, G. & Perkins, D. 1989 'Rocky roads to transfer: Mechanisms of a neglected phenomenon' *Educational Researcher* 24(2)

Solomon, N. 2000 'De-schooling vocational knowledge' in C. Symes & J. McIntyre (eds) *Working Knowledge* Buckingham: Open University Press

Sork, T.J. 1996 'Negotiating power and interests in planning: A critical perspective' in R.M. Cervero & A.L. Wilson (eds) *What Really Matters in Adult Education Program Planning: Lessons in negotiating power and interests* New Directions for Adult and Continuing Education No. 69, San Francisco: Jossey-Bass

——2000 'Planning Educational Programs' in A.L. Wilson & E.R. Hayes (eds) *Handbook of Adult and Continuing Education* San Francisco: Jossey-Bass

——2001 'Needs assessment' in D.H. Poonswassie & A. Poonswassie (eds) *Fundamentals of Adult Education: Issues and practices for lifelong learning* Toronto: Thompson Educational

Sparks, B. 1998a 'The politics of culture and the struggle to get an education' *Adult Education Quarterly* 48(4), 245–59

——1998b 'Repeat performance: How adult education reproduces the status quo' *Journal of Adult Education* 26(1), 3–15

——2002a 'Adult literacy as cultural practice' in M. Alfred (ed.) *Learning and Sociocultural Contexts: Implications for adults, community, and workplace education* New Directions for Adults and Continuing Education 96, San Francisco: Jossey-Bass

——2002b *The Struggles of Getting an Education: Issues of power, culture, and difference for Mexican Americans of the Southwest* DeKalb, IL: Educational Studies Press

Sparks, B. & Peterson, E. 2000 'Adult basic education and the crisis of accountability' in A. Wilson & E. Hayes (eds) *Handbook of Adult and Continuing Education* San Francisco: Jossey-Bass

Spence, W.G. 1909 *Australia's Awakening: Thirty years in the life of an Australian agitator* Sydney: The Worker Trustees

Spencer, B. 1998a *The Purposes of Adult Education: A guide for students* Toronto: Thompson Educational

——1998b 'Distance education and the virtual classroom' in S.M. Scott, B. Spencer & A. Thomas (eds) *Learning for Life: Canadian readings in adult education* Toronto: Thompson Educational pp. 243–53

Spender, D. & Sarah, E. (eds) 1980 *Learning to Lose: Sexism and Education* London: The Women's Press

Spronk, B. 1994 'Distance learning for participatory development: A case study' *Canadian Journal of University Continuing Education* 20(2), 9–22

Stata, R. 1996 'Organizational learning: The key to management innovation' in K. Starkey (ed.) *How Organizations Learn* London: Thomson International Business pp. 316–34

Stephenson, P. 2002 *The Double Bind and the Double Burden: Implications for the professional education and practice of indigenous environmental health practitioners* Doctoral thesis, Faculty of Education, University of Technology, Sydney

Sternberg, R.J. 1988 *The Triarchic Mind: A new theory of human intelligence* New York: Penguin

Stevenson, J. 1986a 'Adaptability: Theoretical considerations' *Journal of Structural Learning* 9, 107–17

——1986b 'Adaptability: Experimental studies' *Journal of Structural Learning* 9, 118–39

——1994 'Curriculum and teaching in TAFE' in J. Stevenson (ed.) *A Collection of Conference Papers Presented by John Stevenson* Brisbane: Centre for Skill Formation Research, Griffith University pp. 11–28

——2000 'Working knowledge' *Journal of Vocational Education and Training* 52(3), 503–19

Stewart, D. 1947 'Pioneering the WEA in Australia, 1: The beginning' *Australian History,* xxix(1), 5–7

Stokes, T.F. & Baer, D.M. 1977 'An implicit technology of generalisations' in *Journal of Applied Behaviour Analysis* 10: 349 & 367

Stromquist, N.P. 1997 *Literacy for Citizenship* Albany, NY: SUNY Press

—— 2001 *Knowledge and Power in Feminist Politics: The experience of CIPAF* Unpublished MS Los Angeles: Rossier School of Education, University of Southern California

Suchodolski, B. 1976 'Lifelong Education: Some philosophical aspects' in R.H. Dave (ed.) *Foundations of Lifelong Education* Oxford: Pergamon Press & Hamburg: UNESCO Institute for Education

Sutherland, J. 2002 'An approach to learning at, for and through the workplace: A trade union case study' in K. Evans, P. Hodkinson & L. Unwin (eds) *Working to Learn: Transforming learning in the workplace* London: Kogan Page

Sweden, Government Bill 1995–97: 222

Swieringa, J. & Wierdsma, A. 1992 *Becoming a Learning Organization: Beyond the learning curve* Wokingham, UK: Addison-Wesley

Taksa, L. 1983 *'Defence Not Defiance': Social protest and the NSW General Strike of 1917* Unpublished honours thesis, Sydney: University of NSW

——1991 '"Defence not defiance": Social protest and the NSW General Strike of 1917' *Labour History* 60 May, 16–33

——1992 'Spreading the word: The literature of labour and working class culture' in J. Shields (ed.) *All Our Labours: Oral histories of working life in twentieth century Sydney* Sydney: NSW University Press

——1993 *All a Matter of Timing: The diffusion of scientific management in New South Wales prior to 1921* Unpublished PhD thesis, Sydney: University of NSW

——1994a 'Oral history and collective memory: Labour rituals and working class memory' *Oral History Association of Australia Journal* 16, 46–52

——1994b 'Work, struggle and repose: Oral history and working class culture in Australia' *Labour History* 67, 110–27

——1995 'The cultural diffusion of scientific management: The United States and New South Wales' *Journal of Industrial Relations* 37(3), 427–61

Taylor, J. 1996 'The Solidarity Network: Universities, computer-mediated communication and labour studies in Canada' in T. Harrison & T. Stephen (eds) *Computer Networking and Scholarly Communication in the Twenty-First-Century University* New York: SUNY pp. 277–90

——2002 'Union e-learning in Canada' in B. Spencer (ed.) *Unions and Learning in a Global Economy: International and comparative perspectives* Toronto: Thompson Educational

Taylor, P.V. 1993 *The Texts of Paulo Freire* Buckingham: Open University Press

Taylor, S., Rivzi, F., Lingard, R. & Henry, M. 1997 *Educational Policy and the Politics of Change* London: Routledge

Tegel, K. & Dockett, S. 1995 '"Tanya has to fix them—she alives them with a stick": Critical thinking in early childhood' in S.E. Chen, R. Cowdroy, A. Kingsland & M. Ostwald (eds) *Reflections on Problem Based Learning* Sydney: Australian Problem-Based Learning Network pp. 297–317

Tennant, M. 1999 'Is learning transferable?' in D. Boud & J. Garrick (eds) *Understanding Learning at Work* London: Routledge

Terkel, S. 1974 *Working: People talk about what they do all day and how they feel about what they do* New York: The New Press

Thelen, K. 2000 'Why German employers cannot bring themselves to dismantle the German Model' in B. Iversen, J. Pontusson & B. Soskice (eds) *Unions, Employers and Central Banks* New York: Cambridge University Press

Thelen, K. & Kume, I. 1999 'The effects of globalization on labour revisited' *Politics and Society* 27(4), 477–8

The Railroad

The Railway Union Gazette

Thompson, J. 1983 *Learning Liberation: Women's response to men's education* London: Croom Helm

———1995 'The Great Tradition—A personal reflection' Paper presented to the *Social Action and Emancipatory Learning Seminar*, University of Technology, Sydney 18-20 September

———1997 *Words in Edgeways: Radical learning for social change* Leicester: NIACE

———2000 *Stretching the Academy* London: NIACE

Thompson, P. & McHugh, D. 1995 *Work Organizations: A critical introduction* London: Macmillan Business

Thompson, P. & Warhurst, C. 1998 (eds) *Workplaces of the Future* London: Macmillan

Thurbin, P. 1994 *Implementing the Learning Organization: The 17-day learning program* London: Pitman

Thurow, L. 1996 *The Future of Capitalism* Sydney: Allen & Unwin

Tisdell, E.J. 1995 *Creating Inclusive Adult Learning Environments: Insights from multicultural education and feminist pedagogy* Columbus, OH: ERIC Clearinghouse on Adult, Career, and Vocational Education

Torres, C.A. 1998 *Education, Power, and Personal Biography* New York: Routledge

Tough, A. 1979 *The Adult's Learning Projects: A fresh approach to theory and practice in adult learning* Toronto: OISE

Trades Union Congress 1998a *Leaders in Learning: Four union initiatives in helping members access learning* London: Congress House

Tuijnman, A. & Boström, A.-K. 2002 'Changing notions of lifelong education and lifelong learning' *International Review of Education* 48(1/2), 93-110

Tyler, R.W. 1949 *Basic Principles of Curriculum and Instruction* Chicago: University of Chicago Press

Usher, R. 1987 'The place of theory in designing curricula for the continuing education of adult educators' *Studies in the Education of Adults* 19(1), 26-36

———1989, 'Locating adult education in the practical' in B. Bright (ed.) *Theory and Practice in the Study of Adult Education* London: Routledge

———1996 'A critique of the neglected epistemological assumptions of education research' in D. Scott & R. Usher (eds) *Understanding Educational Research* London: Routledge

Usher, R. & Bryant, I. 1989 *The Captive Triangle: Adult education as theory, practice and research* London: Routledge

Usher, R. & Edwards, R. 1994 *Postmodernism and Education* London: Routledge

Usher, R., Bryant, I. & Johnston, R. 1997 *Adult Education and the Postmodern Challenge: Learning beyond the limits* London: Routledge

Varela, F.J., Thompson, E. & Rosch, E. 1991 *The Embodied Mind: Cognitive science and human experience* Cambridge, MA: MIT Press

Vavrus, F. 2002 'Constructing consensus: The feminist modern and the reconstruction of gender' *Current Issues in Comparative Education* 4(1) (http://www.tcrecord.org)

Vinkour, A. (1976) 'Economic analysis of lifelong learning' in R.H. Dave (ed.) *Foundations of Lifelong Education* Oxford: Pergamon Press

Vogel, S. 2001 'The crisis of German and Japanese capitalism' *Comparative Political Studies* 34(10)

Von Glaserfeld, E. 1995 *Radical Constructivism: A way of knowing and learning* London: Falmer Press

Vygotsky, L. 1978 *Mind in Society: The development of higher psychological processes* Cambridge, MA: Harvard University Press

——1987 *The Collected Works of L.S. Vygotsky* R.W. Rieber & A.S. Carton (eds) New York: Plenum Press

Waddington, S. 2002 'Reflecting on policy' in J. Field (ed.) *Promoting European Dimensions in Lifelong Learning* Leicester: NIACE

Wadsworth, Y. 1997 *Do It Yourself Social Research* (2nd edn) Sydney: Allen & Unwin

Wain, K. 1986 *Philosophy of Lifelong Education* London: Croom Helm

——2003 *The Learning Society in a Postmodern Age* New York: Peter Lang

Walker, J. 1988 *Louts and Legends: Male youth culture in an inner city school* Sydney: Allen & Unwin

Wallerstein, N. 1983 *Language and Culture in Conflict: Problem posing in the ESL classroom* Reading, MA: Addison-Wesley

Walters, S. (ed.) 1997 *Globalization, Adult Education and Training* London: Zed Books

Waterhouse, P., Wilson, B. & Ewer, P. 1999 *The Changing Nature and Patterns of Work and Implications for VET* Adelaide: NCVER

Waters, M. 1995 *Globalisation* London: Routledge

Watkins, K. 1991 *Facilitating Learning in the Workplace* Geelong: Deakin University

Watson, L. 1999 *Lifelong Learning in Australia: Analysis and prospects* Discussion paper No. 1 Canberra: The Lifelong Learning Network, University of Canberra

WEA 1914–1921 *Annual Reports*

——1919 *Adolescent Education: Report of a conference promoted by the WEA of NSW in October 1919* Sydney: WHB Printing

Weedon, C. 1987 *Feminist Practice and Post-structuralist Theory* Oxford: Blackwell

Weil, S. 1988 'From a language of observation to a language of experience: Studying the perspectives of diverse adults in higher education' *Journal of Access Studies* 3, 17–43

——1989 'Access: Towards education or miseducation? Adults imagine the future' in O. Fulton (ed.) *Access and Institutional Change* Buckingham: SRHE & Open University Press pp. 110–43

Welton, M. 1987 'Vivisecting the nightingale: Reflections on adult education as an object of study' *Studies in the Education of Adults* 19, 46–68

——1993 'In search of the object: Historiography and adult education *Studies in Continuing Education* 15(2), 133–48

——2001 *Little Mosie from the Margaree: A biography of Moses M. Coady* Toronto: Thompson Educational

Welton, M.R. (ed.) 1995 *In Defense of the Lifeworld: Critical perspectives on adult learning* Albany, NY: State University of New York Press

Wenger, E. 1998 *Communities of Practice: Learning, meaning and identity* Cambridge: Cambridge University Press

West, L. 1996 *Beyond Fragments: Adults, motivation, and higher education— a biographical analysis* London: Taylor & Francis

Whitehead, A.N. 1967 *The Aims of Education* New York: The Free Press

Whitelock, D. 1974 *The Great Tradition: A history of adult education in Australia* Brisbane: University of Queensland Press

Whiting, M. 1994 'The education of adults in Schools of Arts in colonial New South Wales' in P. Candy & J. Laurent (eds) *Pioneering Culture: Mechanics Institutes and Schools of Arts in Australia* Adelaide: Auslib Press

Wickham-Crowley, T. 1992 'Democratic organisation for social change: Latin American Christian based communities and literacy campaigns' *Social Forces* 71(2)

Wikelund, K. 1989 *Social Aspects of Literacy Acquisition and Use* Portland, OR: Northwest Regional Educational Laboratory

Wildemeersch, D., Jansen, T., Vandenabeele, J. & Jans, M. 1998. 'Social Learning: A new perspective on learning in participatory systems' *Studies in Continuing Education* 20(2), 251–64

Williams, R. 1977 *Marxism and Literature* Oxford: Oxford University Press

——1981 *Culture* Glasgow: Fontana

Williamson, B. 1998 *Lifeworlds and Learning: Essays in the theory, philosophy and practice of lifelong learning* Leicester: NIACE

Willis, P. 1978 *Learning to Labour: How working class kids get working-class jobs* London: Saxon House

——1988 *Patrons and Riders: Conflicting roles and hidden objectives in an Aboriginal development program* Adelaide: Centre for Research in Education and Work, University of South Australia

Wilson, A.L. & Cervero, R.M. 1997 'The song remains the same: The selective tradition of technical rationality in adult education program planning theory' *International Journal of Lifelong Education* 16(2), 84–108

Wong, L. & McBride, S. 2003 'Youth employment programs in British Columbia: Taking the high road or the low road?' in M. Cohen (ed.) *Training the Excluded for Work: Access and equity for women, immigrants, first nations, youth and people with low income* Vancouver: UBC Press

Woods, D. 1994 *Problem-Based Learning: How to gain the most from PBL* London: Donald Woods

Wright, N. 1990 *Assessing Radical Education: A critical review of the radical movement in English schooling 1960–80* Milton Keynes: Open University Press

Yang, B. 1999 'How effectively do you use power and influence?' in M. Silberman (ed.) *The 1999 Training and Performance Sourcebook* New York: McGraw-Hill

Yeatman, A. 1990 *Bureaucrats, Technocrats, Femocrats* Sydney: Allen & Unwin

——1993 'Corporate managerialism and the shift from the welfare to the competition state' *Discourse* 13, 3–9

——1998 (ed.) *Activism and the Policy Process* Sydney: Allen & Unwin

Young, I.M. 1990 *Justice and the Politics of Difference* Princeton, NJ: Princeton University Press

——1997 'Asymmetrical reciprocity: On moral respect, wonder and enlarged thought' in *Intersecting Voices: Dilemmas of gender, political philosophy, and policy* Princeton, NJ: Princeton University Press

Youngman, F. 1986 *Adult Education and Socialist Pedagogy* London: Croom Helm

Zack, M. 1999 'Managing codified knowledge' *Sloan Management Journal* 40(4), 45–69

Zuber-Skerrit, O. (ed.) 1996 *New Directions in Action Research* London: Falmer Press

Zuss, M. 1994 'Value and subjectivity in literacy practice' in B. Feldman, R. Weber & A. Ramirez (eds) *Literacy Across Languages and Cultures* Albany, NY: State University of New York Press

NAME INDEX

328

SUBJECT INDEX